In Remembrance of
Emmett Till

IN REMEMBRANCE OF
EMMETT TILL

Regional Stories
and Media Responses
to the Black Freedom Struggle

DARRYL MACE

UNIVERSITY PRESS OF KENTUCKY

Scholarly publisher for the Commonwealth,
serving Bellarmine University, Berea College, Centre College of Kentucky, Eastern
Kentucky University, The Filson Historical Society, Georgetown College, Kentucky
Historical Society, Kentucky State University, Morehead State University, Murray State
University, Northern Kentucky University, Transylvania University, University
of Kentucky, University of Louisville, and Western Kentucky University.
All rights reserved.

Editorial and Sales Offices: The University Press of Kentucky
663 South Limestone Street, Lexington, Kentucky 40508-4008
www.kentuckypress.com

Library of Congress Cataloging-in-Publication Data

Mace, Darryl, 1975–
  In remembrance of Emmett Till : regional stories and media responses to the Black
freedom struggle / Darryl Mace.
    pages cm
  Includes bibliographical references and index.
  ISBN 978-0-8131-4536-5 (hardcover : acid-free paper) —
  ISBN 978-0-8131-4538-9 (PDF) — ISBN 978-0-8131-4537-2 (ePub)
  1. Till, Emmett, 1941-1955—Death and burial—Press coverage. 2. Lynching—
Mississippi—Press coverage. 3. Trials (Murder)—Mississippi—Sumner—Press
coverage. 4. Mass media—Political aspects—Mississippi—History—20th century.
5. Journalism—Political aspects—Mississippi—History—20th century. 6. Memorials—
Political aspects—Mississippi—History—20th century. 7. African Americans—Civil
rights—Southern States—History—20th century. 8. Southern States—Race relations—
History—20th century. 9. Racism—United States—Public opinion—History—20th
century. 10. Public opinion—United States—History—20th century. I. Title.
  E185.93.M6M24 2014
  364.1'34—dc23   2014010708

To the love of my life, Nikki Mace.
I thank God every day that he brought us together.
Thank you for your constant support and for reading
countless drafts of this manuscript while it was still
in a very rough format.

Contents

Preface

Fourteen-year-old Emmett Louis Till left his mother's Chicago home on August 20, 1955, to vacation with his great-uncle Moses Wright and his family in Mississippi.[1] Till spent several uneventful days playing with his cousins and learning to pick cotton. At the end of the week, he and some relatives traveled to the nearby whistle-stop town of Money, Mississippi, to shop. Reports about what happened differ, and each story has contributed to the Emmett Till lore, but it is commonly agreed that Till bought bubble gum and then whistled at Carolyn Bryant, a white woman who was tending the Bryant family store while her husband was out of town making deliveries. Three days later, in the predawn hours of Sunday morning, August 28, Roy Bryant, J. W. Milam, and likely others traveled to Mose Wright's house in Leflore County and kidnapped Emmett Till. They allegedly took him to the Sunflower County plantation managed by Milam's brother, Leslie, and proceeded to beat him without mercy. Sometime during this process, Till was shot in the back of the head.[2] Later, the perpetrators took the body to the Tallahatchie River and dumped it into the water along with a seventy-five-pound cotton gin fan, which was tied to the body with barbed wire.[3] On August 31, a fisherman saw Till's feet sticking up out of the water and contacted the Tallahatchie County sheriff's office. The sheriff, H. C. Strider, in turn, retrieved the body and attempted to bury it in an unmarked grave at a local cemetery.[4] Till's relatives stopped the burial and ensured that the body was returned to Chicago, where his mother, Mamie Till-Mobley, insisted that the pine box containing her son's remains be opened. She inspected the body and confirmed that it was indeed that of Emmett Till.

Subsequently, Mamie Till-Mobley held a public open-casket wake and funeral. Her efforts memorialized the lynching and turned the public's critical eyes toward the state of Mississippi. Bryant and Milam, who had been questioned and arrested on August 29, 1955, were indicted by a grand jury and stood trial on the charge of murder. During the brief trial, the jury heard testimony from black Mississippians who, fed up with business as usual, risked life and limb by naming white perpetrators in a white-on-black crime. Equally endangered, the black Chicagoan Mamie Till-Mobley traveled to the heart of Dixie to testify for the prosecution. The defense presented testimony from Sheriff Strider and expert witnesses, all of whom claimed that the body was too decomposed to have been in the river for only three days and that it was too large to be that of a fourteen-year-old boy. The defense also called Carolyn Bryant to the witness stand, but the presiding judge, Curtis Swango, dismissed the jury during her testimony and later ruled that it would not hear her account of the incident. Finally, both sides rested, and the jury retired to discuss the case. After roughly an hour of deliberation, it returned a verdict of not guilty, but Bryant and Milam still faced kidnapping charges. In November 1955, the two men appeared before a grand jury in Leflore County on the charge of kidnapping, but they were never indicted. They returned to their lives after the trial.

This brief historical narrative only scratches the surface of the intrigues, deceptions, horrors, and legacies surrounding the case. To this day, there are many conflicting stories circulating about the death of Emmett Till. Surely, very few, if any, living persons know exactly what happened throughout the saga. Amid the countless assertions and outright lies about events surrounding the lynching, it is nearly impossible to find the actual, objective truth as many scholars would define it. However, the argument that I present in this book rests on the assumption that any "truth" that we might find about the incident is of necessity subjective and that the many people who were influenced by the lynching and the subsequent events created their own memories of the case. For most, these memories, and, thus, their "truth" of Emmett Till, were based on the actual coverage, and their recollections of the coverage, in national and local print media sources. Doubtlessly, the Till lynching engendered an unprecedented media firestorm with regard to race relations in the United States. The death of Emmett Till brought the full weight of the legacy of institutionalized slavery, Jim Crow segregation, and vitriolic white supremacy to bear on the consciences of countless Americans of all races. It fully opened the eyes of many to the untenable situations that racial politics created in this country and inspired a generation of activists to challenge the system of white racial hegemony wherever it existed.

This book lives as a legacy to the too-short life and tragic death of that fourteen-year-old boy. It stands as a memorial to the countless activists who, emboldened by his death, leaped into the struggle for civil rights. It underscores how regional stories and racial dispositions framed the coverage of, and responses to, his lynching. And it remains a tribute to the work of Till's relatives (especially his mother), civil rights organizations, and the black press to honor his death, commemorate his life, galvanize a generation of activists, and push for civil rights for all Americans.

Introduction

While never referred to as *the crime of the century,* the kidnapping and lynching of Emmett Louis Till captured the country's imagination and sent waves of outrage through the public.[1] It engendered a visceral response from many progressive-minded individuals, and the comprehensive coverage by the regional and national press emboldened a generation of activists—dubbed *the Emmett Till generation*—to speak out and act out in remembrance of Emmett Till. Till was not the first black male murdered in the South, but because he was a youth and a northerner his death fanned the flames of regionalism and regional tension in this country. More importantly, his August 1955 murder occurred in the wake of the May 1954 *Brown v. Board of Education of Topeka, KS* (*Brown*) decision making segregated public schools illegal and the May 1955 *Brown v. Board of Education of Topeka, KS II* (*Brown II*) decision mandating the integration of public education "with all deliberate speed," decisions that shaped responses to his death.

Further framing reactions to the *Brown* decisions, amid Cold War tension after World War II mainstream media and the federal government struggled to present the United States as a unified "homogeneity of varying regions." Despite the backlash in response to integration and the growing schisms around civil rights, the fear of the spread of communism led many Americans to bond together behind their desire for a strong and unified country. While acknowledging unique regional identities, many chose to see America as a single "fabric woven of regional patterns and forces."[2]

Amid general unification behind the banner of anticommunism, Emmett Till's brutal murder served as a floodlight reilluminating regionalism and placing center stage all the vitriolic hatred that remained as a legacy of slavery, white supremacy, and segregation. Even given the horrific nature of the crime and the national climate after the *Brown* decisions, Till's death likely would not have garnered the worldwide attention it received were it not for his family, the black press, and civil rights organizations. These individuals and groups, led by his mother, Mamie Till-Mobley, continually underscored the saliency of the Emmett Till lynching in the national narrative on race relations. Mamie Till-Mobley allowed the world to see the gruesome images of her son, and civil rights organizations and black news outlets lambasted the state of Mississippi for fostering an environment that allowed such a crime to occur.

Attempting to explain the lynching in the contexts of American race relations and Cold War geopolitics, mainstream and black news outlets presented stories of Till that contained unique regional biases. By and large, these press reports acknowledged the saliency of the lynching and underscored issues their authors felt readers would find most important. Americans' impressions of the Till lynching, and in many ways their dispositions toward civil rights and integration efforts, were shaped by the coverage of the Till crisis they found in local newspapers and national publications. The Emmett Till saga struck a chord with many people, and, unwilling to let the brutal murder go unchallenged, they leaped into the burgeoning modern civil rights movement.

Unlike the climate of the antebellum period of the 1830s–1850s, when slavery caused regional identities to play out neatly in a North/South divide, regionalism in the 1950s was fluid and based on a myriad of factors. Certainly, as seen through articles, editorials, and letters to the editor selected for publication in the regional and national press in response to the Till lynching, regionalism involved people defining their locale with reference to other regions of the country. This type of regionalism, a phenomenon I refer to as *situational regionalism,* was not static; rather, it was a response to people's views of the place in which they lived and how their locale compared to the rest of the nation. Therefore, the regional map that developed in response to the Till lynching often did not conform to traditional regional boundaries.[3]

Using situational regionalism as a lens through which to view the Till lynching, I provide in this book a textual analysis of the coverage of the lynching, the home-going ceremonies for Till, the trial, the posttrial reactions, and the memorials of Till found in the mainstream and black press.[4] Through this analysis it is clear that the regional press strategically highlighted aspects of the Till saga that best helped them frame their regional perspective on American race relations, and, through their letters to the editor, readers both supported their local paper's coverage and, when necessary, challenged the staff to intensify their reporting efforts.

Adding to and helping shape these regional narratives was the national press coverage found in mainstream and black weeklies and monthlies. Admittedly, outlets such as the *Pittsburgh Courier,* the *New York Times,* the *Washington Post, Jet,* and the *Chicago Tribune* often covered the news from both regional and national angles; however, with the Till lynching each took on a distinctively regional disposition. Through the cataloging and study of similarities in the tone and the messages found in articles, editorials, and letters to the editor from over one hundred print media sources, five distinct regions emerged. Not surprisingly, given the clear racial implications of the Till case, within each of the five regions the black press forwarded more pointed and critical reflections on the Till saga than did their mainstream counterparts.[5] In their unique, regionally specific ways, these black media outlets followed the calling of America's first black paper, *Freedom's Journal,* whose editors, Samuel E. Cornish and John B. Russwurm, noted that black papers should present stories from a black perspective since "we [black people] know our condition better than anyone."[6]

Throughout the coverage—including the Emmett Till lynching, the trial of Roy Bryant and J. W. Milam, reflections on the verdict, and the Emmett Till memorials—journalists, editors, and publishers negotiated questions of race and racial justice by comparing and contrasting their locale with other areas of the country. They vilified people from other areas of the country while promoting the region in which they themselves resided as the true measure of the "ideal" America. Mississippi, as the epitome of racist society and the location of Till's murder, was the gauge by which each region measured its own race relations.[7]

In this book, I highlight the mainstream newspapers with the highest circulation rates. The only anomaly, Hodding Carter's *Delta Democrat-Times,* did not have a large circulation; however, its location in Greenville, Mississippi, a town two hours away from Sumner, where the trial was held—made it an important part of the press coverage. Additionally, I examined coverage from over fifty small-circulation papers from small towns across the country. In every case, these smaller operations used newswire service reports that mirrored the coverage found in papers from the big cities nearest these small outlets. Expanding on previous works on the Emmett Till lynching, this study interrogates coverage from over one hundred newspapers and magazines from across the country and, where appropriate, contextualizes the coverage and editorial decisions using artifacts (personal correspondence, editorial commentary, and archival resources) from these media outlets. By broadening, recasting, and contextualizing (through number of sources, dates of coverage, and editorial commentary) the base of media outlets that covered the lynching, this book illuminates the multitude of responses to the event. Moreover, the use of textual analysis, as opposed to content analysis, shifts the investigation from the quantity and placement of Till coverage to a more nuanced examination of regionalism and racial themes found within it. Further expounding on previous scholarship, this work takes the story of Emmett Till far beyond the lynching and the trial of his murderers. Emmett Till's death underscored the untenable racial situation in this nation, which had been laid bare by the 1954 *Brown* and 1955 *Brown II* decisions. I use the regional and the national interpretations of the lynching, and the links between the lynching and the *Brown* rulings, to foreground how the brutal death galvanized the Emmett Till generation and how its efforts live on as a memorial to a boy who died too young and too innocent.

This work does not pretend that all Americans who lived in the 1950s based their interpretations of Emmett Till on the coverage in their local papers. Nor does it assume that they all cared to follow the coverage of Emmett Till in their local papers. Regardless, it is impossible to deny the fact that discourse around the Emmett Till lynching, and all heavily covered events, is forwarded, guided, and influenced by "people in the know"—those who follow media coverage of highly publicized news stories. Therefore, simply by participating in conversations around a breaking news story, whether they follow the story in the media or not, individuals are influenced by media bias. Equally important is the fact that "mass media . . . transfer the salience of items on their news agenda to the public agenda." This "transfer of salience" occurs through two interrelated mechanisms. First, through *priming*, media outlets report on certain issues while excluding others, thus shaping their readers' views of the events in question. Second, *framing* directs the focus to some aspects of reality while distracting attention from other factors, which could lead the reader to draw different conclusions. Journalists' stories about Emmett Till *primed* preconceived regional notions of race and gender and *framed* readers' reactions. Simultaneously, the public response, seen through letters to the editor, internal press documents, and the solidification of and transitions in the tenor of Till coverage, reinscribed regionalism and regional dispositions toward race relations. In the case of Emmett Till, the print media coverage continued to breathe life into the incident and to shape interpretations of it. That coverage as consumed by those living in 1955 persisted as a legacy to the national and regional importance of the death of Emmett Till, galvanized the Emmett Till generation, and remained a lasting memory of the death of a boy.[8]

Racially motivated deaths before Emmett Till's did not generate the same level of national prominence because they seemed like a case of southern white men taking care of their "Negro problem." Even lynchings after Till's never gained the same national exposure. The deaths of Mack Charles Parker, Herbert Lee, and Medgar Evers failed to stir the national conscience like Till's because Parker was a convicted rapist and Lee and Evers were seen as subversives. Emmett Till's brutal murder was different because he did not fit the mold of a lynch victim. He was too young, too northern, too innocent, and too representative of the population *Brown* and *Brown II* was supposed to protect.[9]

The Till lynching, a reminder for many Americans of the wretched consequences of slavery and the dehumanization that white-supremacist-sanctioned Jim Crow racism engendered, shone a floodlight on the realities of the southern black condition and particularly the condition of black Mississippians. Mississippi, the quintessential Deep South state, became the pariah, the metaphor for all that was wrong with American race relations. Mississippians were the "other," the proof that poverty, ignorance, and cultural backwardness could neither coexist with nor foster progressive civil rights inclusivity. Many Americans outside Mississippi, particularly those from outside the Deep South region, took pride in the fact that they were not from the state and looked on it with voyeuristic fascination. Surely, as Joseph Crespino put it, "the more vulgar the racism in Mississippi, the more interesting it was to American readers."[10]

Many outside the Deep South saw Mississippi through the lens of James Silver's "closed society." It was "the poorest, least industrialized southern state with the highest percentage of African-American residents . . . the South on steroids, the South in all of its gothic horror and campy, absurdist charm." Till's death and the growing civil rights movement thrust the state into national prominence as a symbol of the worst of the South: "a grotesque relic of racism, poverty, ruralism, and violence." White citizens learned this disposition toward race relations at a young age, and they appeared in the rhetoric of state leaders, especially during periods of increased outside criticism. Mississippi, deemed "the most southern place on earth" by James Cobb, was the model of white supremacy, for, despite the geographic and cultural differences found in the state, race forced an uneasy alliance of white citizens, a white narrative and ideology that crossed geographic, socioeconomic, and cultural boundaries. Mainstream newspapers from outside the Deep South region adopted a disposition in opposition to Mississippi's and consistently juxtaposed their locale with the state, the nation's quintessential other; however, this disposition of opposition was manifested differently in different regions and led to regionally unique stories of Emmett Till.[11]

Surfacing with the Till lynching (and becoming increasingly clear throughout the 1960s) was a second metaphor according to which "America is Mississippi writ large," for the entire country had a racial problem. During the coverage of the Till saga, many in the black press embraced this metaphor and argued, as Crespino put it, that "when push came to shove the vast majority of white Americans shared their deep hostility to racial integration; that if white Americans in other parts of the country were in their shoes, they would act the same way that white southerners acted." Again, while the theme "America is Mississippi" permeated the coverage in many of the black media outlets, differences in the regional stories and racial and gender messages produced regionally diverse stories of the Till lynching.[12]

In response to increasing scrutiny and the prevalence of the moniker *other*, Deep South mainstream newspapers embraced a third metaphor, one identified by Crespino, whereby Mississippi served as the innocent scapegoat for all the country's racial ills.[13] To the employees and readers of these newspapers, the Deep South region boasted the best race relations in the country, and those outside the locale condemned it in order to hide their own inadequacies when it came to racial harmony. Crespino's three metaphors both reinforced and complicated images of Mississippi and the Deep South.

While this book focuses on regionalism and regionally engendered racial messages, each chapter begins with an investigation of national narratives as seen through such mainstream publications as *Time, Newsweek, Life,* the *Daily Worker,* and the *Nation* and the black publications *The Crisis, Ebony,* and *Jet.* This work demands a framing of the national press for two reasons. First, no study of Emmett Till is complete without an analysis of *Jet,* which during the Till lynching read more like a midwestern than a national publication. Second, readers from across the country were increasingly garnering their news from both local and national print media sources.

It is imperative to study Emmett Till through the lens of print media coverage because the mid-1950s was the highpoint of per capita newspaper circulation. Additionally, magazine circulation was also high, especially the new Johnson Company publications *Ebony* and *Jet.* Adding to the importance of print media sources was the fact that television news lasted only fifteen minutes; therefore, the networks could not cover the Till lynching in as much detail as the print media could. By all accounts, there were more print media employees at the trial than radio and television employees, so the former had the advantage of sheer numbers. For all these reasons, Emmett Till scholars have focused almost exclusively on the print media coverage of the event, and this text continues that scholarly focus.

Chapter 1 sets the stage for the lynching of Emmett Till by using Till and his family to illuminate the legacies of racism, Jim Crow, lynching, regionalism, World War II racism, Cold War race relations, and *Brown.* It places Till's family within the long history of the Great Black Migration, showing how a northern upbringing offered Till a worldview that was foreign to the gender and racial mores of the Deep South. As part of the Great Black Migration, Till's family exists as a case study of a centuries-long battle blacks had waged against oppressive race relations. Dissonance between Chicago race relations and Mississippi race relations combined with growing racial tensions in the wake of the *Brown* decisions sets the stage for the brutal murder of this fourteen-year-old boy. Throughout, chapter 1 points up how black media outlets underscored the growing racial tensions and the white backlash against integration efforts. It makes clear the fact that the Till lynching was part of a longer legacy of racial conflict in this country, a conflict that the black press covered in great detail. As part of the case study, it traces the legacy of white supremacist leaders in Mississippi who laid a foundation on which Emmett Till's childish actions one August evening appeared to white Mississippi as an affront to the fundamental sanctity of white womanhood. In response to his actions, Bryant and Milam brutalized and murdered Emmett Till in the sweltering heat of an August night.

Chapter 2 opens with the August night incident in Bryant's Meat and Groceries where Emmett Till wolf-whistled at Carolyn Bryant, and it traces the subsequent events through the lynching. Analysis then links the wolf-whistle prank and the resultant murder to the broader fights for racial justice in the country. By highlighting when and in what manner regional and national news outlets introduced the kidnapping and murder, this chapter illuminates the ways in which media coverage utilized the Till lynching as a barometer measuring regional dispositions toward racial and gender norms. This analysis predicts how these dispositions solidified and proliferated during Emmett Till's home-going ceremonies.

Emmett Till's home-going events—from the return of his body to Chicago through the wake and funeral services—are the subject of chapter 3. Included in this chapter are pinpoint analyses of what aspects of the return of the remains and the funeral services national and regional news sources chose as salient (i.e., Mamie Till-Mobley's grief, NAACP involvement, Communist attempts to infiltrate the services, attendance at the funeral, and doubts about the identity of the body). By foregrounding, obscuring, and whitewashing elements of the saga, national and regional news sources framed the events and the actors in ways that fanned existing dispositions toward gender and race. Analysis in this chapter foreshadows the ways in which the press used Mississippi as a foil by which to articulate a region's unique dispositions toward race relations. Publications across the country put the entire state of Mississippi on trial; in most cases, Mississippi was deemed guilty of being the epicenter of racial brutality.

Key to the analysis in chapter 4 is a study of how print media outlets presented their final framing of Mississippi and the Deep South on the eve of the trial. Across most of the country, those publications that chose to offer pretrial coverage depicted the state along the lines of the NAACP pamphlet "M Is for Mississippi and Murder,"[14] where this Deep South state was cast as the epitome of southern racial oppression. Much of the examination in this chapter focuses on the national and midwestern press, both of which sent reporters to Mississippi well ahead of the trial to set the scene for their readers. This chapter underscores the negative framing of Mississippi and points up the growing attacks on Roy Bryant and Milam as prototypically racist white Mississippians. In these environs, Bryant and Milam were assured acquittal, and analysis in chapter 4 foreshadows how this guaranteed exoneration served only to intensify the scrutiny the South would feel as the entire region underwent a trial by print.

As seen in chapter 5, trial coverage brought even greater scrutiny of Mississippi racial mores. Central to this chapter is a study of how national and regional news outlets chose to cover the trial (i.e., the Associated Press newswire, the United Press newswire, embedded reporters, stringer reporters, editorials, letters to the editor) as well as what aspects of the trial and the milieu each outlet found salient. This chapter also covers the dispute between Mamie Till-Mobley and the NAACP that led to a severing of ties between the two parties. Through their framing of the trial, regional and national press put Mississippi mores under scrutiny as Tallahatchie

County shepherded Bryant and Milam through a farcical criminal proceeding. By pointing up the outrage resulting from this case, an outrage fueled by press coverage of the saga, this chapter contextualizes the galvanization of the Emmett Till generation.

For many of these activists, Emmett Till's death was the seminal event that thrust them into a burgeoning movement for racial justice. Chapter 6 analyzes the posttrial reaction, covering the period from September 24, 1955, through the responses to the January 24, 1956, publication of "The Shocking Story of Approved Killing in Mississippi"—Bryant and Milam's confession to the lynching of Emmett Till.[15] Key to the analysis in this chapter is an investigation of trial attendees' firsthand accounts of their experiences covering the Emmett Till trial. Out of fear for their safety, these biographical recollections came out only after the attendees left Mississippi. Also included in this chapter is an investigation into continued efforts on the part of the Deep South mainstream press, particularly the *Jackson (MS) Daily News,* to discredit the Till family through disparaging reports about trial witnesses, the NAACP, Mamie Till-Mobley, and Emmett's father, Louis Till. Despite relentless attempts to defame black people and assuage white guilt, Emmett Till's brutal murder galvanized the Emmett Till generation to speak out against racial injustices. The work of these activists continued to breathe life into the Emmett Till lynching and, in many ways, made necessary the outpouring of efforts to memorialize Till, thus ensuring that his legacy lived on far longer than his murderers lived.

So much of what has happened through recent years around the memory of the civil rights movement has been in remembrance of the death of Emmett Till. Chapter 7 looks at what happened to the key actors in the Till trial and analyzes the myriad memorials that have sprung up to commemorate the life and death of Emmett Till. Key to this study is the use of media sources to show how the public remembers Till. Although many of the actors do not continue to garner attention outside their region of residence, the Emmett Till lynching perseveres as an integral part of the national narrative on race relations. Emmett Till thus remains a lens through which we can analyze and interrogate media responses to other murders with racial motivations.

1

Emmett Till's America

"If Jesus Christ bore our sins, then Emmett Till bore our prejudices." Mamie Till-Mobley issued this poignant proclamation during a 1989 interview with Studs Terkel. Having grown up in the Church of God in Christ (COGIC) faith tradition, Till-Mobley often used her religion and her faith to make sense of turbulent times in her life. Surely, no event was more turbulent than the brutal 1955 lynching of her fourteen-year-old son, Emmett Louis Till. Her family had a strong connection with the COGIC faith tradition. When the COGIC founder, Bishop Charles Harrison Mason, split from the Church of God, he moved to Mississippi and stayed with Till-Mobley's great-grandmother. Subsequently, the great-grandmother and her family became the first converts to the new COGIC. The tenets of this faith tradition were passed down to Till-Mobley, and she subscribed to the church's teachings. Much to her dismay, around the time of Emmett Till's murder, Till-Mobley's work hours made it difficult for her to attend church.[1]

After the lynching, Mamie Till-Mobley was having difficulty resolving her son's murder in her mind until a "divine" presence told her: "Mamie, it was ordained from the beginning of time that Emmett Louis Till would die a violent death. You should be grateful to be the mother of a boy who died blameless like Christ. . . . Have courage and faith that in the end there will be redemption for the suffering of your people and you are the instrument of this purpose. Work unceasingly to tell the story so that the truth will arouse men's conscience and right can at last prevail."[2] For Mamie Till-Mobley, and arguably for many others who followed the saga in their local and the national press, her son's murder *was* the death of innocence. Countless individuals and organizations entered into the fight for black equality in remembrance of him. Emmett Till was led like a lamb to the slaughter. He was wounded for the two-century-long transgressions of racial slavery and bruised for the century-long iniquities of Jim Crow's white supremacy. His lynching marked a clarion call to justice, and print media outlets across the nation and the world joined his family and civil rights–minded organizations in exposing the horror that resulted from the plague of racism. Truly, through his stripes, Till laid bare the malignant tumors of racial hatred that for too long had suffocated the national ethos of democracy, freedom, and equality.

Mamie Till-Mobley was no stranger to the effects of racism on the lives of African Americans. Born Mamie Elizabeth Carthan on November 23, 1921, in Webb, Mississippi, at the age of two she moved with her mother, Alma Smith Carthan, to a Chicago suburb. The two joined Mamie's father, Willy Nash Carthan, who had migrated to Summit, Illinois (known by natives as Argo), several months earlier to secure work and housing.[3]

Like so many other African Americans who participated in the Great Black Migration, the Carthans left Mississippi in search of greater access to economic and social advancement as well as to escape the untenable racial violence that beset their home state of Mississippi. Reflecting on the push factors that drove the Carthans from the Deep South, Mamie Till-Mobley pronounced that "just about any place else would have been better than Mississippi in the 1920s": "All kinds of stories came out of Mississippi with the black people who were running for their lives. . . . There had been talk of a lynching in Greenwood, Mississippi."[4] While none of the black press sampled confirmed any lynchings in Greenwood in the months surrounding Till-Mobley's January 1924 departure for the Chicago suburbs, Mississippi did register five lynching deaths in 1923, tying the state with Florida as the lynch leaders that year.

Five, a relatively small number, signified a marked decline in the number of lynch murders in Mississippi as well as in the country, and the black-owned and -operated *Broad Axe* (Chicago) quoted NAACP secretary James Weldon Johnson's assessment that "agitation for a federal anti-lynching law and . . . the Northward migration of Negroes by the hundreds of thousands" were most responsible for this welcome decline. In Johnson's estimation, the migration "has borne in on the South that lynching will have to be stopped if the best labor the South can get for its plantations and industries is to be retained." In 1923 and 1924, the Carthan family added their names to the swelling list of black families fleeing the yoke of Mississippi racial oppression for the hopes of a brighter future in northern cities.[5]

Lynching was an all-too-common experience for blacks across the

Deep South, and nowhere was this form of terrorism more woven into the political and social fabric than Mississippi. Mississippi senators and governors held to the Theodore Bilbo model of supporting segregationist and white supremacist policies. Born in 1877, the same year as the end of Reconstruction, Bilbo grew up in a South that idolized "redeemers" in white robes who terrorized and disenfranchised African Americans. Serving Mississippi over four decades as state senator, lieutenant governor, governor, and U.S. senator, he gained the most attention in this last duty because he consistently thwarted efforts to improve the condition of black Americans.[6]

Exemplifying his obstructionist agenda, in 1938 Bilbo blocked voting on a national antilynching bill by participating in a filibuster, and he was such a virulent racist that he supported those black nationalists calling for the colonization of Africa by African Americans. His motivations far from altruistic, Bilbo supported colonization because he wanted to rid his state and the entire United States of what he perceived as a Negro problem. The black press took issue with his blanket dismissal of an entire race, and papers like the *Kansas City (KS) Plain Dealer* called the senator out for suggesting that black Americans were anything but American.[7]

In the wake of World War II, as the seeds of black efforts toward racial advancement began to show minimal signs of fruition, Bilbo shifted his tactics from obstruction to outright racial warfare. While running for reelection in 1946, he boldly demanded unimaginable terrorist attacks on black voters, charging every "red-blooded white man to use any means to keep the niggers away from the polls." Continuing this unveiled call for violence, the senator bellowed: "You know and I know what's the best way to keep the nigger from voting. You do it the night before the election. I don't have to tell you any more than that. Red-blooded men know what I mean." It was clear Bilbo's call to action worked across Mississippi. As Michael Klarman has noted, "crosses were burnt in Jackson. In Biloxi, a sign at a street intersection warned blacks to 'vote at your own risk.' In Pucket, Mississippi, four whites beat a black man and threatened to kill him for attempting to register. Whites brandishing pistols repulsed Medgar Evers and four other black veterans from the polls in Decatur, Mississippi." Despite the fact that black people outnumbered white people in several Mississippi counties, or perhaps precisely because of this fact, only three thousand African Americans were registered to vote in 1946. Of those registered, few were able to cast their ballots. Aggressively lambasting Bilbo's white supremacist electioneering, the NAACP and black newspapers, including the *Kansas City Plain Dealer,* the *Arkansas State Press* (Little Rock), and the *Negro Star* (Wichita, KS), initiated a successful campaign to have Bilbo unseated from Congress in 1947.[8]

Sent to Washington in 1941 to fill the Senate seat left vacant by the death of Pat Harrison, James O. Eastland forwarded equally racist policies. Over the course of thirty-six years, Eastland fought to maintain white rule in his home state. He labeled the 1954 *Brown v. Board of Education* decision a Communist plot. During the 1955 Emmett Till saga, his office disclosed to Mississippi's rabidly racist mainstream press, the *Jackson News,* that Emmett Till's father, Louis Till, had a questionable military record. Furthermore, furious over the enormous outpouring of support Mamie Till-Mobley received during her son's wake and funeral and the shocking photographs of Till's mutilated body that appeared in the black press, Eastland led the effort to make events like Till's open-casket funeral illegal. During the civil rights era, Eastland resurrected the "Lost Cause" rhetoric employed in the wake of the Civil War—an argument that lauded valiant southern efforts to maintain the regional status quo in the wake of the insurmountable forces of outside aggression—as a justification for white supremacy, racial oppression, and lynching. This neo–Lost Cause exacerbated already tense race relations and created a climate of hatred that bred extralegal violence and murder.[9]

Given the culture of racism that fostered and sanctioned such a legacy of racist leaders, it is no wonder that the Carthans joined so many blacks in leaving the Deep South state. As was customary, Willie and Alma Carthan brought their daughter, Mamie, north along the rail lines riding the Illinois Central to greater opportunity in the Chicago suburbs. The Carthans were but three of the more than seventy-five thousand black Mississippians who moved to Illinois between 1910 and 1930 as part of the Great Black Migration. The migration affected the midwestern region more than any other area of the country. Race relations in this region shifted as more African Americans moved to its cities and immediate suburbs searching for employment, housing, and opportunity. Midwestern states saw a massive influx of southerners beginning with the war mobilization in the second decade of the twentieth century. Between 1910 and 1920, the black population increased by 308 percent in Cleveland, 611 percent in Detroit, 148 percent in Chicago, and 114 percent in Milwaukee. Throughout the twentieth century, automobile production in Detroit, food processing and distribution in and around Chicago and Milwaukee, and industrial development in Cleveland transformed these small outposts into major urban hubs.[10]

From 1917 through the early 1940s, African Americans poured into mid-western cities. Much of the reason for the massive growth in the midwest-ern black population is attributable to the fact that black papers, led by the *Chicago Defender,* published job postings and letters from recent migrants. Illinois was uniquely positioned for this population boom because the state, and specifically the city of Chicago, lay on the hub of two railroads and served as a processing and distribution mecca for the food industry. As the twentieth century progressed, increased contact between the races would continue to breed animosity in all midwestern cities. These issues coalesced into what Thomas Sugrue called an *urban crisis.*[11]

Mamie Carthan came of age in and around one of these urban cruci-bles. While she did not grow up with the overt racism and segregation that beleaguered her native Mississippi, covert discrimination circumscribed her daily life, and the regional stories of black migrants forged the racial dispositions in these midwestern industrial hubs. Reflecting in 1956 on the difficulties of being black in Chicago and across the integrated North, Till-Mobley told the *Chicago Defender* that the teachers at her integrated school did little to encourage her academic success even though she "was the first Negro student to make the 'A' honor roll and was the fourth col-ored graduate there." Moreover, the lack of African American teachers to serve as role models made her feel that her goal of becoming a teacher was unobtainable.[12]

Despite these and similar shortcomings, the midwestern region, and really the entire North, still held infinitely more promise for black people than did the Deep South. For this reason, Mamie remembers her mother always encouraging relatives to move from Mississippi to the Midwest. In fact, she described her mother's home as "the Ellis Island" or "the Under-ground Railroad" of Chicago. Whatever the shortcomings of their adopted hometown, Mamie and her mother, Alma, believed that it was "more than five hundred miles and at least a hundred years away from Mississippi."[13]

One of the main reasons black migrants, like Alma Spearman and the *Chicago Defender* publisher John Sengstacke, viewed the Midwest as infinitely better than the Deep South was the employment opportuni-ties found there. Companies like the Illinois Steel Works, Ford Motors, Dodge Motors, and Packard Motors actively pursued black workers. Even as early as 1919, these companies employed thousands of blacks in "all lines" of work.[14]

Entrepreneurs like Henry Ford spent time and money courting African Americans, and one of his plants housed a largely integrated workforce.

His loyalty to the black community, including funding various initiative and uplift programs in the ghettos where, regardless of socioeconomic status, blacks were forced to live, endeared him to African Americans and ensured that they would support him in his business dealings.

Doubtless, large corporations courted and supported black workers in large part because they were barred from membership in unions and their presence on shop floors weakened the union base. Those corporations reasoned that, because they had no union ties and were simply trying to make a living, African Americans would make ideal strikebreakers. Not surprisingly, when black workers decided to support not their employers but their union, those employers quickly ceased their community assistance programs. As a case in point, the close tie between Ford Motors and black workers continued until the 1941 strike, when, as noted in the *Kansas City Plain Dealer,* Congress of Industrial Workers (CIO) officials praised "colored workers," who "have had a decided change of heart[,] joining the CIO in great numbers since the strike." Despite this show of loyalty, the United Auto Workers, a division of the CIO, felt no loyalty to its African American members and did little to assist them. Moreover, after the 1941 strike, black workers saw declining support from their employers as many automotive companies (in particular Ford Motors and General Motors) turned to automation as a means to cut their increasingly unionized (and, thus, more vocal, less loyal, and more expensive) black work force.[15]

As if the unions' snubs were not enough, once they left the shop African Americans like Willie Carthan encountered discriminatory living conditions. With a new influx of black migrants to the North during World War II, cities faced serious postwar overcrowding issues. Exacerbating these problems was the fact that the federal government promised housing and opportunity for returning veterans. As with most policies in that era, the benefits were largely seen only in the white community. African American veterans were not given access to favorable housing; moreover, because of housing segregation, the homes they did find available for purchase were in the overcrowded black ghettos. Adding insult to injury, many of these ghettos were shrinking, owing to urban renewal projects that invariably meant infrastructure improvements requiring the demolition of existing housing in the black communities.

Even with the GI Bill's promise of low-interest mortgages, black veterans were unable to invest in property that would appreciate in value and increase family wealth. Redlining, or the race-based valuation of property on the part of the Federal Housing Authority (FHA), exacerbated a depreciation of housing values in African American neighborhoods. Put simply, the FHA lowered the property value of residences in and around communities that were predominantly inhabited by people of color. Thus, no one wanted to buy houses in areas where African Americans lived. Since blacks could buy property only in segregated ghettos, and since redlining led many urban whites to leave neighborhoods adjacent to these ghettos, homes owned by blacks continued to decline in value while homes in all-white communities saw unprecedented increases in value. Excluded from the suburban dream, many black families turned to whatever government housing remained in the black ghettos.[16]

Tensions that workplace and housing discrimination engendered led to a rise in northern race riots that Roberta Senechal attributes to the pressures of the Great Migration. The influx of African Americans like the Carthans meant increased racial interaction on the factory floor and in public spaces like parks and beaches. The racial animosities and tensions resulting from the migration notwithstanding, blacks, like Mamie's family, still found infinitely more acceptable lives in the Midwest than they did in the Deep South. Life in the covertly racist Midwest still surmounted potential death in the overtly and violently racist Deep South. Blacks in the Midwest, and anywhere outside the South, had much more opportunity to voice their discontent than they would have had in states like Mississippi. For this reason, countless black newspapers and magazines sprang up in the North with the goals of telling the news from the black perspective and spotlighting events that were salient to the black community. Black outlets also existed in the South, but, through both disposition and language used during the Till saga, it is clear the black press outside the South felt more comfortable than their southern allies in voicing their opinions.[17]

Emmett Louis Till was born and raised in this "better land," in these "better racial conditions." He was a product of midwestern racial values and, thus, did not and could not understand what it was like to be black in Mississippi. For this reason, his mother perpetually feared allowing him to go down South to visit his Mississippi relatives. It turns out that her fears were valid, but the reality was that countless African American families made a habit of sending their young people to the Deep South to summer with family. Succumbing to his relentless begging to be allowed to visit Mississippi kin in the summer of 1955, Mamie Till-Mobley acquiesced and agreed that Emmett could ride the Illinois Central down South to Mississippi to stay with her uncle Moses Wright. Till was not the only Illinois cousin to make that fateful journey. His cousin and close friend Wheeler

Parker joined him on that summer vacation, but Emmett was the only one who crossed the unwritten line of racial etiquette and the only one who lost his life as a result.

Emmett Till was not the first African American male murdered in the South, but his death was anomalous because he was a youth and a north-erner, and his murder, which occurred in the wake of the 1954 *Brown v. Board of Education* decision, fanned the flames of regional tension in this country. *Brown,* which outlawed segregation in public schools, was a pro-gressive advancement in response to the long history of racism and racial oppression. However, it led to a potent and violent conservative back-lash that centered on the fear that integration would lead to young white women engaging unwillingly or willingly in sexual relationships with black men. Segregationists argued that miscegenation would weaken the white race because African Americans were "inherently inferior." Addi-tionally, because black men were seen as "hypersexual," they posed a spe-cific threat to white women. The origins of these arguments trace back to the colonial period and were brought to life again through the popular works of Thomas Dixon and D. W. Griffith and the widely accepted schol-arly works of William Dunning and Ulrich B. Phillips. The irrational fears that these racist ideologies created led to a rash of race-based attacks, and Mississippi found itself the epicenter of the racial violence.[18]

After *Brown,* Mississippi in fact saw a small outbreak of lynchings. On May 7, 1955, the Reverend George Lee, a prominent minister, a cofounder of the NAACP chapter in Belzoni, and an activist in the black voter-registration effort, was shot to death. Later that year, Lamar Smith was lynched in Brookhaven, shot after casting his ballot in an election. These two deaths caused some uproar, but, unlike Till, both Lee and Smith were southern adult males who had a history of activism. Their murders did not reach the national prominence that Till's did because they seemed like cases of southern white men taking care of their Negro problem. No news source outside the Deep South offered as much copy space to the Lee and Smith lynchings as they did to Till's murder. Even lynchings after Till's never gained the same national exposure. The deaths of Mack Charles Parker, Herbert Lee, and Medgar Evers, for example, failed to stir the national conscience as did Till's because Parker was a convicted rapist and Lee and Evers were seen as subversives. While Medgar Evers's death did cause a media firestorm and his life continues as a legacy to civil rights activism, few papers outside the Deep South covered these murders in as much detail as they afforded that of Emmett Till. Till's death was different because he did not fit the mold of a lynching victim. He was too young, too northern, too innocent, and too representative of the population *Brown* was supposed to protect.[19]

Writing about white southerners' blatant disregard for—and in fact open defiance of—*Brown,* Pete Daniel argued that in response to the call for racial equality in the twentieth century, southerners resurrected the Lost Cause argument, claiming that outsiders were interfering and disrupting southern race relations. In many ways, southerners embraced their otherness, and, as James Cobb argued, white southerners were "steadfastly and often blindly resisting what they saw as northernization for well over a century."[20]

This response stemmed from the idea of control. White southerners feared losing control of the black population—hence the *Brown* backlash in the face of the much-needed economic growth that integration and racial equality could provide. White men created the specter of miscegenation and the "rape complex" to justify extralegal efforts to control black men. In the archaic southern patriarchal structure, the control of white women was equally paramount, and for white men interracial sex signaled a loss of their hegemony. Not surprisingly, the rape complex and the violence that resulted from it were more pronounced where the black population was the greatest. Despite the massive outmigration of the early part of the twentieth century, the state of Mississippi still housed the largest black population in the nation.[21]

The disproportionately large black population combined with growing pressures for integration led Dewey Grantham to reason: "The epochal Supreme Court decision of 1954 in *Brown v. Board of Education* provoked a movement of massive resistance to public school segregation. Resistance to this movement dominated southern politics in the late fifties, and fostered an intensified politics of race." After *Brown,* most white southern tolerance for the NAACP disappeared amid a "counter-movement . . . to deny the legitimacy of the new definition of values that the integration movement espouse[d] and to prevent the followers of this movement from gaining any greater measure of control."[22]

Movements championing integration and countermovements grounded in strict segregationist principles made for compelling theater, and, from the mid-1950s through the 1970s, media outlets increasingly shone a spotlight on the issues of race in American society. These press reports highlighted flashpoints where American ideals of democracy and equality conflicted with American practices of exclusion and discrimination. Moreover, these contentious hot spots where racial mores trumped national morality were framed as distinctly regional phenomena.

This was the case with the Emmett Till lynching, with newspapers from various regions of the country weighing in on the affair and creating a new and temporary regional focus, *situational regionalism*. Unlike sectionalism ("the idea of separatism and isolation; of separate units with separate interests"), regionalism assumed that the United States is a "homogeneity of varying regions" rather than a loose conglomeration of disparate and irreconcilable ideologies. Despite the backlash to integration and the growing schisms around civil rights, most Americans, regardless of regional affinity, did not lose sight of their desire for a strong and unified country. Adding to the complexity, collective impressions of people's own locale as well as other regions of the country developed within a comparative framework wherein specific regions were defined with reference to other regions of the country. Espousing "regional solutions . . . for the social, economic or political problems" illuminated by the Till lynching, print media outlets framed the saga by highlighting aspects that they felt spoke to their readers' disposition toward race relations. Certainly, the mid-1950s were a time of incredible social, political, and cultural turmoil, and this era engendered a new, fervent resurrection of regionalism.[23]

The regionalism that arose during the Emmett Till coverage was not static; rather, it can be viewed as an evolving ideological response both to people's views of the place in which they live and to how their locale compares to the rest of the nation. Viewed in this manner, the ideological map that developed in response to the Till lynching can be seen as unintended and as not always conforming to what would have been expected given traditional regional boundaries. As we have seen through the Till saga, the regional print media coverage promoted outlets' home turf as the true measure of ideal America while vilifying other areas of the country. Emmett Till scholars have focused almost exclusively on the print media coverage of the saga—a saga that began with Emmett Till's childish actions one August evening. Heightened racial tensions led white Mississippians to view those actions as an affront to the fundamental sanctity of white womanhood, and in response Roy Bryant and J. W. Milam brutalized and murdered Emmett Till in the sweltering heat of an August night.[24]

2

August Nights

When, on August 31, 1955, a fisherman spotted Emmett Till's feet break-ing the surface of the Tallahatchie River, some print media outlets from across the country sprang into action reporting on the event: yet another senseless murder of a black male in the Mississippi Delta. The Till lynch-ing tested the limits of tolerance for racial oppression in the post–World War II era, an often-referenced subject, given national efforts to cham-pion the merits of American democracy over Soviet totalitarianism. Truly, as Mary Dudziak identified the problem, "during the Cold War years, when international perceptions of American democracy were thought to affect the nation's ability to maintain its leadership role, and particularly to ensure that democracy would be appealing to the newly independent nations in Asia and Africa, the diplomatic impact of race in America was especially stark."[1]

As was the case throughout American history, in the midst of the Cold War, African American individuals and groups seized on contemporary rhetoric to scrutinize the nation's race relations and, thus, transferred the salience of the Till lynching into mainstream conscience as seen through heightened coverage by mainstream media outlets. During America's fight for national independence, black people employed revolutionary ideals like democracy and natural rights to lobby for the end of the institution of enslavement. Throughout the antebellum period, African Americans invoked the Bill of Rights as proof that they should enjoy equal citizen-ship. Even Homer Plessy, the unfortunate namesake of the 1896 *Plessy v. Ferguson* Supreme Court decision that solidified segregation as the national policy on race relations, used the Fourteenth Amendment to the Constitution to argue for the rights of blacks to ride alongside whites on the Louisiana rail system. Efforts toward civil rights in the Cold War era offered a spin on long-standing black critiques of American democracy. Amid this anti-Communist environment, the public dismissed as subversive open indictments of the American people as a whole. In response to this climate, individuals and organizations had to focus their attack on subsets of the population whose actions threatened to taint the national narrative of progress in the area of race relations. The national narrative followed Dudziak's argument: "If segregation only existed in particular areas of the country, it would have been easier for the federal government to characterize it as a regional phenomenon." Open indictments of the entire nation found in the rhetoric of Paul Robeson, W. E. B. DuBois, and Josephine Baker failed to garner much popular support during the first decades of the Cold War, and these prominent voices met ridicule and scorn. Surely, as Dudziak notes, through McCarthyism and entities like the House Un-American Activities Committee "the government took steps to silence alternative voices, such as Paul Robeson's, when they challenged the official narrative of race and American democracy." In lieu of blanket accusations, which had found a more welcome audience in the 1930s, prominent civil rights organizations and individuals involved in the struggle turned to regionalism as a means to point up racial woes during and after World War II. These activists foreshadowed James Silver's metaphor of the Deep South, and particularly Mississippi, as a *closed society.* Situational regionalism, read more specifically during this era as efforts to blame the Deep South for all the nations' racial woes, opened the door for criticism of race relations without implicating all Americans in efforts to impede racial progress.[2]

Framing impediments to racial progress as uniquely regional, during World War II and in the postwar years African Americans fought for and realized measurable gains, and by 1955, laws and judicial decisions had challenged disenfranchisement, dictated equal employment, mandated integrated public education, and assimilated whites and blacks in the armed forces. Despite these advances, all was not well with respect to race relations in the United States. Segregation was prolific, disenfranchisement ruled the day, and African Americans continued to struggle against untenable racism and dehumanizing conditions. Given the persistence of these oppressive circumstances, it should come as no surprise that in the Deep South, Till's whistle, an innocent August night prank, engendered a senseless beating and lynching of the boy pictured in figure 2.1.

To differing degrees, newspapers and magazines chose to relate Till's death to the national race relations climate. Within the nationally acceptable narrative, which evolved out of Cold War efforts to regionalize racism, the Till case became a barometer measuring regional dispositions toward

Figure 2.1. P. M., Sketch of Emmett Till (n.d.). *Daily Worker* and *Daily World* Photograph Collection, Tamiment Library and Robert F. Wagner Labor Archives, New York University.

racial and gender norms. This early reading predicted the ways in which these dispositions solidified and proliferated during Emmett Till's funeral ceremonies, the trial of Roy Bryant and J. W. Milam, and the coalescing of the Emmett Till generation.

Only three national outlets, *The Nation, Newsweek,* and *Jet,* reflected on events that occurred before Till's funeral, but these outlets underpinned the saliency of the crime, highlighting the fact that it marked a watershed moment in American race relations. For them, Emmett Till was too young, too northern, too innocent, and too representative of the young black people whom the Supreme Court's 1954 *Brown v. Board of Education* and 1955 *Brown v. Board of Education II* decisions were supposed to protect. Polling data from Gallup showed that the *Brown II* decision—the Supreme Court ruling that desegregation must occur with "all deliberate speed"—was viewed as the most important event of 1955, and Americans doubtlessly drew links between the Till lynching and *Brown* and *Brown II.*[3]

Framing the lynching within the context of such growing racial angst, the national weekly *The Nation* unabashedly recorded: "The kidnap-slaying in Mississippi of Emmett Louis Till . . . is dramatic evidence of the existence of 'a state of jungle fury' in the Deep South which has been mounting in intensity for nearly a year." Characterizing the fury was "the stepped up campaign of the White Citizens Councils against the Supreme Court ruling that segregation in the nation's schools is unconstitutional." Clearly rejecting the need for immediate action necessitated by the violent and racially motivated nature of the Till lynching, Tallahatchie County sheriff H. C. Strider embodied a southern culture of indifference by guessing that "he might get around to making an investigation once it had stopped raining." His unresponsiveness transformed into outright deception as he worked to prove "his theory that the National Association for the Advancement of Colored People (NAACP) might have 'planned and plotted' the murder for propaganda purpose." Unconvinced by Strider's ruse, *The Nation* article drew distinctions between this regional narrative forwarded by the local sheriff and the NAACP national narrative. It surmised that "national opinion clearly supports the petition of the NAACP," a document in which NAACP executive secretary Roy Wilkins lambasted the "wanton killing" as a "logical and inevitable culmination" of Mississippi's reign of terror and accused white citizens councils, housed in southern states, of waging a "thinly-gloved effort to 'persuade' Negroes to . . . forego their demand for civil rights."[4]

Accentuating *The Nation*'s condemnation of southern racial mores, the national magazine *Newsweek* concluded: "Emmitt [*sic*] Louis Till was the victim of a crime which had aroused the Negroes of Chicago more than any crime against a member of their race in recent years." Indeed, Chicagoans joined with many in the Midwest to bemoan the lynchings and other atrocities reported in John H. Johnson's Chicago-based black magazine *Jet*. Quoting Dr. T. R. M. Howard, a black Mississippi physician and civil rights activist, *Jet* staff pointed up regional variations in race relations, arguing: "If this slaughtering of Negroes is allowed to continue, Mississippi will have a civil war. Negroes are going to take only so much." Howard's remarks came to the magazine as part of *Jet*'s "stringer system." As Simeon Booker, a *Jet* journalist, described that system: "In all the rural areas of the South . . . people . . . would submit articles or ideas every week and . . . the press would pay for the best ones." Serving as boots on the ground, these stringers "not only became informers for the articles"; they also served as contacts and guides when outside reporters entered a community. Stringer stories allowed the magazine to localize the reporting process. At the same time, since locals saw the names of friends and family in the article bylines, stringers helped publications like *Jet* develop "a huge new audience in an area that had been forgotten." The stringer system also facilitated the transfer of salience as locals offered emotional analysis of events, thus helping raise their profile in the national narrative.[5]

The Johnson Publishing franchise, which printed *Jet* magazine, afforded at least some journalists the freedom to choose which stories they wanted to cover extensively. Capitalizing on this journalistic freedom, after the discovery of Till's body Simeon Booker and the photographer David Jackson adopted the Till story as their own and documented, in articles and photographs, every aspect of the Till saga. Booker even recalled staying "up all night" with Mamie Till-Mobley "waiting on the body to come in from . . . Mississippi." Such efforts allowed *Jet* to humanize the ghastly story and prime the indignation of people—white and black alike—across the country and around the world. Although *Jet* was a national publication, its staff covered the Till saga in a hometown style that connected readers emotionally with the slain boy and his family. Americans responded instinctively to the heinous crime that emboldened the Emmett Till generation, many of which point to *Jet*'s decision to circulate the gruesome photograph of the disfigured body as the impetus for their protest. The issue in which that photograph appeared sold so many copies that, for the first time in the magazine's history, it had to reprint the edition.[6]

Surely, Emmett Till's murder struck a chord with the public. His youth, or more likely his age combined with the fact that he was native to Chicago, prompted staff at the *Chicago Tribune* and the *Chicago Sun-Times* to join *Jet* in offering vivid images and comprehensive reporting that generated passionate reactions among their readers. Both these mainstream Chicago papers recounted the discovery of the body in striking detail. As the *Tribune* noted, "[Till] was found today in the Tallahatchie river near Pecan point, about 25 miles north of Greenwood and 12 miles north of Money." Accompanying the rich geographic depictions were accounts from H. C. Strider, the racist sheriff, that underscored the heinous nature of the crime and, given Strider's lack of cooperation in the prosecution of the murderers, framed the closed society that sanctioned such a brutal slaying. According to the *Tribune*'s account of Strider's description of what was found when the body was retrieved, Till's murderers attempted to anchor his body in the water using barbed wire and a cotton gin fan wheel "approximately a foot and a half in diameter [and] 150 to 200 pounds." Efforts to hide the corpse failed, however, and Till's body surfaced, complete with "a bullet hole one inch above his right ear . . . [and] the left side of his face . . . beat up—plumb into the skull." The *Tribune,* the *Sun-Times,* and the *St. Louis Post-Dispatch* were the only media outlets—mainstream or black— to print Strider's initial, outraged statement, which would eventually prove to be significant, given that he later testified that the body was too old and too decomposed to have been that of Emmett Till. Others who witnessed firsthand Till's broken and battered corpse buttressed the sheriff's initial outrage at the state of the body. The *Jet* journalist Simeon Booker poignantly recalled viewing Till's remains at the Chicago funeral home, stating: "When they opened the casket in the funeral home . . . I remember a piece of his skull fell off. And my photographer went over and reached over and picked it up and put it back on before he shot a picture." These first-person accounts notwithstanding, Sheriff Strider would soon change his interpretation of events leading up to and including Till's murder.[7]

Strider's cover-up came as no surprise to NAACP officials, who felt it imperative to utilize the Till atrocity to further the causes of racial equality and racial justice. Carefully avoiding blanket indictments of white Americans, the NAACP pounced on the murder and Strider's deception to highlight the racial fever that had surfaced in the South since the 1954 *Brown* decision. Roy Wilkins, the organization's executive secretary, followed the strategy of his predecessor, Walter White, in casting American racial woes as a regional rather than a national epidemic. This strategy had long served the NAACP, and in the 1940s and 1950s, the federal government even commissioned White to mediate disagreements between black and white soldiers and promote national progress on issues involving race relations. Many in the mainstream press addressed the NAACP's regionally focused efforts, noting how Wilkins proclaimed that Till's death qualified as a lynching, a racially motivated murder perpetrated by three or more individuals. Wilkins further asserted "that Mississippi was determined to keep segregation 'by murdering children' if necessary." While most print media outlets at least mentioned Wilkins's lynching accusation, those in the Midwest, including *Jet,* offered their readers the most extensive coverage of NAACP efforts.[8]

Relentlessly pressing the case for racial justice, the NAACP, America's most prominent civil rights organization, raised awareness about the lynching and pushed for vigorous prosecution of the murderers. Allying with NAACP efforts, *Jet* built on its initial coverage of Roy Wilkins, highlighting his wire to Mississippi governor Hugh White, in which he lamented: "We cannot believe that responsible officials of a state will condone the murdering of children on any provocation." Furthering its comprehensive involvement in the Till case, the NAACP also joined with Till's mother, advising her through the saga, and promoting her numerous speaking engagements. Mamie Till-Mobley's poignant commentary underscored the saliency of this murder by personalizing the monstrous nature of this crime, and the midwestern press transferred this saliency by offering the most copy space to covering her efforts.[9]

Both the *Chicago Sun-Times* and the *Detroit News* quoted Till-Mobley as saying in reaction to her son's death: "Someone is going to pay for this. The entire state of Mississippi is going to pay for this." While versions of her call to arms appeared in other mainstream and black press, that found in midwestern papers used the phrase *is going to pay* instead of the *should pay* that was part of almost every other regional paper's coverage. The *Chicago Tribune* printed Till-Mobley's recollection of preparing her son for his trip to the South: "I told him he would have to watch what he said, and how he said it. . . . I told him to avoid trouble . . . and stay out of towns as much as possible."[10]

Without question, the midwestern press was at the vanguard of the racially progressive mainstream treatment of the Till saga. Readers of this region's daily newspapers found full and uncensored coverage of the NAACP responses to Till's death, pointing up the growing tensions between the civil rights group and Mississippi elected officials. Moreover, these newspapers accentuated NAACP efforts to frame Till's death in the broader context of the Cold War position of the United States as the defender of democracy and freedom. Citing William Huff, the Chicago lawyer who served as Till-Mobley's NAACP liaison, the *Chicago Tribune* offered: "The United States is being observed by 'countless millions of the darker people of the world,' and such an act of violence constitutes 'wholesome food for the enemies of our country.'" Similarly, the *Milwaukee Journal* quoted Huff saying, "Those who commit such dastardly acts are themselves enemies to our country." Put simply: "What better ammunition could we give the Communists. . . . Common decency demands that the murderers be brought to justice and this sort of thing stopped."[11]

As midwestern press employees supported the NAACP vision that Emmett Till was emblematic of broader regional racial issues, these papers cast Hugh White as part of the problem, noting that in response to Roy Wilkins's lynching proclamation the governor "scoffed 'They're in the press all the time, that gang.'" White's outright rejection of NAACP efforts to link Till's death to the broader national battles for racial justice evoked storied images of southern whites dismissing, through filibuster, lobbying, and violence, pleas to end the heinous practice of lynching.[12]

Further exemplifying midwestern mainstream press efforts to link white southerners with the long history of irrational and vitriolic racism, the *Detroit News* said of the white citizens' councils: "[They] may not be the old Klan in a bedsheet. It looks more like a new one in a tuxedo." The material the newspaper quoted, which came from a statement issued by the NAACP representative Medgar Evers, was simply another instance of midwestern mainstream newspapers transferring the saliency of these events by offering their pages as a platform for the NAACP's war on the scourge of institutionalized racism. Typifying this initiative, the *Detroit News* further explicated the links between Till's lynching and *Brown*, noting that "the 260 citizens councils in the defiant state of Mississippi [were] Ku Klux Klan in dinner jackets" vehemently rejecting the integration mandate handed down by the highest court in the land.[13]

Governor White, who represented the dinner-jacketed so-called better people of Mississippi, frequently vocalized his complicity in the fight against integration, and midwestern mainstream papers framed nearly every statement from him as completely irrational. Responding in the press to accusations of racial violence and injustice levied against his state, White proclaimed: "If any violence of any kind occurs in Mississippi it will be started by the NAACP." Although the governor did not acknowledge it, violence, in the form of Emmett Till's lynching, had already occurred, and the *Detroit News* blamed the so-called better white people of Mississippi, who, along with their governor, insisted: "We're just not going to have integration in Mississippi, Supreme Court or no Supreme Court. Our people won't stand for it." This palpable intransigence on the part of the old southern guard spilled over the pages of midwestern mainstream papers and offered rich and moving commentary on the state of race relations in at least some southern locales. Coverage found in midwestern dailies established a disposition of objection to the vile and cancerous racism currently plaguing Mississippi; however, it was the midwestern black press that best traced the historical narrative of racial violence, placing the Till lynching within the annals of southern racial oppression and white supremacy.[14]

Mattie Colin and Robert Elliot, reporters for the *Chicago Defender,* best highlighted the saliency of the crime, emphasizing: "Even Mississippi's Gov. Hugh White, traditionally silent on such matters, promised a complete investigation and full prosecution of persons responsible." Of course, initially, at least, prosecution seemed unlikely given the current state of public opinion. Elsewhere they wrote:

> The blood of "Bo" Till is on the hands of the five candidates for governor who campaigned on an anti-Negro platform in the recent elections. They charged the atmosphere of the state for acts of violence.
>
> We accuse these rabble-rousers [of] contributing directly to the murder of "Bo" Till and the lynching of American reputation for decency and respect for law and order in the eyes of the entire world.

And they ended with a call for government intervention: "It is up to the administration in Washington to begin action once and for all to end the crime of lynching that has degraded our nation." This was not the first such call. The organized struggle to abate lynch murders dated back to 1882, the year the Tuskegee Institute began to catalog lynching deaths. In response to such extralegal killings, in 1921 Leonidas Dyer, a Republican congressman from Missouri, introduced the most well-known antilynching legislation, and three times, in 1922, 1923, and 1924, the bill made it through the House of Representatives only to have old guard southerners stall it in the Senate through filibuster.[15]

Pressed by the NAACP, Congress in the 1930s readdressed antilynching legislation in the form of the Costigan-Wagner Anti-Lynching Act, and southern legislators again banded together to defeat the bill. Mississippi's own Theodore Bilbo was one of the leaders of the 1938 filibuster of this legislation, delivering long and vividly racist diatribes designed to stall the legislative process long enough for the bill to expire before it could come to a vote. Bilbo ignited a racist firestorm when he said of the Costigan-Wagner Act: "If you succeed in the passage of this bill, you will open the floodgates of hell in the South. Raping, mobbing, lynching, race riots, and crime will be increased a thousandfold." He further warned: "Upon your garments and the garments of those who are responsible for the passage of the measure will be the blood of the raped and outraged daughters of Dixie, as well as the blood of the perpetrators of these crimes that the red-blooded Anglo-Saxon White Southern men will not tolerate." As part of the successful filibuster, Bilbo essentially predicted that violence inevitably would result from civil rights legislation.[16]

Buoyed by the defeat of the Costigan-Wagner legislation, Bilbo spent nearly a decade intensifying his vitriolic rhetoric. His vile war on black America reached a head when, leading up to the 1946 election, the senator issued a plea for open violence, urging: "I call on every red-blooded white man to use any means to keep the niggers away from the polls." By this time, the nation had reached its limits, and the Senate ended Bilbo's national political career by refusing to seat him when the new Congress entered into session in January 1947. Although Bilbo lost his congressional soapbox, others would fill the void and continue his clarion call for the oppression of African Americans at any cost. Given this pedigree of racism, it should come as no surprise that white southerners, and specifically white Mississippians, would be the champions of segregation, racial oppression, and the defense of lynching.[17]

Indeed, in the eyes of the *Defender* journalist Mattie Colin, Emmett Till proved that the Old South closed society still existed in Mississippi. Consequently, she asked of Mississippi:

> Could it be possible that one of the poorest economic states in the Union, who should thank Negroes for their agricultural contribution for the meager wealth that it has, is still fighting the civil war? Could it be possible that in Mississippi's blind frenzy to continue to humiliate Negroes, they cannot observe their lack of public health education, in which the so-called poor white trash suffer along with the Negroes? Could it be possible that they are in a dream world, thinking that "Cotton" is still KING, and therefore cannot see the forest for the trees?

For the midwestern black press, this forest was the growing need to address America's racial tension in the wake of the *Brown* decisions, and Till's death represented what Abel Meeropol's poem "Bitter Fruit" identified as a tree marking, in the words of the *Cleveland Call and Post,* "Mississippi's reign of terror against Negroes following the Supreme Court's decision on segregated schools." As Meeropol himself put it:

> Southern trees bear a strange fruit,
> Blood on the leaves and blood at the roots,
> Black body swinging in the Southern Breeze,
> Strange fruit hanging from a poplar tree.

Meeropol's poem, later adapted into Billy Holiday's 1939 hit single "Strange Fruit," captured the regional focus of America's racial dilemma. Clearly, Meeropol's and Holiday's visions of lynching, articulated through the midwestern black press analysis of Till's death, did not resonate across the country, for some regions invoked a different narrative of the Emmett Till lynching.[18]

Belying pointed condemnations of the Deep South in the midwestern black and mainstream press, northeastern mainstream outlets initially contextualized the murder as a response to some social *ill* perpetrated by the fourteen-year-old youth because they had yet to comprehend the saliency of the lynching within the national narrative on race relations. As if excusing the murder, the *Pittsburgh Post-Gazette* charged: "[Till] whistled the two notes of the wolf call at Mrs. Roy Bryant." The *Philadelphia Evening Bulletin* and the *New York Times* alleged that Till made "ugly remarks" to Carolyn Bryant. Joining its regional competitors, the *Philadelphia Inquirer* indicated that the youth "made some *obscene* remark to Mrs. Bryant." Admittedly, *Bulletin* staffers acknowledge that it was unusual in 1955 for any paper in the Philadelphia area to cover a race story in depth.[19]

The NAACP national leadership was also rebuked by the northeastern mainstream papers, which framed the organization as intemperate and intrusive. The *Inquirer* and the *Bulletin,* although using different news wire sources for their articles, made Wilkins's August 1955 press release look biased by framing it as a "bitter statement." Moreover, the *Pittsburgh Post-Gazette,* while not calling Wilkins's statement *bitter,* engaged in a similar qualifying practice. It quoted Ed Cochran, the president of the Greenwood, Mississippi, NAACP chapter, as offering a "milder outlook" where he "urged his people to keep calm" because he had "not lost faith in a trial by jury." By not acknowledging the perceived or real coercion that could have led a black Mississippian like Cochran to issue a "milder" outlook, the *Post-Gazette* minimized Wilkins's actions by framing an intra-NAACP dispute between the southern insider Cochran and the outsider Wilkins.[20]

The nation's most recognizable newspaper, the *New York Times,* which in many cases was more accurately viewed as a national media outlet, in the case of the Till saga followed a northeastern regional disposition of cautious reaction. Choosing not to print any of the NAACP's press releases, the *Times*'s editors instead included statements from the National Urban League, a more conservative civil rights organization. Following the cues of the *Pittsburgh Post-Gazette,* the *New York Times* framed an intraorganizational squabble by highlighting the objections of one Edwin E. Dunaway to the statement released by the league at its yearly convention. Dunaway, a white Arkansan, "objected to the part that said: 'The kidnap-lynching in Mississippi was compounded by a tragically irresponsible attitude of substantial elements of the state and its leaders.'" He protested because he felt that the league could express its "outrage without a blanket indictment of the people of Mississippi." While Dunaway's racial and regional dispositions could have had an effect on his views, by omission the *New York Times* refused even to consider race or region as a mitigating factor in his decision to object to the organization's condemnation of Till's lynching.[21]

Correspondence between the *New York Times* publisher, Turner Catledge, and the paper's southern desk reporter John Popham highlights how the *Times* chose to approach the Till case with a sense of caution. Responding to Popham's anxieties that the *Times*'s "handling of the Till case may be the last time anyone is going to be able to get out and get decent respect for balanced coverage," Catledge expressed significant concern. This distress led the publisher to visit the Deep South, and he came away "not only depressed but frightened," for he felt that race relations in the South "had deteriorated so rapidly . . . that it is impossible to measure the extent of it." In his estimation, "emotion has taken place of all reason . . . [for] these damn citizen's councils are also applying economic pressure where it really hurts and people with any sense of decency and justice are running for cover." Despite viewing firsthand the growing racial antagonism in the Deep South, Catledge defended his paper's moderate disposition toward problems in the region. He wrote Popham on the topic: "I think your idea of coverage from our standpoint is the right one for the time being." Such a response was emblematic of the *Times* and other northeastern mainstream publications' slow-motion coverage of civil rights issues "at a time when the movement and resistance to it were spreading and accelerating."[22]

Like the *New York Times,* the *New York Post* did not cover the NAACP's statements; however, this more liberal Big Apple newspaper offered an ironic quote that accentuated the persistence of racial oppression in the South and positioned the paper as the most cynical news voice in the Northeast. Freely using racist epithets, the Leflore County deputy sheriff John Cothran lamented: "The white people around here feel pretty mad about the way that poor little old nigger boy was treated. . . . Northerners always think that we don't care what white folks do to the niggers down here, but that's not true. The people around here are decent, and they won't stand for this." From the introduction of slave codes in the South beginning in the 1640s, *decency* has meant masking the dehumanization of people of African descent with the thin veil of paternalism and employing violence and intimidation to maintain white supremacist doctrine. For many white people acculturated in such environs, Emmett Till was simply another "poor little nigger boy."[23]

As usual, for the black press transferring the saliency of the event to its readers and offering a counternarrative to mainstream efforts at objective and nonjudgmental reporting were paramount. Unlike their regional mainstream counterparts, the northeastern black newspapers railed against the racially charged culture of white supremacy that condoned vile epithets and sanctioned lynching. However, at this early stage, their coverage did not match, in either scope or scale, the reports from their midwestern compatriots. Northeastern black outlets focused their attention and efforts on defending the NAACP—not surprising, given the disparaging depiction of it in northeastern mainstream papers. Opposing the anti-NAACP disposition of the mainstream press of their regions, black papers like the *Philadelphia Tribune* set about linking "the barbaric practice of lynching" with Mississippi's efforts to "defeat public school integration." Of the 1955 Mississippi lynchings of the Reverend George E. Lee and Emmett Till, the *New York Amsterdam News* noted: "Neither of these tragic crimes can be classified as incidents of passion and violence that just happened." Instead, "public officials have gone about the State encouraging disorder by their repeated denouncements of the recent U.S. Supreme Court decision on segregation in the public schools," and "white citizens have stressed racial hatred in their various councils and states [*sic*] rights groups set up to protect white supremacy." For northeastern black press employees, Emmett Till died a gruesome death because his northern mind could not comprehend the violent and vitriolic racism in Mississippi. Hammering home this point, the *Pittsburgh Courier* alleged that Emmett Till was "sacrificed on the altar of a fallacious 'White Supremacy' doctrine" because, despite his mother's warning, he "couldn't believe that any place in America was so barbaric . . . such a throwback to the 'Savage Age' that they would take a life for naught." Surely, these black press reports foreshadowed what was summed up in the two-word title of Nina Simone's 1964 hit "Mississippi Goddam." *Courier* staff, including the executive editor, P. L. Prattis, the white staff writer James Boyack, and the columnist and social critic George Schuyler, joined their fellows at other papers in employing the often-referenced contrast between northern progress and southern entrenchment.[24]

The contrast did not elude members of the southeastern region's mainstream press—attempting to nuance the narrative of white southern racial views, these papers framed southeastern states as reformist and allied with like-minded Deep South elites in a movement against Old South racial mores. Buoyed by a cadre of progressive southeastern white publishers, newspaper staff from this region offered a narrative of their region challenging the ensconced racial oppression found in the Deep South. However, these publications refused to support the NAACP. As such, they missed the importance of pointing up civil rights organizations as a way to combat the vile racism of the Deep South. In truth, the regional interest in racial segregation was more salient to them than the promotion of the founding principles of democracy and equality. In the eyes of the scholars Gene Roberts and Hank Klibanoff, these journalists "would write and speak with proselytic power and majesty of the newly converted," and they "could be relied on to push for national unity." While this may be the case, Roberts and Klibanoff also credit them with "rising above" regionalism when in actuality they reinscribed southern regional narratives of racial oppression.[25]

As a rule, the southeastern mainstream press focused its criticism on the poor white people who clung desperately to violent means of racial oppression and the NAACP, which goaded those poor whites into acts of violence. To that point, the *Charlotte Observer* editorialized: "There's little you can say about the death of Emmett Louis Till except that it was murder in its most sickening form—heartless, emotional, inflamed, senseless, stupid." Adding to the despicable nature of the crime, the *Observer* editorialist lamented: "Somebody killed a 14-year-old child because he whistled at a white woman. Because he happened to be black. Because he was a Negro from Chicago, visiting in Mississippi during a time of racial awareness. Because of a grotesque combination of time and circumstance, chance and impulse." Grasping the obvious connection between the lynching of Emmett Till and the *Brown* decisions, the editorial continued: "Murder is never pretty. This one could have happened anywhere and it would still have been ugly. That it happened in Mississippi—when it did, as it did—gives it a shameful connotation. There will be other murders in the South before the desegregation issue is settled unless southerners generally take a good long look at where they are heading." Under the tutelage of the integrationist C. A. McKnight, at least some of this paper's staff had taken this reflexive step, and they were encouraging others to do the same. As the *Observer* pointed out, whites were not trying to mediate the growing animosity. Instead: "The Ku Klux Klan is stirring. Citizens Councils are organizing. 'Patriot' groups are waving the banner of white supremacy." In this untenable climate, the Till death had even greater implications because it was emblematic of the irrational elements of the white citizenry. Focusing on this key issue, the editorial concluded: "We don't know who murdered Louis Till. It seems absurdly clear, however, that he died as a victim of prejudice. It isn't a reasonable way for a human being to die, or a civilized mood to kill in."[26]

While southeastern mainstream news outlets like the *Charlotte Observer* offered gripping condemnation of Till's murder, the region's four dailies—the *Washington Post,* the *Richmond Times-Dispatch,* the *Charlotte Observer,* and the *Atlanta Constitution*—judged the NAACP to be part of the problem and criticized its statements and actions. Even though they could go as far as condemning the murder, they could not ally with the NAACP and other civil rights organizations, for, in their minds, that alliance would mean they themselves were complicit in the fight for integration. Framing the NAACP as an organization of race baiters, southeastern mainstream papers accused the organization of stepping into the Till case and hurling demands on the white officials in Mississippi. To that point, the *Washington Post* employed a clear rhetorical attack, claiming that the NAACP "branded" the *lynching* moniker on the case and that this would only fuel racial tension. The only case where southeastern mainstream papers offered supportive analysis of the black actors in the Till saga came in their coverage of Mamie Till-Mobley. Along with the midwestern mainstream press, the *Chicago Tribune,* the *Chicago Sun-Times,* the *St. Louis Post-Dispatch,* and the *Milwaukee Journal* all printed her charge: "Someone is going to pay for this. The entire State of Mississippi is going to pay for this." The *Observer* chose to print this additional reaction of Till-Mobley's: "I can't think; I just can't think. I'm frozen. He didn't do anything to deserve that." This pathos-riddled appeal aside, southeastern mainstream papers honored what they saw as courageous efforts on the part of better whites in the Deep South to mete out justice against Till's murderers.[27]

Exemplifying the privilege afforded to officials of the Deep South state, southeastern papers' reports contrasted allegations of NAACP rhetorical violence with Mississippi's quick response to the crime. The *Richmond Times-Dispatch* staff raved that the Mississippi governor calmed tensions by informing the NAACP that "parties charged with the murder are in jail" and "the court will do their duty in the prosecution." Since the 1940 unification of the relatively liberal *Richmond Times-Dispatch* and the relatively conservative *Richmond News Leader* under the ownership of the Bryan family, both papers' staffs endeavored to serve their respective samplings of the Richmond population; however, the publishers had the ultimate say over the tenor of reporting. When it came to issues of civil rights, the Bryans mandated that both papers lean toward a conservative and segregationist stand, even though the *Times-Dispatch* editor, Virginius Dabney, had won a Pulitzer Prize in 1948 for his editorial attacks on segregated public transportation and poll taxes in Richmond. The Bryans' biases were particularly apparent when it came to the *Brown* decision. They dictated that the *Times-Dispatch*'s Dabney, a native Virginian who had worked his way up the ranks of the paper since joining the team in 1928, remain silent on the Supreme Court ruling. Conversely, the *News Leader*'s conservative editor, James Jackson Kilpatrick, had free reign to rail against the decision. Since the Till lynching was so closely aligned in time and circumstance with the desegregation decision, it was only natural that the Bryan family would push *Times-Dispatch* staff to take a moderate, if not conservative, view of the lynching, and reports from the supposedly liberal source stand as a hallmark to this publishing manipulation. Similarly, a review of the *News Leader* from September 1 to September 30, 1955, reveals that the newspaper offered no coverage of the lynching and scant coverage of the trial.[28]

The *Charlotte Observer* went even further in justifying Mississippi governor Hugh White's reaction by printing the same release offered in the *Times-Dispatch,* under the title "Boy's Slaying Brings Wrath of Governor." As was the case with the Richmond papers, publishers' directives limited the *Observer*'s C. A. McKnight's editorial freedom. In 1954, while directing the pro-*Brown* Southern Education Reporting Service, McKnight not only promoted integration but also pushed the hiring of African American teachers. However, in the newsroom during the 1950s and 1960s, southern newsmen like him and Harry Ashmore, the prointegrationist executive editor of the *Arkansas Gazette* (Little Rock), had to moderate their views on integration in order to maintain their jobs, forward a slow push for change in the racial hierarchy, and prevent riots among both the white population and the black. McKnight, who returned to Charlotte, North Carolina, in 1955 as the editor of the *Charlotte Observer,* toed this line. In Charlotte, he encountered ideological conflict with the publishing team of John S. Knight and James L. Knight, who supported segregation and lamented "the American Negro . . . pushing a little too far and much too fast" for equality. McKnight's integrationist leanings came in conflict with the segregationist ethos of his paper's publishing team, and, over the course of a decade, he would fight increasingly for the recognition of black equality in all aspects of life.[29]

Despite the concessions around racial equality achieved in the 1960s, during the Till saga the *Charlotte Observer* went even further than the *Richmond Times-Dispatch* in justifying Governor Hugh White's reaction to the lynching. Clearly, the title "Boy's Slaying Brings Wrath of Governor" supported claims made by Mississippi officials. As such, while the *Observer* and *Times-Dispatch* articles were identical, the *Observer* title raised the bar of support for the governor, arguing that he was infuriated over the murder of Emmett Till and that, in this enraged state, he was going to do everything in his power to ensure that Till's death was vindicated.

In framing similar to that of the Richmond and Charlotte papers, the *Atlanta Constitution* noted: "Gov. Hugh White ordered local officials today to 'fully prosecute' two white men for the abduction-slaying of a Chicago Negro teen-ager who allegedly leered and whistled at the wife of one of the suspects." Additionally, "he instructed authorities here to 'press the case' against storekeeper Roy Bryant and his half-brother, J. W. Milam." Framed as they were by the *Atlanta Constitution* staff, the governor's directives showed his concern about the legal process, but his insistence on two perpetrators negated the lynching claim, which necessitates at least three killers. Moreover, the *Constitution* editors did not interrogate White's accusation that Till leered and whistled at a white woman. Given the *Constitution* editor Ralph McGill's approval of the cautious and nonjudgmental coverage offered by the *New York Times*'s John Popham, it should come as no surprise that the Atlanta mainstream daily forwarded an analysis that praised Mississippi officials' handling of the Till case. However, all was not well in Mississippi, and, while the southeastern main-stream press lauded White and other state officials for openly promoting vigorous prosecution, they never questioned the governor's failure to offer any state resources to the ill-equipped and unmotivated Tallahatchie County sheriff.[30]

Similarly, Mississippi state officials, including the district attorney who prosecuted the case and the special prosecutor appointed by the governor to assist in the trial, simply accepted Sheriff Strider's lies about the identification of Till's body. District Attorney Gerald Chatham said of Strider's deception: "When we took over the case, I was assured by Stanny Sanders [district attorney for the adjoining district] that there is no question of corpus delicti." Without questioning the sheriff's motives or evidence, "Chatham said Strider's statement complicated the issue" because now he "would certainly have to prove the death." The *Richmond Times-Dispatch* shared Chatham's blind faith, for it failed to question Strider's motives. As they defended Mississippi's reaction to the lynching, the *Charlotte Observer,* the *Washington Post,* and the *Richmond Times-Dispatch* gave credence to the sheriff's accusations, which they reprinted: "The body we took from the river looked more like that of a grown man instead of a young boy. It was also more decomposed than it should have been after the short stay in the water." Adding fuel to the raging animosity this region's mainstream press felt toward the NAACP, a position forwarded by the publishers rather than the editors, the *Observer* mimed Strider's conclusion: "The whole thing looks like a deal made up by the National Assn. for the Advancement of Colored People." Clearly, the titles "Doubts Body That of Till" and "Sheriff Says Body Found May Not Be Chicago Boy," printed in the *Observer* and the *Times-Dispatch,* respectively, buttressed the sheriff's argument.[31]

Refusing to countenance regional mainstream support of Mississippi officials and condemnation of the NAACP, editors of southeastern black newspapers accentuated the barbarism that necessitated action on the part of the civil rights organization. Perhaps no paper stated the issues more plainly than the *Norfolk (VA) Journal and Guide* when it printed: "Now that the nation has learned that residents of Mississippi will even lynch 14-year-old boys in their effort to keep the flag of white supremacy flying high, officials of the state are 'passing the buck' onto the already heavily-weighted shoulders of the NAACP."[32]

As the only major black daily newspaper, the *Atlanta Daily World* was out front of the saga. From day one of its coverage, the *Daily World* left no doubt about its sentiments on the matter, offering analysis of the press releases from the NAACP's Roy Wilkins and William Henry Huff. For the latter, unlike other papers, the *Daily World* printed an additional portion of the statement where the NAACP legal counsel accused: "Those who do nothing toward bringing such criminals to justice are themselves parties to the crime." Since lynching was a real danger confronting most blacks, particularly in the South, the southeastern black press could readily identify with Till's lynching and see a disturbing pattern of continuity. Moreover, by deeming the unresponsive and indifferent Deep South officials as parties to the crime, *Daily World* staff added their names to the list of perpetrators. Essentially, the paper framed Till's death as a postmortem lynching by implicating Sheriff H. C. Strider, Governor Hugh White, and District Attorney Gerald Chatham in the crime. Till's death was unlike the morbid fairground spectacles of the past, however. A *Daily World* editorial proclaimed: "Traveling from the early scenes of yesterday's enactment of the orgies of rope and faggot, we come to a new order meant to obtain the same objective as the old. This underground course is nevertheless as much a violation of one's civil rights as the other." In fact, the paper argued that time and place made this "new order" worse than the old: "We now come to this sad pass of seeing this ugly head of lynching move again above the troubled waters of this cold war in which we find ourselves engulfed."[33]

While the Cold War was changing the global context, the southeastern black press brought home the fact that Mississippi remained the epitome of racism and cultural backwardness. Setting the pulse for the C. A. Scott–published *Atlanta Daily World,* the paper's managing editor, William Gordon, maintained that "'you can get lynched quicker in Mississippi than any other state,' is still a familiar saying by those who knew of this state, the background of its political temperament, the geography, and the mentality of the people who run the state." Immorality reigned in Mississippi, and, in Gordon's estimation, the state's political leaders had committed unprecedented crimes against humanity and, therefore, "should get down on their knees, not on Sundays, but each day and give thanks that the Almighty has not broken wrath against them." As Gordon noted: "The killing of a 14-year-old boy in Mississippi means just another notch added to the gun of 'lynch law' in the state."[34]

Accentuating the barbarism, the *Daily World* noted: "Since 1882, Mississippi has led the country in lynchings, holding the record of more than 11 percent of all in the country. Only three years, since 1932, has the state been without a lynching." While taking conservative stances on some race issues, including civil protest and the negative effects of housing integration on black businesses, Scott directed his paper to be unapologetically critical when it came to lynching. The *Daily World* wanted its readers to understand the political, racial, and historical context in which the Till lynching occurred. In its view, Mississippi was through and through the heart of the closed society, and civil rights organizations like the NAACP were right to lambaste it for its torrid past, intemperate present, and hazy future.[35]

Truly, responses varied by region, but Till's murder drew at least a modicum of indignation in the national press and regional outlets from the Midwest, the Northeast, and the Southeast. Significantly, confrontational dispositions toward Deep South racism did not infuse western mainstream newspaper coverage. As was the case with southeastern mainstream papers, the NAACP found neither sympathy nor support in the pages of western regional mainstream papers. Instead of condemning or qualifying statements from the civil rights organization, western dailies almost exclusively chose to avoid references to it altogether. Notably, only the *Daily Oklahoman* (Oklahoma City) printed Wilkins's accusatory statement about maintaining white supremacy "by murdering children." Moreover, the *Seattle Times* painted Till's death as anomalous rather than characteristic of the state of race relations and racial oppression in Mississippi, stating: "The last previous established case of lynching in the United States occurred in 1951." In a reversal of the motif found in the midwestern press, the West chose to downplay the lynching as the exception rather than the rule of Deep South racial norms.[36]

Early coverage of the Emmett Till lynching in the western mainstream newspapers presented a picture of southern officials aggressively investigating the murder. *Seattle Times* and *Los Angeles Times* articles quoted Governor White as saying: "I have called upon the district attorneys of Tallahatchie and Leflore Counties to make a complete investigation and fully prosecute the guilty parties." Shaping the tenor of the coverage, the former, a paper owned by the Blethen family, privileged local stories over national, while the latter, part of the Norman Chandler–headed Times Mirror Company, took a conservative stance on all issues including race relations.[37]

The Palmer Hoyt–edited *Denver Post* was generally more liberal than either the Seattle or the Los Angeles mainstream papers, but this liberalism did not emerge during coverage of Emmett Till. Instead, the *Post* offered editorials in support of Mississippi whites, like the one that trumpeted: "The local district attorney has brought charges against the accused slayers of the boy and Governor White of Mississippi has joined Governor Stratton of Illinois in denouncing the violent outcome and demanding a full investigation." Accentuating the argument that promoted Mississippi officials' judicious handling of the case, a *Seattle Times* article asserted that Chicago mayor Richard J. Daley felt that "the full force of our country's law enforcement agencies, both state and federal, will see to it that whoever committed this terrible crime is brought to justice." Actually, Daley's statement was part of a longer letter to President Eisenhower asking for federal intervention in the case, but, exhibiting a disposition of indifference, western dailies promoted half facts over incisive coverage of the Till lynching.[38]

Representative mainstream newspapers from the West consistently highlighted the belief that white Mississippians could handle the case without any outside intervention. To that end, the *Denver Post* argued, "There is every reason to believe the case will be handled properly and justly through the regular processes of the courts." This view rested on the premise that "there is impressive evidence that the principle of anti-discrimination is making rather remarkable headway—even in the deep south which has developed a surprising number of spokesmen for racial equality." Perhaps the *Post* and the *Seattle Times* counted citizens council members among the ranks of these morally reformed southerners—a notion that their southeastern mainstream counterparts rejected—for both papers quoted a response to the Till lynching from Robert Patterson, the White Citizens Council executive secretary. In Patterson's estimation, the murder had nothing to do with citizens council efforts to maintain segregation. His rationale? "'One of the primary reasons for our organization is to prevent acts of violence.'" As western mainstream papers refused to deal with the obvious racial implications of Till's murder and the natural link between the lynching and the NAACP's fight for integration, Patterson's statements appeared as an honest assessment of the racial climate in Mississippi.[39]

The misrepresentation of the racial climate found in western mainstream papers prompted the western black press to speak out in protest and, thus, to transfer the salience of the event to their readers, who could not find such pointed commentary anywhere else. From the very beginning of its coverage of the Till case, the *Los Angeles Sentinel* left no doubt that it was supremely suspicious of Mississippi officials who claimed that they were shocked at the lynching of Emmett Till and promised an investigation of the murder. In an editorial entitled "An Investigation, Then What?" the *Sentinel* asserted: "It is magnanimous of Gov. Hugh White of Mississippi to promise an investigation into the brutal kidnap-slaying of 14-year-old Emmett Louis Till, but if the results of similar probes by the governor are any barometer, his findings will fall far short of satisfaction." Moreover, the paper argued, "That Governor White is horror-stricken by young Till's murder somehow doesn't ring true. He was elected on the promise to fight integration with his last gasp, and is surrounded by officials similarly dedicated." In the opinion of the *Sentinel,* the most important question that begged for an answer was "What happens when the murderers face an all-white jury of their peers. Will they get the usual polite wrist-slapping?" Even in these early days of coverage, the answer was painfully evident to the *Sentinel.*[40]

The *Sentinel* staff saw through the obvious lie that the lynching of Till was simply the byproduct of white men's outrage over a black male violating the sanctity of white womanhood. This was structural violence. As the paper maintained: "We suspect there is more behind the sordid slaying than the indignation of outraged men or a Negro violation of the 'sanctity' of white womanhood, since neither premise, nor the lad's alleged actions, justify such actions. What then was actually behind the lynching?" The answer was clear: "The wanton murder is the latest in a series of terror tactics designed to put 'the fear of God' in the hearts of Mississippi Negroes who are at last demanding their rights." Despite acute white racism and discrimination as well as violence launched against them in Mississippi, blacks were pushing for equality, and the *Sentinel* applauded their efforts. Couched in the white concern with black demands for equal rights was the monumental *Brown v. Board of Education* decision outlawing public school segregation. In the *Sentinel*'s estimation, there was no difference between poor whites and the so-called better people of the South. Consequently, "White Mississippians—from top officials to the lowest sharecropper—are challenging the law in the only manner they know how—trial by terror."[41]

Buttressing this indictment of southern whites as backward and criminal, one angry letter from an African American New Yorker, Elizabeth Hines, blasted: "Your great grandfathers should have told you that you came from the jails of England and Ireland, as criminals and murderers. Our background can be traced all the way back to King Solomon, King Tutt and King Nebuchadnezzar." Although blanket generalizations, the historical connections in this letter held some validity, and, in light of her history lesson, Hines asked: "How could you class yourselves as a superior race than the Black race?" Finally, she played on white southerners' all-consuming fear of black retaliation, asking: "Suppose we get as ignorant as you are and start lynching white men of the South as you are doing to my people in the South." Above all, white southerners feared that they would have to redress centuries of brutality and oppression directed toward African Americans, and, as Emmett Till's name was added to the annals of senseless violence in defense of white supremacy, his murder only enhanced these fears.

More than any other locale, the Deep South needed to atone for racial violence. Refusing to admit to the long legacy of vitriolic racial oppression, the Deep South mainstream press sought dispensation and attempted to reform the region's image by announcing that most southern whites, specifically those in Mississippi, did not condone the murder of Emmett Till. Underscoring this point, an editorial in the *Memphis Commercial Appeal* asserted, "Mississippi and Tallahatchie County are proceeding in lawful manner to solve the recent murder of a young Negro and to bring those responsible to justice. It is regrettable that such a tragedy occurred." Additionally, the *Appeal* noted: "The crime against the Negro was a terrible thing. . . . [W]e want to see justice done." The paper was also convinced that "the State of Mississippi and its people will see to it that it is done in a manner that the law prescribes—on the basis of incontrovertible evidence and with reasonable speed." The *Delta Democrat-Times* (Greenville, MS) chimed in by asserting: "We have met no Mississippian who was other than revolted by the senseless brutality of the kidnap-slaying of the 15-year-old [*sic*] Negro youth near Greenwood this past weekend." It called for those guilty of such a savage crime to be prosecuted fully. The *Vicksburg (MS) Post* (as quoted in the *Jackson [MS] Daily News*) concurred with the *Appeal* and the *Democrat-Times*. In the opinion of its staff: "The ghastly and wholly unprovoked murder . . . cannot be condoned, nor should there be anything less than swift and determined prosecution of those guilty of the heinous crime. We must not stand by and let this crime go unpunished."[42]

Deep South papers also employed testimonials from residents to drive home their argument that racial harmony was a hallmark of their culture. For example, in Money, Ben Roy, a white merchant, said: "Nobody here, Negro or white, approves of things like that. It's too bad this had to come at a time when there is so much talk about racial tension." Ruben Neal, a white service station operator, added: "I hate that this happened in our neighborhood." Moreover, "In Greenwood, 10 miles south of Money, Sam Ezell, a white citizen of that city, called the slaying 'the worst thing that could have happened to disturb racial relationships.'" William Street wrote in the pages of the *Commercial Appeal*: "People of both races have always trusted each other. Why, there are only a few white people in Sumner who would hesitate to leave their children with a trusted Negro woman." Furthermore, he noted: "Sumner folks are friendly and go out of the way to make visitors feel at home. There is an atmosphere often evident in small towns where everybody knows everybody else. They all join hands to welcome strangers. . . . If any tension was felt by either race, it wasn't evident." The *Delta Democrat-Times* also promoted the illusion of harmony between the races in Mississippi by zeroing in on a story in which a young white girl, Dianne Kearney of Money, Mississippi, saved the life of a black nurse.[43]

Offering credence to the belief that Bryant and Milam would find summary justice, the *Jackson Daily News* argued that black people enjoyed more leniencies in the Deep South penal system than whites. The 1954 acquisition of the paper by the racist Mississippi Publishing Company owners T. M. and R. M. Hederman, who also owned the rival *Jackson (MS) Clarion-Ledger,* offered the *Daily News* editor Frederick Sullens the ideological and financial mandate to heighten the white supremacist coverage he had firmly established prior to the buyout. With Till, the Hederman cousins, who were close friends and ardent supporters of Senator James Eastland (D-MS), along with Sullens, who had garnered respect and praise from segregationist politicians like Eastland and Walter Sillers Jr. (a Mississippi politician and ardent racist), joined forces in offering the most callous and vitriolic analysis of the saga.[44]

According to the *Daily News,* "Three Leflore county Negroes have been charged with rape in the last two years, one of them against a 12-year-old white girl, and none received the death sentence." The paper asserted: "No threat of violence occurred in any of the three cases, even including the 12-year-old child." Digging through the history of Mississippi court decisions to find proof that whites could be convicted of a crime against blacks, the *Delta Democrat-Times* pointed out: "Contrary to published reports, Mississippi has executed at least one white man for the murder of a Negro. A white storekeeper, Mel Cheatham, was hanged in the courthouse yard here 65 years ago for the slaying of Negro Jim Tillman." Of course, the main point of the article was to counter the views advanced by individuals the *Democrat-Times* dubbed "'rabid-minded, trigger-happy newsmen' which 'unjustly cast a shadow upon the state of Mississippi racial-wise.'"[45]

Despite the obvious fact that African Americans rarely, if ever, received justice in Mississippi, whites continued to argue to the contrary. Numerous white citizens went so far as to maintain that there was a double standard of justice in the state that favored African Americans, and an editorial in the *Jackson Daily News* epitomized this notion: "It has been a kindly double standard and one calculated to let the Negro live with as few overlapping regulations from a society he is ill-equipped to meet as a social equal as possible. . . . It is virtually an unwritten law that Negro justice is substantially softer than white law." Furthermore, "A Negro in New Orleans can get away with murder and people shrug their shoulders and say 'they are just niggers.'" The author did not advocate the enslavement of African Americans; nevertheless, he concluded: "The vast majority [of blacks] are simply not ready to assume equality. They do not have the background or the years of tradition and breeding to make normal, wholesome citizens. Their equality must necessarily be a gradual processing, evolving to a place of equality in society." Accordingly, "In the meantime, we are destroying our own standards by this ridiculous system of allowing the Negro to have his cake and eat it, too."[46]

The bloated list of extralegal murders perpetrated against African Americans in the Deep South refuted any claims of preferential options for blacks in this region; however, Percy Green, the editor-publisher of the black newspaper the *Jackson (MS) Advocate,* did little to challenge mainstream opinions on the matter. Rather, his leadership defended Deep South racial oppression and framed Wilkins's lynching accusation as a "bitter statement in regard to the people of Mississippi." Mirroring the outrage toward lynching found among the publisher and editors of their parent paper, the *Atlanta Daily World,* the *Birmingham World* and the *Memphis World* approached the Wilkins statement in a different manner. Because they were headquartered outside Mississippi, the threat to these two papers was a little less than that to the *Advocate;* however, like the *Advocate,* these two subsidiaries of W. A. Scott's *Atlanta Daily World* hesitated to call Till's death a *lynching.* The headline in both papers read: "Battered Body of Boy, 14, Found in River in Miss." Within the article, the only reference to the crime as a lynching came in the often-quoted Wilkins statement.[47]

While they shied away from the *lynching* moniker in articles, in their editorials the *Birmingham World* and *Memphis World* staff consistently expressed their belief that this crime qualified as a lynching. Both papers printed an editorial entitled "The Mississippi Lynch-Murder" in which it was charged: "The kidnap-murder of a young teenager in Mississippi last week was nothing short of a lynching." In a separate editorial, the *Memphis World* added to this commentary, arguing: "The outright lynch-murder of Emmett Louis Till . . . should call up all hands on deck of justice, for in the gruesome act, the state and the nation have been . . . disgraced."[48]

The August night wolf-whistle prank, which precipitated the August night brutalization and murder of Emmett Till, generated countless pages of September daily and weekly news copy. In the wake of the lynching, the national and regional press worked to inform readers of the facts behind the case, and, through this process, they established their publications' disposition toward this murder. These dispositions pointed up existing racial tension, already inflamed by *Brown v. Board of Education,* and attitudes toward the Supreme Court decision framed the lynching in the context of regional and national perceptions of race relations. These perceptions held significant meaning in the Cold War era, during which Americans readily labeled *Communist* anything they saw as subversive or contrary to national principles of democracy. Media framing of Till's lynching, and the responses to his murder, presaged the dispositions through which press outlets would view subsequent events in the Till saga.

Beginning with the return of the body to Chicago and the home-going services for this victim of Mississippi racial violence, national and local print media sources stepped up their coverage of the lynching drama and in earnest framed the narrative of Emmett Till as a commentary on American democracy. This was due in no small part to efforts by Mamie Till-Mobley, the NAACP, and the black press to keep Till's death in the forefront of people's minds and to transfer the salience of the event into the national narrative on race relations.

3

Home Going

Emmett Till's brutal 1955 murder exposed the malignant cancer of racial hatred rapidly metastasizing across the South in the wake of *Brown v. Board of Education.* Untreated, this tumor threatened to disfigure and permanently discredit U.S. Cold War efforts at home and abroad. Through interest and disinterest in the case, domestic print media sources positioned themselves in relation to the senseless killing. By foregrounding, obscuring, and whitewashing elements of the saga, national and regional news outlets framed the events and the actors in ways that bolstered existing dispositions toward gender and race. Moreover, these approaches demarcated the importance of the lynching in the psyches of media outlet leaders as well as what aspects of the events these leaders and their staff felt were the most salient. In much the same way as the image of Emmett Till sacrificed at the feet of a Ku Klux Klan–hooded Abraham Lincoln substitute (see figure 3.1), this framing foreshadowed the ways in which the media juxtaposed regional dispositions with perceptions of Mississippi racial norms. Through the process, the entire state of Mississippi was put on public trial.

African American individuals and groups understood the hypocrisy of promoting democracy abroad while relegating a significant portion of American citizenry to second-class status; thus, they worked continually to position Emmett Till's death within the broader milieu of American race relations. At the forefront of these efforts stood Mamie Till-Mobley, who, alongside her relatives, the black press, and the NAACP, underscored the importance of Till's death with respect to the growing movement for racial equality. Unlike the Scottsboro Boys cases of the 1930s and 1940s—referred to here as the collective defense and conviction appeals of nine black boys accused of the rape of two white women in Scottsboro, Alabama—with Till the NAACP took the lead in the defense of a black youth accused of the inappropriate treatment of a white woman. In the Scottsboro cases, the NAACP did assist; however, the defense of the nine

Figure 3.1. *Another Sacrifice to Jim Crow*. Political cartoon, September 12, 1955. Laura Gray Political Cartoons, Tamiment Library and Robert F. Wagner Labor Archives, New York University.

wrongfully accused black males largely fell to the pro-Communist International Labor Defense (ILD). Referring to Communists' civil rights effort in the 1930s and 1940s, Stephen Lawson noted: "From its defense of the Scottsboro Nine in the early 1930s to its support of organizing sharecroppers in Alabama and factory workers in North Carolina in the 1930s and 1940s, the [Communist] party played an important role in the black freedom struggle."[1]

Thanks to Scottsboro, the NAACP had learned that efforts to protect black males from allegations of impropriety levied by white women could be successful. When in 1955 press reports from the Deep South and the West attempted to dismiss Emmett Till as a stereotypical black brute intent on raping white womanhood, the organization made sure it was at the vanguard of efforts to defend Till's image and use his death to forward racial justice. Of course, the rampant anticommunism of the 1950s also precluded Communist organizations like the ILD from taking charge of the Till case, and the NAACP most effectively used Cold War politics to fight for racial justice. As Lawson underscored, "in casting aside the radical economic ideology of the [Communist] Popular Front, groups such as the NAACP succeeded in using America's anticommunist foreign policy and the corresponding need to win allies in emerging Third World nations to pry civil rights measures from the national government."[2]

It had to be the NAACP leading the call for racial justice in the Till saga, and, in the wake of the *Brown* decisions, the NAACP continued to be a thorn in the side of white southerners by doing all it could to see that those responsible for Till's death were held accountable. The organization used the tragedy to recruit new members, solicit funds for its campaign for greater civil rights, and highlight the magnitude of racism and racial violence in the South. Till was a logical tool for the NAACP, and through the lynching it was able to confirm the existence of unrestrained white supremacist violence. Moreover, his death validated NAACP legal arguments found in *Brown;* if Americans could stomach the brutal lynching of this fourteen-year-old boy, then segregation had decimated the nation's moral compass.

Through his death and the efforts to memorialize his suffering, Emmett Till emerged as a beacon of light exposing the deep darkness of racial injustice. He became the rallying point for a generation of activists and decades of protest. His death continued to unite people well beyond the historical confines of the modern civil rights movement. His sacrifice on the altar of racial oppression led eventually to the Federal Civil Rights Law (1964), the Violent Crime Control and Law Enforcement Act (1994), the national apology for lynching (2005), and the Emmett Till Unsolved Civil Rights Crime Act (2007). Till's significance was due in large part to the print media coverage of the gruesome affair, reporting armed by Mamie Till-Mobley's decision to give the press free and open access to images of and stories about her slain son. Truly, this coverage brought to bear the untenable racial oppression that plagued the nation at home and damaged the national image abroad.

Through words and images, the national news outlets that covered Till's home going pointed up the level of outrage invoked by his death. Capturing the fury, *Newsweek* included an image of the masses gathered outside Chicago's Roberts Temple Church of God in Christ waiting to view the body. Along with *The Nation, Newsweek* reported that over 10,000 people attended the home going. *Jet,* the Chicago-based black national magazine, put the number at over 600,000 across the three-day period encompassing the wake and the funeral service.[3]

Whatever the attendance, all reports agreed that the mourners waited hours to see what a journalist for *The Nation* described as a boy "badly beaten, his teeth knocked out, one side of his face nearly unrecognizable, [with] a small bullet hole through his temple." *Newsweek* affirmed the battered state of the body, and, using the words of one of the bishops presiding over the home-going ceremony, the staff writer explicitly linked Emmett Till to all who suffered from racial oppression. Referencing the words of Jesus, Bishop Louis H. Ford of St. Paul Church of God in Christ intoned: "For as much as ye have done unto one of these my little ones . . . ye have done unto me." Doubtlessly, many at the home going felt a visceral connection to this murdered boy, and *The Nation* warned: "National attention should focus on Chicago, not Mississippi. . . . In situations of this kind, where there has been a succession of acts of violence, a time usually comes when one additional act is enough to tip the scale." It was feared that Till's lynching was the tipping point: "From reports of the memorial services for young Till in Chicago, it seems clear that the Negro community there is aroused as it has not been over any similar act in recent history." Truly, Emmett Till's death moved many to attend his home going and witness firsthand the visage of southern racial brutality. *The Nation* and *Newsweek* captured in words and images much of the indignation felt by funeralgoers, but no group illuminated the passionate responses to or elucidated the salience of the lynching like the midwestern press, a regional confederation of newspapers to which I append the Chicago-based *Jet.*[4]

Out front in the coverage of events in Chicago even preceding Emmett Till's home going, the *Chicago Sun-Times* reported: "Mrs. Bradley [Mamie Till-Mobley] is waiting at the home of her mother, Mrs. Alma Spearman, 1626 W. 14th, Chicago, for the body of her only son to be shipped home for burial. The body will arrive in Chicago at 9 A.M. Friday at the Illinois Central Station and be taken to the chapel at 4141 Cottage Grove." The *Sun-Times,* whose publisher, Marshall Field III, championed through column space and financial support black uplift efforts, testified that the remains could be returned because "Crosby Smith, an uncle of the Till boy, . . . interrupted a hasty burial of the body." "They were getting ready to spill the boy into [the two-foot grave]," Smith said, without even embalming the body. Only after some insistence—dangerous given the existing racial animosity—did Smith stop the burial: "They let me have the body, I got it embalmed and made arrangements with the railroad to bring it here." As was the case with Mamie Till-Mobley and other relatives, Crosby Smith felt it essential to memorialize Emmett Till's short life and untimely death, and he risked life and limb, insisting that white Mississippi law enforcement release Till's body. This resolve on the part of Smith, Till-Mobley, and others underscored the salience of the Till case and doubtlessly led papers like the *Chicago Sun-Times* to cover the unfolding events. As they did with Till's infamous visit to Bryant's Meat and Grocery and his subsequent abduction and murder, midwestern media outlets offered unrivaled details of the home going, effectively keeping Emmett Till in the midwestern public narrative. Included in their coverage were the arrival date and time and the address of the funeral home, presenting readers ample opportunities to pour out their sympathies to the grief-stricken mother and her family.[5]

Not to be outdone by its competitors, the *Chicago Tribune* provided addresses and minibiographies of two of Till's older relatives, both of whom were in Mississippi with the boy. Till's cousin Wheeler Parker was described thusly: "Wheeler Parker, 16, of 7524 W. 64th st., Argo . . . a pupil at Argo Community High school." A later *Tribune* article identified another of Till's cousins as "Curtis Jones, 17, of 1252 S. Racine av., a Crane Tech senior and a second cousin of Till." With these reports, the paper emphasized the hometown connection to the murder, and, by offering contact information, the staff prompted readers to send condolences to Till's family.[6]

Offering unmatched regional reporting on Till's home going, the *Chicago Sun-Times* detailed the slain youth's September 2, 1955, arrival in Chicago. Journalists covering the homecoming found Chicago's Central Station engulfed in anguish and grief. Headquartered in Till's home city, the *Chicago Sun-Times* presented some of the most gripping recollections of the scene when the "Illinois Central R.R.'s Panama Limited pulled in" to the station. A *Sun-Times* journalist recounted, on seeing the engine enter the depot: "Mrs. Mamie E. Bradley . . . jumped from her wheelchair . . . [and] sprinted across three sets of tracks to the baggage car in which the body lay in a pine box." As attendants lifted the meager coffin from the train: "[Till-Mobley] fell to her knees and sobbed hysterically. 'My darling, my darling . . . I would have gone through a world of fire to get to you.'" The mother was not alone in her grief. "Weeping relatives formed a ring, and a hearse backed into the scene," the *Sun-Times* testified. Despite the din of trains and the sobbing masses, the reporter heard Till-Mobley's voice again ring out: "My darling, my darling . . . I know I was on your mind when you died. Oh my baby. You didn't die for nothing."[7]

Mamie Till-Mobley intended to uncover why her son had died and ensure that he *had* died for something. Despite promises to Mississippi officials that she would not examine the remains, when the body arrived at the funeral home she demanded to see it. Although the *Sun-Times* journalist framed Till-Mobley in traditionally gendered terms, picturing her as "hysterical" and sobbing loudly, the mainstream press defied gender norms by noting that she faced up to male authority figures who urged her to leave the casket unopened, and the *Sun-Times* emphasized that she was at the forefront of every decision involving her son's home going. Ascribing her agency that belied typical 1955 gender conventions, the paper lauded her for having the presence of mind to show the world what had happened to her son. Following every aspect of Till's home going, its journalist recounted: "'Open it up,' Mrs. Bradley shouted, 'Let the people see what they did to my boy.'" Without her timely decision, her son's death would not have emboldened a generation of activists, for these civil rights champions from across the country would not have seen the decimated remains of Emmett Till as captured in photographs printed in *Jet*'s September 15 edition. Without these nationally circulated images, Till's death may have evoked a visceral reaction only within a small subset of the population. With these photographs posted prominently in barbershops, hair salons, and churches and on coffee tables across the nation, Till's brutalized visage became a rallying point for a cadre of disillusioned Americans fed up with the unacceptably slow pace of racial uplift in the nation and the hypocrisy of deplorable domestic race relations in an era during which America promoted democracy abroad.[8]

Sensing the magnitude of the situation and its readers' need to learn every detail, the *Chicago Sun-Times* took pains to describe the gruesome state of the body: "Condition of the boy's face indicated a beating far more brutal than first reported in dispatches from Mississippi. Almost all the boy's teeth were knocked out. The entire right side of the face was caved in. There was a small bullet hole through the temple." Doubtlessly, coverage like this contributed to the outpouring of support that Mamie Till-Mobley received and probably led many to view the body and offer their condolences. The large crowds that descended on the wake became another prominent story in papers across the country, but in no region was this event covered in as exhaustive detail as in the Midwest. Marking this shift to the second phase of Till's home going, the *Chicago Tribune* emerged as the torchbearer, offering the most thorough coverage of the home-going services.[9]

Describing the opening of what would become a roughly seventy-two-hour home-going ritual, a journalist for the *Chicago Tribune* wrote: "More than 5,000 persons attended the wake for the slain teen-ager yesterday and last night in the chapel at 4141 Cottage Grove av." Of the crowd the following day, the paper reported: "More than 2,500 persons in Roberts' Temple of the Church of God in Christ, 4021 S. State st. . . . Another crowd estimated at 2,000 waited outside the church. . . . More than 40,000 persons viewed the body in the afternoon and night." The *Tribune*'s Clay Gowran stated of the estimated tens of thousands who attended the home going: "Throngs continued yesterday to file past the bier of Emmet [*sic*] Louis Till in Roberts' Temple of Church of God in Christ, 4021 State st. Church attendants said crowds continued unabated thru the day." The enormous turnout, which necessitated the lengthy vigil, revealed the salience of this event for many, and the *Chicago Tribune* dedicated its pages to highlighting how, despite palpable outrage, a sense of order reigned over the somber scene.[10]

Not surprisingly, given the tenuous Cold War situation and Communists' desires to use any means of discrediting the image of the United States, the Communist Party published and attempted to distribute several treatises capitalizing on the Till lynching. These statements lamented that Till's death was symptomatic of the historically abysmal race relations in this country, and the party called on the federal government to act. Of the Mississippi response to the Till lynching, the Communist Party USA wrote: "Local authorities cannot and will not cope with this emergency. The governor of the state, its district attorneys, sheriffs, senators and congressmen are all in league with the Dixiecrat conspirators who created the crisis." Deeming the 1955 political climate untenable, it urged: "Only immediate and firm intervention of the Eisenhower Administration can restore law, order, and decency to Mississippi. Only the federal government can bring to heel the racist insurrectionists who thumb their noses at the Constitution and Supreme Court of the United States."[11]

As the *Tribune* estimated, the seditious literature and the Communist Party action plans around the Till lynching mandated that demands be made for federal prosecution of "Ku Klux lynchers and their accomplices, the Mississippi officials." Fearing the negative effect of such literature, the city of Chicago dispatched police officers to monitor the home-going services. Preempting potential reports that the police presence represented an attempt by the mayor to stop a riot before it started, the *Tribune* pointed out that the move was simply a precaution against possible Communist agitation. The *Sun-Times* concurred, reporting: "The police department, suspecting that extreme left-wing groups might try to exploit the racial aspects, . . . assigned Sgt. Frank J. Heimowski of the police anti-Communist security detail . . . to mingle with the crowds."[12]

In fact, the *Sun-Times* asserted: "Inflammatory literature issued by 'the Communist party of Illinois-Indiana, Claude Lightfoot, chairman,' was passed out, and the literature was ill-received." As was the case with reports on Mamie Till-Mobley, which challenged existing gender norms, the midwestern mainstream press defied existing racial narratives in the western, southeastern, and Deep South mainstream press by foregrounding black efforts to disassociate with Communist activities during Till's home going.[13]

Parroting coverage in the Chicago mainstream papers, one Wisconsin mainstream daily, the *Milwaukee Journal,* also observed funeral attendees policing themselves. In reference to possible riots, the paper assured readers that this was not a riot situation: "[The funeral attendee] Archibald Carey, a former alternate delegate to the United Nations, . . . warned that another wrong would not make up for the murder." Carey continued: "Revenge . . . is not for us to seek, and will not correct the evil that has happened." Further highlighting the clearheadedness of funeral attendees, the *Journal* quoted Carey saying: "A mob in Chicago is no better than a mob in Mississippi." As was the case throughout the history of blacks in America, African Americans were able to calm their emotions and rationally plan the best course of action. In this situation, the best option was allowing Mamie Till-Mobley and the NAACP to handle the case. To that end, the NAACP used the somber occasion to collect money to fund the fight against lynching. One *Sun-Times* journalist maintained, "The Rev. Cornelius Adams of the Greater Harvest Baptist Church sat at a table a few feet from the boy's body, collecting money for a fund set up by the National Assn. for the Advancement of Colored People. 'Contribute your money so that this will not happen again,' he intoned."[14]

The focus on the Reverend Adams, a Baptist minister, is particularly noteworthy because his message of unity around racial uplift showed that Till's home going was much more than a denominational celebration of the boy's life. This funeral was an interreligious effort to ensure that Till's death found vindication. The services mirrored growing interdenominational cooperation, a hallmark of the modern civil rights movement as seen in the work of groups like Church Women United (CWU) and later embodied in organizations like the Southern Christian Leadership Conference (SCLC). Of the former, Bettye Collier-Thomas noted that it was "designed to shape government decisions on policies affecting education, labor, housing, and segregation." The CWU, the SCLC, and interfaith groups like them used the denominationally based doctrines of their faith as lenses through which their members embraced faith in the way that the theologian James Fowler would define it, as a shared center of value and power. In Fowler's context, and in the modern civil rights movement, the goal of racial uplift within a democratic nation like the United States served as a common faith that transcended denomination, race, and creed. Even in the shadows of this brutal race-based lynching, this faith in racial uplift unified funeral attendees behind a belief in democracy rather than communism as the key to racial equality and universal human rights.[15]

Armed with a faith in American democracy as the medium through which they could bring about a solution to American racial woes, funeral attendees were undeterred by Communist efforts outside the church, and, by all accounts, funeralgoers joined with Till's relatives in ignoring the party's propaganda. Rather than succumbing to Communist pressures, they chose to sit vigil memorializing the glorious life and intolerable death of this fourteen-year-old boy. Continuing to connect its readers with the Till family, the *Tribune* went so far as describing the seating arrangements at the viewing: "Till's mother sat in the second row . . . and got up at one time to view his body. In the front row were other relatives, including George T. Smith, 1119 W. 61st st., an uncle of Till; Mrs. Alma Spearman, Till's grandmother, and Mrs. Moses Wright of Money, Miss." (The latter was the great-aunt with whom Till stayed during his trip to Mississippi.) Moreover, the family friend and eventual husband of Mamie Till-Mobley, "Genie Mobley Jr., 66031/2 Cottage Grove av.," was introduced as "a barber who had cut the dead youth's hair for years" and who "identified him [Till] by his hairline." Gene Mobley's identification of the body reinforced Mamie Till-Mobley's claims, the veracity of which became increasingly important once Tallahatchie County sheriff H. C. Strider voiced doubts about the identity of the corpse.[16]

When Mamie Till-Mobley heard about the sheriff's statement, she said: "I positively say it is my son lying there [i]n the church. If the state of Mississippi says he is not my boy, the burden of proof rests upon that state. I will say that as long as there is a shadow of doubt, I will not have the body interred." As was the case with respect to the decision to open the casket, the *Tribune* challenged gender conventions, depicting Till-Mobley as decisive and clearheaded. Despite her grief, she took charge of the situation and made critical choices that furthered the memory of her son and helped bring the realities of Deep South white supremacy to the public's attention. She was a determined individual who was willing to postpone the burial, and, thus, any sense of closure she might obtain, in order to prove that this body was her son's. Mamie Till-Mobley did postpone her son's interment, but not because of challenges from the racist Mississippi sheriff. Rather, the love and support that poured out to her through the tens of thousands, or hundreds of thousands, who came to view her son's body led her to delay the service until everyone who wanted to had the chance to pay their respects to the slain boy.[17]

The strain of the extended wake took a toll on the grieving mother, and both the *Tribune* and the *Sun-Times* reported on Till-Mobley's fragile emotional state during the funeral. A sympathetic *Tribune* journalist reported that she "collapsed and had to be assisted to a seat after she looked for the last time at her son's body." However, this collapse was contextualized as much more than a weak woman's maternal instinct: "Several others of the 18 relatives of the boy also broke down as they passed the casket. . . . [C]hurch officials estimate that at least one out of every 10 persons who viewed the body fainted." For that reason "special nurses were kept in attendance." The *Sun-Times* validated the *Tribune* coverage, further breaking down gender stereotypes: "Men shielded their eyes and three women fainted at the sight of the boy's crushed head." As *Jet* reported, even the white Church of God in Christ minister the Reverend Luke Ward fainted at the sight of the gruesome remains. Still, after seeing the throngs, Till-Mobley decided to delay the burial. "They came here to see my boy,' she said, 'and they'll see him." This selfless action allowed tens, or hundreds, of thousands of people to see firsthand the brutal consequences of the centuries-old white supremacist ideologies, and through this experience they internalized the salience of this event in the annals of American race relations. According to this antiquated hegemonic ideology, Till deserved to die for his wolf-whistle, because, through unwarranted fears in words and beliefs, Americans had forwarded a narrative of black males as hypersexual brutes singularly focused on the sexual conquest of white women.[18]

While the midwestern mainstream papers offered detailed, personal, and heart-wrenching accounts of Emmett Till's home going, the midwestern black press zeroed in on the long history of reasons why black people should leave the American South. As such, these publications most effectively placed the lynching in the context of civil rights endeavors to break down long-standing stereotypes of black people. Reinforcing midwestern mainstream angst over Till's home going, during the second week of coverage midwestern African American papers intensified their attacks on the state of Mississippi and the Deep South. Couched in their condemnation were arguments as to why black people had left, and should continue to leave, Mississippi. On this point, Marty Richardson of the *Call and Post* wrote: "The Cleveland [NAACP] membership drive this year is geared around the contention that 'What is happening in Mississippi is a sample of what will happen in the rest of the South.'" The *Call and Post* editorial team of William Walker and Lawrence Payne likely selected Richardson to compliment James Hicks's coverage of the Till saga precisely because he was a veteran of civil rights reporting who, while covering the 1934 lynching of Claude Neal, spent three days eluding a lynch mob. His expertise combined with Hicks's gripping narrative reporting style lent validity to the paper's stories of Till. If, therefore, Richardson and Hicks argued the conditions of white supremacy and racial hatred that led to Till's death were symptomatic of the entire South, then this region, dubbed a "closed society" by James Silver and "the most southern place on earth" by James Cobb, was not safe for any African Americans. Throughout the twentieth century, de jure racial oppression in the South and job prospects elsewhere served, respectively, as powerful push and pull factors fueling the migration from South to North of millions of blacks between 1915 and 1970.[19]

In focusing attention on the horrendous experiences of Moses Wright and other blacks in Mississippi, both the *Defender* and the *Call and Post* buttressed the argument that black people should leave the Deep South. For example, one *Defender* editorialist asserted: "Mose Wright [Till's great-uncle, with whom he was staying when he was abducted] . . . declared early this week that he is leaving Mississippi 'as soon as possible.'" The fact that "Wright and most of the other Negroes who live in Money are 'scared to death'" served as a push factor. This intolerable fear stemmed from the absolute inability of African Americans to find just conditions in Mississippi. Given this untenable situation, which extended beyond Mississippi, many midwestern black residents were immigrants from the Deep South, so many, in fact, that it is almost certain that the people who attended Till's viewing and funeral had deep connections with the region.

They therefore feared that what happened to Emmett Till could happen to any black person who dared to cross the Mississippi border. Validating this claim, the *Defender*'s Robert Elliott observed: "Most of them [the crowd at the Till services] were thinking it is no crime for a boy to whistle at a pretty woman. They were thinking, 'My son might do it—or yours.' And thinking that, they suddenly felt 'Bo' Till belonged to them. And they came to see him. Many of them talked to him. They all swore they'd never forget him." Sensing the deep connection the public felt with the murdered boy, the midwestern black press promoted NAACP efforts to use his death to lambaste Mississippi racism. As part of this poignant condemnation of the state, these publications forwarded NAACP attempts to combat the culture of fear: a culture made possible through intricate systems of disenfranchisement.[20]

Of the NAACP's work, Ethel Payne of the *Defender* quoted Thurgood Marshall, the NAACP's chief legal counsel, as saying, "If the citizens in the state of Mississippi can get neither protection from within the state nor the federal government, the country is in bad shape." Within the Cold War global context, the United States could ill afford to have foreign countries point out any flaws in American democracy. Even as Till's death shone a light on vile racism in the southern regions of the country, the NAACP and the black press argued that inaction on the part of state and federal officials proved that the entire nation was complicit in the slaying of the Chicago youth. Reinforcing the national implications of the crime, the *Chicago Defender* lamented: "Until the bloody-handed criminals who beat life from his young body are given swift and adequate punishment, the white inhabitants of this benighted town will stand condemned. Until the lynching of Negroes in Mississippi is vigorously suppressed by the Federal government, the white people of the U.S. will stand dishonored in the eyes of the civilized world." In this estimation, crimes like the Till lynching, if unpunished, showed American hypocrisy, for, if senseless murders occurred at home, they most likely affected confidence in America abroad.[21]

In the same vein, the *Cleveland Call and Post* editorialized: "Negro people of Mississippi have every right to look to the Department of Justice to protect them against the growing wave of terrorism. . . . The brutal truth is that, without this federal protection, they will have to breed a race of supermen forthwith or surrender in abject fear to defiant and unlawful southern bigotry." Unconvinced of the likelihood of federal intervention, the editorialist painted a grim picture in which, despite the laudable efforts of black activists and white sympathizers, white supremacy reigned in the South, and black southerners continued in perpetual economic and social slavery.[22]

Through headlining the pull and push factors that fueled the Great Migration, the midwestern mainstream and black press offered readers in their region an interracial narrative that supported Till's family and lambasted southern attempts to discredit the memorialization of his death as a sad consequence of southern racial oppression. Although they pointed up different aspects of the Till saga, these publications exhibited similar degrees of indignation about the senseless and racially charged murder of a fourteen-year-old black boy.

Apparently, this style of coverage, or, more accurately, this disposition toward the lynching of Emmett Till, did not transfer to other regions of the country. Western mainstream dailies offered an alternate analysis of southern racial equality. Clearly supporting dispositions toward race relations first evidenced in their coverage of the initial stages of the Till saga, newspaper staff from this region touted what they perceived as progress in the southern part of the nation, and they blamed racially progressive institutions and individuals for creating a culture of contention that retarded further movement toward equality. This approach was unlike that of mainstream papers from the Midwest, which accentuated the interracial nature of the home-going service and lauded efforts to resist Communist co-optation. Western dailies framed the funeral as an African American affair.

The *San Francisco Examiner* and the *Los Angeles Times,* for example, reported: "Services for a 14-year-old Negro boy slain while vacationing in Mississippi drew thousands of Negroes today to a South Side church where the battered body was placed on view." In actuality, as seen in midwestern accounts, many white people, including one of the ministers at the Church of God in Christ Temple, where the funeral was held, traveled to the South Side to view the body. By framing the funeral and, by extension, Till's lynching as a "Negro" event, the western mainstream papers downplayed the interracial cooperation that was a hallmark of the modern civil rights movement.[23]

As inaccurate as such race-based portrayals of the funeral attendees seemed, more egregious, given the anti-Communist Cold War climate, was the outright acceptance of allegations that Communist subversives guided black efforts and, thus, used Till's death to discredit the United States. Though such allegations were unfounded, western mainstream papers levied charges of NAACP collaboration with Communist subversives, and these accusations further alienated readers in the West. These dailies subscribed to the FBI's, and particularly J. Edgar Hoover's, assumption that the Communist Party had infiltrated and was directing the NAACP.[24]

Even after the death in 1951 of its longtime leader, William Randolph Hearst, the *San Francisco Examiner* remained true to his ethos. Hearst was originally a liberal supporter of Democratic policies; however, personal conflict with the party led him to shift to a conservative ideology. This conservative leaning came across in the coverage of the Till lynching, and, more than the other papers from the region, the *Examiner* seemed intent on flushing out Communist involvement in the Till affair. Most notably, the journalist Alvin Spivak declared: "American Communists grabbed a Mississippi 'lynching' as their biggest issue this week." For this alleged Communist boon, Mamie Till-Mobley and the NAACP bore the brunt of the criticism because they made a media spectacle out of the lynching and, in essence, provided the Communist Party with fodder for its attacks on the entire nation. The *Examiner* in turn applauded Mississippi's white officials for handling the case in a fair and legal manner that afforded the Communists no room to defame America's reputation for democracy and equality.[25]

Presenting a more accurate view of the events surrounding Till's home going, and refuting western mainstream condemnation of the black actors in the saga, the western black newspaper the *Los Angeles Sentinel* published a forceful denial of allegations that the NAACP or Mamie Till-Mobley had any connections to the Communist Party: "Mrs. Bradley said she had received no aid from the Communist party and that she hopes the prosecution of her son's murderers will be an aid to the people of the United States 'and not a help to the communists.'" Because Till's death occurred in the immediate wake of Wisconsin senator Joseph McCarthy's infamous witch hunt for alleged Communists—the House Un-American Activities Committee still held hearings to try and condemn Communist subversives—people challenging the status quo were likely to find their views characterized as anti-American. Recognizing that a cold war was raging across the globe, Till-Mobley had the shrewdness to understand the importance of quieting any inclination that she or the NAACP had connections with or sympathized with the Communist agenda.[26]

Southeastern and northeastern mainstream newspapers chose to eschew altogether any analysis of the Communist presence at Till's wake and funeral. In fact, these publications were notably disinterested in covering most aspects of the slain youth's home going, from his return to Chicago to his burial. This lack of reporting obscured the paramount

importance of the home going, whitewashed Mamie Till-Mobley's decisive actions throughout it, and ignored attempts on the part of Communists
to use it to promote their agenda.

Black press from the Southeast and the Northeast did not offer much
more analysis than their mainstream counterparts presented. In fact,
only the *Philadelphia Tribune* and the *Pittsburgh Courier* approached
the level of detail of the train station scene provided in the midwestern
press. Accounting the arrival in Chicago of the body, these two northeastern black papers corroborated reports in the *Sun-Times*. Moreover, the
Courier journalist, Theodore Coleman, broadened the context of Till's
home going and ascribed even greater agency to Mamie Till-Mobley's
words: "[Her] 'agonized cry' can easily become the opening gun in a war
on Dixie, which can reverberate around the world." Of note, coverage
in the *Philadelphia Tribune* marked another high point for Till's mother,
an article there depicting her insisting "that the casket be opened when it
arrived in Chicago, although it had been sealed when it left Mississippi."
These critical exceptions notwithstanding, in the case of reporting on Till's
home going, the southeastern and northeastern press typified their regions'
dispositions toward the Emmett Till lynching. These publications' lack of
coverage is indicative of their framing of the home going, not as part of
the broader national struggle for civil rights, but as a regional, midwestern
phenomenon.[27]

Deep South mainstream newspapers also ignored the home-going services, choosing rather to play up southern responses to the Till saga. These
mainstream publications quickly hailed the grand jury indictment of Roy
Bryant and J. W. Milam as confirmation that Mississippians valued justice, even in a case of white-on-black crime. To that end, an editorial in
the *Jackson Daily News* proclaimed: "The two accused men have been
arrested and indicted with all due speed. The case will be tried through
established procedures by a Mississippi judge and jury." Clearly race bait-
ing, the *Daily News* presented the indictment as a slap in the face of the
NAACP and other outsiders who had hoped for a no bill—that the two
would not face indictment. In the Jackson paper's estimation, these outsiders would have taken advantage of a no bill to promote selfish and reck-
less political agendas. Proud of its Deep South brethren, the *Daily News*
asserted:

The National Association for the Advancement of Colored People took a blow Tuesday when a Tallahatchie County Grand Jury

returned an indictment against two men accused of kidnapping and murdering Emmett Till, the 14-year-old Negro boy. NAACP didn't expect an indictment, even as the radical organization of Northern do-gooders and Negroes didn't anticipate the characteristic Southern reaction of shock toward the violence of the crime. NAACP obviously didn't want the reaction which made that organization and its leaders liars. They said the South condoned such actions. It was plain that the South does not. NAACP was disturbed by the arrest of the two men accused of the crime. It would have suited NAACP propaganda purposes better had no arrests been made. Then the Mississippi law enforcement officers would have conformed to the distorted portrait NAACP agitators painted of them for the equally distorted Chicago and New York press. NAACP has taken a stunning blow from this action in Mississippi by Mississippians.

Jackson Daily News staff were proud of the grand jury action, for, clearly, Mississippians did take charge of the legal proceedings. However, the indictment notwithstanding, subsequent events would reveal that the inhabitants of this region supported a prosecutory strategy that in effect offered the defendants an immunity bath, proving that blacks could not receive justice in the case of white-on-black crime.[28]

Headlining the injustice prevalent in this Deep South locale, many Mississippi officials voiced their belief in the innocence of the defendants and Carolyn Bryant. Their families were the most ardent defenders of the accused, and the *Jackson Daily News* used this support to cast aspersions against the case against Bryant and Milam. As the paper saw it: "The mother of two white men accused of murdering a Negro boy over a wolf whistle vowed to 'stand by them' today despite the outrage of the nation, the state and her own neighbors." Similarly, the *Memphis Commercial Appeal* said of J. W. Milam: "His children all 'worshipped' their father." Another *Commercial Appeal* article reported: "'I know he's innocent,' said Raymond Bryant of 1433 South Willett, whose brother, Roy Bryant, is being held for the killing. . . . 'The family has had several grocery stores in Mississippi through the years and we've never had any trouble with Negroes before,' Raymond Bryant said. He charged that it was 'all a matter of politics.' Mr. Bryant said police had 'no proof to go on,' in the case and that the authorities had 'only circumstantial evidence' against his brother."[29]

Even more than the accused, Carolyn Bryant, who by all accounts was complicit in the kidnapping, found favorable coverage in the pages of Deep South mainstream papers. The *Birmingham News* noted: "Authorities apparently have abandoned the search for Mrs. Roy Bryant. . . . Dist. Atty. Stanny Sanders of Indianola, Miss., said Friday there were 'no plans at present for picking up Mrs. Bryant.'" Likewise, "Leflore County Deputy Sheriff W. A. Shanks said the sheriff's office didn't believe Mrs. Bryant was 'involved in the crime.' . . . 'We know where she is and feel sure we can pick her up if needed.'" The day after the *Birmingham News* article, the *Jackson Daily News* reported: "Officers have not questioned Bryant's pretty, brunette wife, in her early 20's, who was believed to have stayed in the car with an unidentified man when Bryant and Milam whisked Till from the home of his uncle in the Money, Miss. community. 'We aren't going to bother the woman,' said Leflore county sheriff George Smith, 'she's got two small boys to take care of.'" Clearly, paternalism protected white women in the Deep South. These "benevolent" white men decided to spare Carolyn Bryant the trial of further investigation because she had to fulfill her maternal duty of raising her children. Ironically, it was paternalistic dominion, taken to the extreme of the power over life and death, that robbed Mamie Till-Mobley of the opportunity to raise her son to manhood.[30]

Although the Deep South mainstream press continued to promote the belief that justice in Mississippi was color-blind, the NAACP knew better and criticized state officials for perpetuating a racist society that made the outcome of the Till trial a foregone conclusion. It also labeled the Till murder a *lynching* and specifically called on Mississippi governor Hugh White and other state officials to assure that those responsible for the crime were brought to justice. Of course, the Deep South mainstream papers promptly attacked the NAACP for its actions, and the *Jackson Daily News* attempted to discredit NAACP criticism of the Mississippi legal process. The paper's staff also maintained that Governor White did all in his power to see that justice prevailed. He ordered the district attorneys of two districts to use all their resources to see that the criminals were adequately punished. Moreover, the *Birmingham News* blasted the NAACP for "its blindness and injustice in charging that 'Mississippi has decided to maintain white supremacy murdering children'": "If the NAACP and other groups want justice, then let them cease throwing stones at the prosecution, the judge and jury."[31]

As a civil rights organization that had been at the forefront of the struggle for black equality for more than forty-five years, the NAACP had an impeccable reputation and had achieved a substantial amount of success in its campaign for black rights. It could count the 1954 *Brown v. Board of Education* decision, which ended segregation in public schools, as its greatest victory. In fact, the NAACP was the oldest and most potent civil rights organization in the country. Always abreast of its role in American society, it served as a watchdog in the Till murder case. It was acutely aware of the tactics of southern whites, and it was understandably concerned that white officials, including the governor, the sheriffs, the district attorneys, and the jury, would not side with justice.

Spearheading these efforts to derail justice in the Till case was the U.S. senator from Mississippi James O. Eastland. Eastland followed in the white supremacist pathway of Theodore Bilbo, and, during his thirty-five-year tenure in public office, he made every effort to suppress black advancement. He labeled the *Brown* decision a Communist plot, and his office disclosed Emmett Till's father's questionable military record. Eastland led the push to make events like Till's open casket funeral illegal, and, during the civil rights era, he resurrected the Lost Cause rhetoric as a justification for white supremacy, racial oppression, and lynching, exacerbating already tense race relations, and creating a climate of hatred that bred extralegal violence and murder.[32]

Buoyed by efforts by elected officials like Eastland, a *Delta Democrat-Times* reader wrote a letter to the editor, stating: "I read that the NAACP displayed the Negro's body in Chicago for three days to collect money and to incite hatred against the people of Mississippi. I certainly hope that the people of this nation catch on to the schemes of the NAACP before it is too late." Of these so-called schemes the *Democrat-Times* asserted: "All the macabre exhibitionism, the wild statements and hysterical overtones at the Chicago funeral of the Till child seemed too well staged not to have been premeditated with the express purpose of (1) inflaming hatred and (2) trying to set off a reaction in reverse in Mississippi, where there had previously been honest indignation."[33]

What Deep South mainstream press employees saw as race-baiting schemes most of the Deep South black press counted as prudent efforts toward racial uplift. Determined not to relegate the lynching debate to its back pages, the *Tri-State Defender* boldly challenged: "It appears that the [Mississippi] Governor was splitting hairs [when he said the crime was a murder rather than a lynching]." Turning to the "experts" at *Webster's Dictionary,* the editorial informed readers that a lynching was a murder by a mob and that a mob was the "disorderly element of the populace . . . a gang . . . criminal set." Without a doubt, Roy Bryant, J. W. Milam, and anyone who was with them at the time of the abduction and murder qualified as a "disorderly element of the populace." The piece ended with a simple rhetorical question: "Satisfied, Governor?" The *Defender* knew that its readership, and likely much of the American public, would see Bryant, Milam, and others present at the murder as an unruly "criminal set," thus making this crime a lynching. The editorial pressured Governor White to come to the same conclusion, do everything in his power to see that the perpetrators were punished, and ensure that such crimes did not continue in his state.[34]

William Gordon, of the *Daily World* syndicate, levied additional pressures on Governor White and the entire state of Mississippi. Skillfully couching his anger in a discussion of how Europeans viewed the American South, he wrote: "[Europeans] don't sit around to wait for pressure from without [before they make necessary changes], they acquire the impulse and the incentive to act on their own." Gordon called on Mississippians to take a proactive approach to the racial crimes within their borders instead of waiting for outside pressure to reach the point at which they would have no choice but to change their ways.[35]

Governor White did not heed these charges, and as the trial approached, it became clear that white Mississippians, from the governor down, would rally behind the accused and allow their bias and dependence on white supremacy to thwart justice. As Roi Ottley wrote in the *Tri-State Defender*, the lynching of Emmett Till and the subsequent coverup was simply the "way of white folks." Ottley recalled: "[Throughout the twentieth century] Negro girls were flogged for allegedly crowding white people in streetcars. Negro boys were beaten for accidentally riding their bicycles on sidewalks. Even Negro attempts to use public parks and beaches caused bloodshed." There was no recourse for African Americans. Even the most innocent action could invoke the wrath of white Americans. In this untenable environment, it should come as no surprise that a simple whistle would lead to a bloodied, beaten, and bullet-scarred body floating in Mississippi's Tallahatchie River.[36]

It was precisely these fluctuating southern social mores that caused the *Tri-State Defender* to proclaim: "The lesson Money, Miss., teaches is that there is no way to avoid trouble in the South, when 'peckerwoods' are bent on creating trouble for Negroes. Moreover, the Negro who genuflects to prejudice will never gain the white man's respect—instead he invites violence." African Americans who insisted on equal rights faced certain violence; however, those who chose to keep quiet invited violence because they did not challenge the supposed supremacy of white men. On the eve of the trial, black newspapers across the region and the nation risked life and limb speaking out against the pending trial in Sumner and the anticipated perversion of justice to be perpetrated by the white citizens of the state. These publications juxtaposed regional dispositions with perceptions of Mississippi racial norms. Through the process, they pointed up the saliency of the events, and they framed a discourse that set the stage for an indictment of the entire state of Mississippi.[37]

4

"M Is for Mississippi and Murder"

The state of Mississippi moved rapidly through the preliminary legal proceedings against Roy Bryant and J. W. Milam, the two men arrested on August 29, 1955, for their involvement in Emmett Louis Till's kidnapping and murder. However, the speed of the legal process could not assuage Mississippi's critics. By the time of the September 6 grand jury indictment on the charge of murder, the state already faced a media barrage from multiple sources lambasting its history of miserably oppressive race relations. With the September 19, 1955, murder trial looming, several media outlets set the stage for an all-out assault on the state's racial mores by characterizing it as the archetype of white supremacy. This coverage highlighted further the saliency of Till's death in the historical narrative of American race relations.

Focusing on the state of race relations in Mississippi, the NAACP printed a pamphlet indicting the entire state and all its citizens for the crimes committed against Emmett Till. The document "M Is for Mississippi and Murder" linked Till's death with the lynchings of the Reverend George Lee and Lamar Smith, and it detailed how Mississippi consistently defied the laws of the country and of God in its unceasing discrimination against and brutality toward blacks. Segregationists' perceived obligation to defy the Supreme Court's 1954 and 1955 integration rulings prompted some to use "gun and torch" to uphold segregation. As cited in the NAACP pamphlet, Mississippians foresaw that this inevitable violence would bring "the stain of . . . bloodshed . . . to the . . . Supreme Court steps." Bloodshed came in the form of Emmett Till's lynching, and, as noted in "M Is for Mississippi and Murder," some, including the *Yazoo Herald* (Yazoo City, MS), placed the blame for this bloodshed squarely in the hands of the nine judges on Chief Justice Warren's Court. For white Mississippians, this was a matter of states' rights. Surely, a significant subset of Mississippi's white population would second White Citizens Council executive secretary Robert P. Patterson's decree that the state could disregard *Brown:* "This is not the United States. . . . This is . . . Mississippi." Those publications that chose to offer pretrial context framed Mississippi along similar lines, casting it as the epitome of southern racial oppression.[1]

National mainstream news sources buttressed the arguments in the NAACP pamphlet. As the freelance journalist and native Indianan Dan Wakefield lamented to readers of *The Nation,* many white Mississippians supported Bryant and Milam and subscribed to Sheriff H. C. Strider's accusations that the entire ordeal was an NAACP conspiracy to discredit the state. In words and actions, the Tallahatchie County sheriff sided with the defendants, and, to Wakefield, it was apparent that little in the South had changed since the days of slavery, since whites still blamed outsiders, particularly progressive blacks, for anything that went wrong there.[2]

Of the stagnant nature of the trial's host town, *Newsweek* said: "[Sumner] was content with its place in the sun, never plagued with growing pains; it was reminiscent in some ways of a bone-tired plantation patriarch who long ago has seen all he wants to see and, thinking back isn't much impressed with what he saw." More explicitly, Mississippi was depicted as an anomaly compared to the rest of the country: "The town never became part of the New South—never wanted to. Its roots remained deep in the delta." Of this environment, the *Daily Worker* white journalist and native Mississippian Rob Hall affirmed: "Segregation wasn't an issue; it was a way of life." The *Worker*'s "Negro Affairs Editor," the black journalist Abner Berry, added: "Like Lady Macbeth, the state's rulers and those who support them are preoccupied with removing from their hands the blood that cries 'Guilty!'" As the trial later proved, casting blame for the sins of two native sons onto others became a preoccupation of white Mississippians.[3]

Shedding additional light on Mississippi's otherness, the *Time* magazine founder and editor in chief Henry Luce sanctioned article titles like "Sumner, Miss. Belongs to the Deeper South." Perhaps the peculiarity of this trial town came through most clearly when a *Time* journalist surmised: "Tallahatchie is not the South, either the Old South or the new, burgeoning industrial South. It is an island, and there are many in the Deeper South, where the law of the land and the will of the community—as expressed in trial by jury or otherwise—are in basic conflict." Although it may have seemed natural in "the most southern place on earth" for these inhabitants to respond to the lynching by defending their white brethren, this rallying point was foreign to most other Americans. Emmett Till's death underscored for countless people the saliency of addressing the cancer of American racial oppression. For this reason, "The feeling created in the US by the Till case indicated that something was going to have to give." Over the next decade, through the efforts of many who were galvanized by the murder, race relations in the United States would begin to change both in law and in practice. Part of the change in practice included federal intervention when local officials were deemed too entrenched in their worldview to challenge systemic oppression.[4]

More than any other region of the country, the Midwest keyed in on Mississippi's systemic ills and pointed to the importance of changing long-standing racial paradigms. On the eve of the trial, the *Detroit News*'s Russell Harris vividly primed memories of slavery and white supremacy: "King Cotton's Delta country starts in the lobby of the Peabody Hotel in Memphis, the saying goes, and runs South 60 miles wide, to Catfish Row in Vicksburg. . . . Tallahatchie County . . . has a population of 30,433. Of that number, 19,355 are Negroes." Paul Holmes, the *Tribune* journalist assigned to cover the trial, further framed: "Here in a rich cotton county of the Mississippi delta region . . . two white men will go on trial . . . before an all-male, all-white jury. . . . Strict segregation . . . is the rule here. . . . Segregation is the cornerstone of this region's society and economy."[5]

Throughout their coverage, Holmes and Harris pointed up the fact that this trial dealt more with the state of race relations in Mississippi than it did the lynching itself, a detail supported by the *St. Louis Post-Dispatch.* By underlining Mississippi's fears of greater outside intervention, and by highlighting the level of support that locals provided to the defendants, the *Post-Dispatch,* the *Chicago Tribune,* and the *Detroit News* presented Mississippi as terrified and trying desperately to hold on to its antiquated system of racial oppression. Enlivening this argument, Paul Holmes penned: "The way of life . . . is going on trial. . . . Planters are downright worried. . . . [T]hey hope the people of the United States are not going to get . . . 'wrong ideas' of Mississippi law or . . . customs." In a very real sense, Bryant and Milam were pawns, "expected to be a . . . trial balloon in the region's resistance to social change." To this commentary, Russell Harris added: "Half way down the strip shabby Sumner sits . . . and pretends that its tensions of fear and hate are not tightening each hour." Despite this false pretense of peace and racial harmony, the *Post-Dispatch* noted: "The trial comes in the race conscious, agricultural delta where Negroes outnumber white persons as much as four to one." Sumner whites loathed the national attention that this trial brought to their town because it shone a spotlight on the system of fear and intimidation used to maintain white supremacy.[6]

Of the fear felt by black locals, Russell Harris pointed out: "Negroes . . . do not talk about the trial, at least to white men." Black people in the Deep South had learned the long, hard lesson of biting their tongues. They negotiated their world and survived by knowing when and to what extent they could challenge their place in society. However, social boundaries were not fixed, and at any time blacks could find themselves hanging at the end of a rope. In this untenable climate, where any action could signal certain doom for local blacks, it was nearly impossible for any outsiders to ascertain the intricate and ever-changing set of racial mores that dictated life in the Delta. One of the problems in this case was that Emmett Till did not understand the extent of racial hatred in this region.[7]

In the wake of the lynching, local blacks remained silent around both northern and southern whites, while white residents complained that the trial was painting their region in a negative light, one that did not correctly represent the good relations between the races. Underscoring the sentiments of many Deep South whites, Whitney Smith, one of the largest planters in Tallahatchie County, told Harris: "Can't understand what you expect to find here. . . . [W]e know and love our colored folk. . . . I got field colored and house colored, and a colored woman nursed my wife before she passed on last year. [The black nurse] [s]lept right in the same room with her." Supporting the notion that all was right with race relations, a white Mississippi newspaperman added: "You know, there's a score or more of colored who hold their own land in the county. . . . They pay taxes and everything." For this newspaperman, the twenty or so African Americans who were able to eke out enough money to purchase their own land were proof that race relations were adequate. Perhaps this distorted vision of reality was best articulated when one white resident remarked: "We don't have race trouble down here . . . that's a Yankee thing."[8]

If these white Mississippians acknowledged problems with southern race relations, they would have to admit that the system needed to change. Smith, and Mississippians like him, did not want any alterations in the status quo, so they continued to blind themselves to the fact that their structure of racial oppression deserved scrutiny from the rest of the country. Much like slavery apologists of the antebellum period, white Mississippians during the Till trial consistently invoked the notion of paternalistic care to argue that segregation and racial inequality protected black people—making race relations in the South better than those in the North.

It was a self-actuated worldview. This patriarchal and white supremacist ideology acculturated whites to view black people as subhuman and, thus, not deserving of equal rights. Tension was inevitable because white southern views did not mesh with the growing black activism in the Deep South region.[9]

White reaction to this rising tide of black activism involved ideological retrenchment as well as vitriolic rhetorical and physical attacks aimed at silencing progressive voices. The saliency of the Till case, and the press coverage that signified the sea change in American response to racial oppression, was not lost on whites in the Mississippi Delta. They joined the burgeoning citizens councils, actively protested the *Brown* decisions, lobbied their congressmen to maintain segregation, supported the defendants in the Till lynching case, and fervently believed that the trial would aid in their battle against desegregation. Efforts to defend the system of oppression led to a snowballing of support for Bryant and Milam in Mississippi. Accustomed to the Mississippi justice system's handling of white-on-black crime, most had no doubt that the jury would acquit the defendants. Articles such as one in the *St. Louis Post-Dispatch* titled "Odds 10 to 1 for Acquittal, 'Intrusion' Resented in Mississippi Murder Trial" supported Mississippians' acquittal predictions.[10]

Half-brothers Bryant and Milam embraced the lopsided system of justice and optimistically awaited the acquittal that they assumed was a foregone conclusion. Having interviewed the accused on the eve of their murder trial, the *Detroit News*'s Russell Harris reported: "[Bryant and Milam] lounged on their prison cots as Carlton [the lead defense attorney] and friends stood by. Carlton was given the jail keys and locked the door carefully behind him when he left." An article in the *Chicago Tribune* further contextualized the suspects' thoughts about their detainment: "Bryant and Milam . . . were in good spirits and apparently unworried about results of the trial, but they professed regret at their temporary confinement . . . [because] [t]he cotton harvest is under way and many persons without cash much of the rest of the year have it now and are spending it." Bryant and Milam's only regret was that they were not free to take part in the harvest's boom economy, because white privilege allowed them to concern themselves with their own finances rather than with the life they had taken.[11]

The social, economic, political, and judicial conditions of black people in Mississippi had changed little since the ending of slavery. While whites basked in their privileged state of hegemony, blacks lived in squalor, worked for scraps, and, through it all, feared for their lives. As was customary in such a totalitarian system, oppressive and segregated ways of life extended to every aspect of the culture, and the *Chicago Tribune* purposefully noted that Sumner and Charleston both served as county seats. Observing strict racial segregation, the jail in Charleston, replete with all the finest accommodations, was reserved for white prisoners, while black prisoners were confined in Sumner's aged and poorly maintained jail. Underscoring this point, the *Detroit News* indicated that "the jail here [in Sumner] was not considered adequate [for whites]."[12]

In contrast to the preferential treatment that the defendants received, Mamie Till-Mobley encountered nothing but obstacles as she prepared to attend the trial. Of the concerns she had for her safety while she was in Mississippi, the *Chicago Sun-Times* reported: "The lawyer, William Henry Huff, promptly said he wanted her [Till-Mobley] to be at the trial if she would be 'adequately protected all the way.'" Till-Mobley agreed, saying that "she would insist on full protection in the South," and adding: "One must be brave, but it is not wise to be foolhardy." Subsequent pieces in both the *Sun-Times* and the *Detroit News* reinforced her apprehensions about her well-being while in Mississippi, but "[Tallahatchie County district attorney Gerald] Chatham was plainly irritated at her insistence on a bodyguard." Putting the matter more bluntly, a *Tribune* journalist questioned why "District Atty. Gerald Chatman . . . called the bodyguard proposal 'absurd.'" He responded publicly: "If they're going to make a farce out of this trial, that's a good way to get about it. . . . We offered her any reasonable protection[.] She won't need any at all, as far as that goes." Having been acculturated in the heart of racism, Chatham could not understand the depth of Mamie Till-Mobley's fears for her safety. He therefore saw her request for guaranteed protection as unnecessary.[13]

Adding to the stress of trial attendance, the *Detroit News* reported, white-owned hotels rejected Mamie Till-Mobley's requests to book a room during her stay in Mississippi. This denial of accommodations was part of the comprehensive and unyielding system of racial segregation. On the eve of the trial, black and white reporters learned fully how entrenched segregation was in these environs, for Sheriff Strider refused to provide acceptable space for black press members at a trial so important to the national narrative on race relations. The *Chicago Tribune* recounted: "Jim Crowism extends to courtrooms here, with a section for Negro spectators, and no Negroes will be allowed inside, except in this section unless they are participating as defendants or attorneys."[14]

MACE, DARRYL, 1975-

IN REMEMBRANCE OF EMMETT TILL: REGIONAL STORIES
AND MEDIA RESPONSES TO THE BLACK FREEDOM STRUGGLE.
                          Cloth   212 P.
LEXINGTON: UNIV PR OF KENTUCKY, 2014
SER: CIVIL RIGHTS AND THE STRUGGLE FOR BLACK
EQUALITY IN THE TWENTIETH CENTURY.
AUTH: CABRINI COLLEGE. MEDIA COVERAGE OF MURDER &
KILLERS' ACQUITTAL KINDLED CIVIL RIGHTS MOVEMENT.
LCCN 2014010708
  ISBN 0813145368   **Library PO#** FIRM ORDERS

                                List   40.00 USD
  8395 NATIONAL UNIVERSITY LIBRAR   **Disc**   14.0%
  App. Date   9/03/14   COLS   8214-08 **Net**   34.40 USD

SUBJ: TILL, EMMETT, 1941-1955--DEATH & BURIAL--
PRESS COVERAGE.

CLASS E185.93   DEWEY# 364.134   LEVEL GEN-AC

YBP Library Services

MACE, DARRYL, 1975-

IN REMEMBRANCE OF EMMETT TILL: REGIONAL STORIES
AND MEDIA RESPONSES TO THE BLACK FREEDOM STRUGGLE.
                          Cloth   212 P.
LEXINGTON: UNIV PR OF KENTUCKY, 2014
SER: CIVIL RIGHTS AND THE STRUGGLE FOR BLACK
EQUALITY IN THE TWENTIETH CENTURY.
AUTH: CABRINI COLLEGE. MEDIA COVERAGE OF MURDER &
KILLERS' ACQUITTAL KINDLED CIVIL RIGHTS MOVEMENT.
  LCCN 2014010708
  ISBN 0813145368   **Library PO#** FIRM ORDERS

                                List   40.00 USD
  8395 NATIONAL UNIVERSITY LIBRAR   **Disc**   14.0%
  App. Date   9/03/14   COLS   8214-08 **Net**   34.40 USD

SUBJ: TILL, EMMETT, 1941-1955--DEATH & BURIAL--
PRESS COVERAGE.

CLASS E185.93   DEWEY# 364.134   LEVEL GEN-AC

Naturally, segregation extended to housing in Mississippi, a fact that offered further ammunition for journalistic attacks on the stark contrast between the lives of rich whites and poor blacks in the state. Sheriff Strider was a classic example of the landed gentry: "[He raised cotton] on 1,500 acres with the help of 35 Negro families who reside on his property as tenants. Seven of the tenant homes, neatly painted, stretch in a row along the driveway to his home. Letters on the roof—one letter to a roof—spell out his name 'S-t-r-i-d-e-r' from the highway. It is pretty impressive." Strider's tattooing of his name on the houses of his black tenant farmers served as a reminder of the subordinate position of African Americans in the Deep South. Just as if he were branding cattle, the lawman placed his mark of ownership on his tenant farmers. Given that tenant farming kept many African Americans in perpetual debt and, thus, unable to escape their situation, the analogy was fitting. Slavery had ended nearly a century before; however, Strider's tenants, and most blacks in the region, were stuck in a system of slavery by another name.[15]

Images of Moses Wright's living conditions represented the other side of Mississippi segregation. The *Chicago Tribune* described his home as "a sun-baked, unpainted, 4 room cabin in the cotton field," while the *Detroit News* emphasized the fact that Wright slept on a sheetless bed in "his empty sharecropper's shack." Portrayals of Wright served to sharply accentuate the privileged life of the obese and gluttonous H. C. Strider—a man who was so much the picture of the patriarchy that he chose to serve the people and allow his black charges to do the work on his plantation. Painting the Deep South as a land of extremes left readers to believe that Wright did not even have enough money to whitewash the outside of his cabin or put sheets on his bed, let alone stencil his name on the roof in letters large enough for passersby on the highway to see.[16]

Most of the cotton money from this region fell into the hands of a few members of the white elite, and they were not willing to help improve the town's halls of justice. Awash in prosperity, the landed gentry felt no obligation to improve Sumner's legal infrastructure, for, as the *Chicago Tribune* observed, the trial venue was "the sagging, gray brick courthouse in Sumner's square." Of the inside of the courthouse, the *Detroit News* reported: "The 'box' in which 12 of them [the jury] will sit is not a box at all, but two rows of chairs bolted to the floor in a corner. Originally these were swivel chairs, but two have been replaced by cane seated straight chairs."[17]

The lack of financial support for the legal facilities was fitting. Because white supremacy ruled in this region, blacks often felt the brunt of the prosecutions. Black people, either through actual crimes committed, attempts to eke out some advances, or outright false accusations, constituted the majority of the defendants in legal cases in the Deep South. Elite white residents therefore felt little urgency to improve the courthouse. Since most of the wealthy residents did not even have to serve on juries, they would see no reason why they should spend their money on a building used by poorer white people to convict even more disadvantaged black people.[18]

The trial of Bryant and Milam set Mississippi justice in stark contrast to that in most of the rest of the country and focused the nation's attention on the social, economic, and political ills of the South. Through the efforts of his family, civil rights organizations, black publications, and Midwest mainstream print outlets, the saliency of Emmett Till's death transferred to the American public. Amid the growing public outrage fueled by individuals and organizations seeking justice for Till, northeastern mainstream papers, which up to that point had offered only moderate criticism of Mississippi, now took on a disposition of utter indignation toward the state. Underscoring the racial injustices in Mississippi's criminal system, the *Pittsburgh Post-Gazette* rebuked: "Rarely, if ever, has a white man been executed in a Mississippi case involving a Negro slaying. And Chatham [the prosecution attorney] made it plain he is not asking the cotton farmers who make up the bulk of any jury here to shatter precedent." Similarly challenging Chatham's defeatist approach to the case, the *Philadelphia Evening Bulletin* questioned why any district attorney would state before the trial that he would not ask for the death penalty and that "a substantial part of the state's evidence is circumstantial." Utterances like these from Mississippi officials led Murray Kempton, a staffer with the *New York Post,* to lament: "The sovereign principality of Tallahatchie County set itself . . . to give a fast trial and a shame-faced acquittal to [Bryant and Milam]." Of the potential jury pool, he added: "Every prospective juryman believes in his heart . . . [that the defendants] dragged a 14-year-old boy out of bed, kicked the back of his head off and threw his weighted body into the river just for being a Negro who had whistled at a white woman." Truly, as the *New York Times* saw it, "the real drama will concern the entire state and its roles as a militant defender of racial segregation practices." Far from the early coverage that minimized the racial aspects of the trial and displayed faith in the legal process, this new set of articles in the northeastern mainstream press captured the saliency of the events, framing the county seat as racist and backward.[19]

Images of a socially, morally, and intellectually backward South abounded as northeastern dailies pointed to the legacy of slavery and the persistence of racism in every facet of this closed society. In stark contrast to depictions of Moses Wright's home as a "cotton field shack" and a "cabin home" was the plantation property, complete with a "headquarters shed," where Till was beaten and murdered. Clearly, the word choices primed memories of slavery. Wright's *shack* or *cabin* invoked images of slave quarters, while Till's murderers reigned over a plantation, the classic symbol of slavery and racial oppression.[20]

White supremacy in this land relied on the persistence of dual societies strictly segregated by race, and northeastern mainstream reporters placed this racially motivated social hierarchy on trial through their coverage of the court proceedings. As an *Evening Bulletin* article pointed out: "Although 63.5 per cent of the population of this county is Negroes, there is not one registered Negro voter. Since one must be a qualified voter to serve on a jury here, there were no Negroes available for duty." Emphasizing the same demographic anomaly, the *Philadelphia Evening Bulletin* editorialized: "This is an amazing and humiliating condition to exist in a part of a nation which prides itself on being the chief supporter of democratic principles in the world's forum." Of this obvious hypocrisy, the *Bulletin* boldly judged: "[Sumner] refuses the vote to Negroes in plain violation of the 15th amendment to the Constitution, which declares no person shall be denied the right to vote 'because of race, color or previous condition of servitude.'"[21]

The fact that there were no blacks registered to vote was not for lack of trying. Many in the Deep South and across the nation had over the years engaged in efforts to increase black access to the franchise. Two such suffrage champions, Charles and Medgar Evers, native Mississippians, World War II veterans, and college graduates, attempted to register black voters beginning with the election of 1946. Part of the reason whites prevented blacks from voting was the fear that by sheer numbers they would dominate Mississippi politics. Blacks outnumbered whites in the state until 1940; by 1950, they represented just over 45 percent of the population and, by 1960, just over 42 percent. Despite these high percentages, on the eve of the 1964 Civil Rights Act, only 6.7 percent of African Americans in Mississippi were eligible to vote because, when African Americans went to the polling stations, armed white citizens met them and turned them away. As the *Evening Bulletin*'s James Kilgallen saw it, "[In the systematic effort to discriminate against blacks] Mississippi resorts to various 'educational' tests as subterfuges to defeat the letter of the law. No one is fooled by them. The fact is that a majority of the people of Tallahatchie county are denied the right of self-government." The Till trial made it clear to the world that black people had no rights in the town of Sumner, in the county of Tallahatchie, or in the state of Mississippi. Mississippi was, as Joseph Crespino saw it, "the South on steroids."[22]

Integration fueled whites' efforts to exonerate Bryant and Milam, and the attacks that this Mississippi community experienced from northeastern black presses were heightened because the locals rallied around the accused. In the words of one journalist, this tiny town was "beset from every quarter by a mounting wave of protests," and these "red-faced Mississippi officials . . . sought to lift the blanket of shame which has been draped over this deep south state."[23]

As the northeastern black press saw it, with the Till case Mississippians elevated their defense of the archaic system of white supremacy that ruled their land, and these publications used every action by Mississippi officials as further proof of the lack of democracy, equality, and freedom in the South. According to reports, Mississippians bonded together and created a protective barrier around Bryant, Milam, and the system of racial oppression that the two men represented. The *Philadelphia Tribune* referred to this phenomenon as "a climate of opinion in which such a brutal insensate murder could be perpetrated."[24]

The *Pittsburgh Courier*'s George F. Brown reflected: "Mississippi culture allowed and encouraged lynching and other race crimes." He cautioned: "Remember, [Till] was conditioned to his way of life just as people in Mississippi are conditioned to their feudal ideas." Brown emphasized that Till did not know the state of race relations. Therefore, "Emmett was not subservient, not cowed by Dixie mores, so he said something to the grocer's wife and whistled—just as he had seen people do on television, in movies, in comic books, on streets." By accentuating Till's youthful innocence regarding the consequences of transgressing against Mississippi racial norms, this analysis added context to his actions. It was precisely this innocence that led many across the country to host rallies protesting the vile crime, and the northeastern black press readily highlighted these mass cries for justice.[25]

In light of the obvious support that Bryant and Milam received from their Deep South neighbors, the *New York Amsterdam News* emphasized a New York rally protesting the Till lynching. Prominent black leaders from labor and civil rights organizations dropped everything to lambaste

Figure 4.1. Roy Wilkins addressing Garment Center Labor Rally for Emmett Till (n.d.). *Daily Worker* and *Daily World* Photograph Collection, Tamiment Library and Robert F. Wagner Labor Archives, New York University.

this gruesome crime against a fourteen-year-old boy that proved democracy was a dream for blacks in white supremacist Mississippi. At a meeting held in Harlem's Williams Colored Methodist Episcopal Church, "A. Philip Randolph, president of the Brotherhood of Sleeping Car Porters, and Roy Wilkins and Dr. Channing Tobias of the NAACP" served as keynote speakers. Rallies like this one and the Garment Center Labor Rally pictured in figure 4.1 persisted throughout the balance of the year as labor and civil rights champions derided the insensate lynching of Emmett Till, which stirred the black community highly, and continued to underscore the saliency of Till's life and death.[26]

White supremacy defined white Mississippians' disposition toward white-on-black violence. Even when a case involved the murder of a young boy, Mississippi racial mores precluded any chance for justice. Choosing to accept this reality rather than adopt a disposition of protest against untenable racial norms, mainstream papers from the West did little to question southern racial conventions. The *San Francisco Examiner,* for example, accepted without challenge statements from Mississippi whites, like: "Sidney Carlton[,] one of the battery of five defense lawyers, declared on the eve of the trial that 'the State's case is rather weak. We are hopeful that we can obtain a directed verdict of acquittal and that the case will not have to go to the jury.'" The prosecuting attorney's clearly stated lack of faith in the case led the *Examiner* to report the next day that both the prosecution and the defense expected a speedy trial. Similarly, the *Denver Post* pointed up statements from other Mississippi officials that predicted a two- or three-day trial because "the state seems to have little evidence." Five days later, another *Post* article noted: "State attorneys privately voice doubt they would get a guilty verdict." All these statements, reproduced without scrutiny in the pages of western dailies, proved that neither Mississippi political and legal officials nor western mainstream papers felt that the jury would convict the defendants. Unlike the mainstream newspapers from other regions of the country that used the assumed impossibility of conviction to challenge the very essence of justice in the Deep South and underscore the importance of the lynching as a barometer of race relations, the western dailies continually argued that the only reason the Till trial would end with a quick acquittal was that the prosecution did not have enough evidence to prove its case.[27]

The pretrial framing of Mississippi race relations in the western mainstream press is revealed as an anomaly when compared to similar coverage in other areas of the country, which by and large blamed Till's death on racial mores in Mississippi. As far as most Americans outside of the South were concerned, *M* truly stood for *Mississippi* and *murder.* It should come as no surprise, then, that, in conjunction with the trial of Bryant and Milam, the vile and violent system of white supremacy that shaped every aspect of life in Mississippi was about to go on trial itself—a trial by print jury.

5

Trial by Print

Over the course of four days in September, Roy Bryant and J. W. Milam, the state of Mississippi, the Deep South, and the nation all went on trial, a trial by print. Four days after the trial began, the shocking saga of brutality and murder that had captured the nation's and the world's imagination reached a climax when, after roughly an hour of deliberation, the jury returned a verdict of not guilty. For many of the reporters, their time in Sumner, Mississippi, following the trial shone a light on the realities of southern racial oppression. Through their trial coverage, national and regional print media outlets reinforced and rearticulated their disposition toward the lynching and Mississippi's ability to ensure justice in a case of white-on-black crime. In effect, the media's coverage of the trial was itself a trial by print of the state of Mississippi, the Deep South, and the nation. This coverage underscored the saliency of the Till lynching in the annals of American race relations, it fueled a visceral public outrage, and it helped galvanize a generation of civil rights activists.

By the start of the trial, most national publications had already deemed Bryant and Milam guilty of murder; therefore, the overwhelming backing the accused enjoyed from their white Mississippi compatriots drew the ire of the staff at news outlets. Only Judge Curtis Swango and District Attorney Gerald Chatham escaped outright condemnation in the pages of *Time* and *Newsweek*. Both publications noted that Judge Swango was a beacon of progress and justice in the dark abyss of Mississippi's white supremacist history. *Time* offered: "Tallahatchie County came into conflict with the tradition of the law in the person of Circuit Judge Curtis M. Swango." District Attorney Chatham and the state-appointed special prosecutor, Robert Smith, also drew kudos. As *Time* saw it: "The prosecutors for the State of Mississippi . . . made an earnest effort to build their case at what can be assumed to be great social cost to themselves." The reason for that "great social cost"? As *Life* observed: "The prosecution was up against the whole mass of Mississippi prejudice."[1]

Surely, the prosecuting attorneys deserved some recognition for battling obstacles throughout the process, but *The Nation*'s Dan Wakefield offered a different perspective, one that made clear the fact that the prosecution's strong case was a result of the courage and determination of black trial witnesses rather than prosecutorial efforts. Commenting on the resolve of black witnesses, Wakefield underscored how Till's great-uncle Moses Wright spoke loudly and clearly while recounting the night of the kidnapping: "He never lost his straightforward attitude or lowered his head." This fortitude came in the face of customarily disrespectful attitudes toward black men, both the prosecution and the defense attorneys refusing to use the title *Mr.* and consistently calling him "Mose" or "Uncle Mose."[2]

Equally affronted by southerners during the trial, and equally praised for her resoluteness, was Mamie Till-Mobley. In typical racist fashion, both sets of attorneys neglected to call her *Miss* or *Mrs.*, and, in an ultimate show of disrespect, the defense counsel received permission from Judge Swango to remain seated while questioning her. Regardless, Till-Mobley showed her strength as well as her resolve to memorialize her son's life and condemn his murderers. Wakefield described her under cross-examination as "answering intelligently, steadily, slightly turning her head to one side as she listened to questions, replying with a slow, distinct emphasis." Chronicling her attention and focus on the stand, Wakefield explained how she turned her head to hear the questions. Most importantly, his description of her answers affirmed her determined assertion that the body found in the Tallahatchie River was that of her son. Mamie Till-Mobley responded to her son's lynching and the racism in Mississippi by going to the Deep South to testify against the murderers, and, in that role, she spoke slowly and deliberately so that there would be no mistaking her beliefs. Moreover, despite the racist lynching of her son, Till-Mobley had the fortitude and forgiveness to say: "I'm not bitter against the white people. . . . The color of a person's skin has never made any difference to me." The public gravitated to her and wanted to show their support, and she "received . . . $1,000 in over 1,000 letters from people all over the country."[3]

The outpouring of support offered Mamie Till-Mobley, which was a sign that the public had internalized the salience of this lynching, was a major topic of coverage in the NAACP's own publication, *The Crisis*. Founded in 1910 under the editorial leadership of W. E. B. DuBois, who charged the periodical with serving as a "record of the darker races," this publication pointed up the groundswell of protest in response to the Till lynching. As *The Crisis* staff saw it, "Not since Pearl Harbor had the country been so outraged as by the brutal insensate lynching of 14-year-old Emmett Louis Till and the unconscionable verdict of the Sumner, Mississippi jury which freed the boy's accused killers." This verdict fueled the fires of indignation in readers of *The Crisis,* which used the opportunity to present clear and poignant indictments of the South. Its editors accused: "The white people of Mississippi are directly responsible for this hideous crime. It is one more casualty in their campaign of reprisal being waged against the NAACP and Negro advancement." *The Crisis* staff, led by the publication's editor, James Ivy, estimated: "The white minds of Mississippi are poisoned with every imaginable lie and slander about Negroes and the NAACP." In the opinion of Ivy and his staff, "These are punitive measures designed to control the Negro, to make him obedient and tractable, to keep him a second-class citizen in his own state."[4]

In Mississippi, second-class status kept blacks disenfranchised and ineligible to sit on the jury that dictated the fate of Bryant and Milam. As a result, the defendants faced a panel of jurors who were all beneficiaries of the racist closed society. Offering exhaustive details about the jury-selection process, the *Chicago Tribune* testified: "There are seven farmers in the tentative jury of 10, some of them neighbors of the men on trial. One of the seven is a former client of Hamilton Caldwell, Tallahatchie county attorney, who sits at the prosecution table as one of a trio." In this small town, the racial implications of the trial, and the fact that all the jurors were white men who directly or indirectly benefited from the patriarchal oppression of African Americans, made a fair trial improbable, if not impossible.[5]

Of the process that empaneled the jurors, the *Tribune* added: "The defense has used up only two of its 12 preemptory challenges. . . . The state employed 11 of 12 challenges. . . . The questioning of these prospective jurors was impressive. It was a questioning that brought the racial issue frankly into the open. It was in effect a soul-searching inquisition into whether the juror, a white man, can sit in judgment on two other white men accused of killing a Negro." Even with this probing inquisition, however, "there was no question asked about a prospective juror's reaction in case the evidence should show the Negro victim had insulted a white woman." The *Detroit News* further pointed up the laxity in the southern legal process: "[The jurors] swore in an atmosphere which appeared incredible to

Northern observers accustomed to the decorum of Northern courts. Judge Swango sipped soft drinks on the bench during much of the day, and the empty bottles strewing the floor clattered together as each prospective juror struggled through the crowded court to his examination."[6]

In contrast to the cramped and debris-ridden spaces afforded to prospective jurors and black attendees, the defendants and their families viewed the proceedings from positions of comfort and accommodation. The *Chicago Tribune* marked these luxuries: "The two defendants came to court with their children in their arms and their wives trailing behind them, followed by an array of 20 to 30 close relatives." The report continued: "Each man sat thru most of the morning [of the first day of the trial] with a child on each knee. . . . The children became bored with the proceedings after a few hours and emitted occasional squawks." This was no mere coincidence; in fact, defense attorneys admitted that the family presence was a clear tactic to garner sympathy from the jury, and the *Tribune* assailed that the defense counsel, C. Sidney Carlton, admitted that he "wouldn't think of even trying a civil case without parading the family." The day wore on: "Leroy [Milam's son] carried a toy pistol with which he snapped shots through the room. Bill [Bryant's son] earnestly kept punching his father's jaw as the father laughed aloud."[7]

Given the nature of the trial, the sight of a "toy pistol" could have offended the prosecution and especially Till's family, but, as Paul Holmes, writing for the *Tribune,* reported, no one made any effort to seize the gun or apologize to the lynch victim's family. All this was customary in a region where enslavement, battles with Native Americans, whites' valuing of honor, and the lack of urban socialization led to the creation of a bellicose culture. In these violent environs steeped with an ardent disregard for the sentiments of black people, the presence of a toy gun during a murder trial in which a firearm was used in the crime seemed ordinary. As only the midwestern press noted, these white children had the privilege of youth, while Mamie Till-Mobley's son died for his August night prank.[8]

Also missing in many other regional accounts of the trial were depictions of the spectacular, almost carnivalesque nature of the trial. The *Tribune*'s Holmes underscored: "Spectators brought lunch and munched on sandwiches while the business of the court droned along. Two were observed with cans of beer which they opened and drank without rebuke from the bailiffs of the court." The *Detroit News*'s Russell Harris mocked: "Along the walls Sumner's young sat, aping the clothing and stance of the land's feudal cotton planters, tried to make single cigars last for hours. The crowd, which grew during the day to several hundred, choked the court-house stairs and broke a window in the press for admittance. The specta-tors laughed at some of the juror dismissals, including the first, a man who said he had not paid his taxes but who, friends called aloud, 'comes under the drunk part.'"[9]

Amid this lax atmosphere, halfway through the first day of the trial the prosecution asked for a recess so that it could search out and question additional witnesses. Detailing the manhunt, Holmes reported: "They were searching the swamplands and the cotton fields tonight for shadow witnesses in the murder trial." Most sought after in this manhunt were Leroy Collins and Henry Loggins, former employees of Milam's, and one Frank Young. Standing in the way of the manhunt was the fact that most black field hands were too wary of repercussions to talk about Col-lins, Loggins, or Young. Eventually, "a few said . . . that neither Collins nor Loggins [had] been seen since Aug. 28 and that Young vanished this week."[10]

While Collins, Loggins, and Young proved impossible to locate, four others were compelled to step forward eventually. Recounting this quar-tets' entrée into the Till saga, Harris wrote: "Four terrified Negroes, dragged from their plantation homes as witnesses in the Emmett Till kidnap-murder case were brought to the courthouse here today." When one of the witnesses, Willie Reed, testified, he was "speaking so softly he frequently could not be heard by the court reporter, three feet away." The inevitable repercussion of testimony at this trial struck terror in the hearts of all Afri-can American witnesses. Threats of violent white retaliation against Afri-can Americans were a staple of the South; despite this fact, these black witnesses risked all to testify that Bryant and Milam were with Till near the time of his death.[11]

Attempting to counter this courageous testimony on the part of black witnesses, Juanita Milam, wife of J. W. Milam, took the stand and testified that "her husband received a battlefield commission in Germany during World War II." The defense also got support from Sheriff H. C. Strider, who swore that the body could not have been that of Till, and bolstered this testimony with similar accounts from Dr. L. B. Otken, a physician from Greenwood, Mississippi, and H. D. Malone, the undertaker who prepared the body for shipment north. Armed with these testimonials, the defense secured from the jury a not guilty verdict on September 23, 1955.[12]

Challenging Mississippi's disposition toward race and gender as it was exhibited throughout the trial, journalists for the midwestern black press excoriated the state for its miscarriage of justice. The *Cleveland Call and Post* columnist James Hicks lamented the fact that Collins and Loggins "were discovered 'missing' as the trial . . . opened." After asking about the disappearance, Hicks learned that locals feared the pair had "either been 'scared out of town' or . . . killed." Similarly silenced were any black voices that might have dared enter the pool of perspective jurors. The county issued jury summonses from a list of names found on its voting registry. Because no blacks in Tallahatchie had broken through the impenetrable wall of disfranchisement, none were eligible to serve on the panel.[13]

L. Alex Wilson, a journalist and editor in the *Defender* newspaper franchise, challenged this system of segregation and, along with others, lamented the deplorable conditions under which black journalists had to practice their craft. The sheriff originally allocated only four seats to black reporters, seats, moreover, that offered only limited opportunity to see the proceedings and hear the testimony. Wilson noted that, although "Strider was advised by this writer that the Negro newsmen might not be able to hear proceedings well from their position," the sheriff did not care. Adhering to southern racism, he would not allow himself to consider the needs of these black professionals, instead responding: "Whenever you are unable to hear just let me know."[14]

Casting his criticism of the segregated conditions a different way, Roi Ottley noted: "If [Moses] Wright was the victim of crude prejudice, so too were the Negro observers. Negro reporters and photographers were labeled 'niggers,' and seated at a Jim Crow table where indeed they had difficulty hearing the proceedings." Black press members from outside Mississippi thus entered a region of the country where white rule shaped every interaction. In fact, Ottley's editorial reminded readers that white Mississippians had perfected white supremacy to the point where it became an international model of oppression: "Few people nowadays remember that back in the 1930's Adolph Hitler sent a mission to the U.S. to study the South's treatment of Negroes, so that he could more efficiently terrorize the Jews."[15]

In these environs, where discrimination and oppression had long since been perfected, "an all-white male jury of sharecroppers demonstrated here Friday that the constitutional guarantees of 'Life, Liberty, and the Pursuit of Happiness' do not apply to Negro citizens of their state." The jury's blatant disregard for justice was the main reason why "Mississippi thus stands in the eyes of the nation today as a place where judgment and fair play have flown to the four winds, and where men either have lost their reason or refuse to recognize it when they are faced by it." Adding salt to the gaping wound on the face of the American justice system, Hicks lamented that the defense's case was based on no substantial evidence. In fact, "It must be stated that never in the history of this reporter's long years of court reporting has he seen a weaker and more inflammatory case based on pure fantasy such as was presented by the battery of five white lawyers who defended the two white men." As if confirming his worst fears, the Mississippi trial led the *Call and Post* journalist to realize, "The hidden factor in the backwardness of this state is the blind spot of racial prejudice in the eyes of its sharecropper people, which prevents them from seeing and thinking straight when they look upon a black face." Everything in Mississippi, from the fields to the courthouse, was determined by the racist legacy of forced servitude and white supremacy. That was why, in the face of obviously damning evidence, Bryant and Milam were able to beat the charges. They were beneficiaries of "the jungles of Mississippi" so perverse that they permitted the criminals to laugh as they mocked the justice system; at the same time the other forty-seven states were "crying for Mississippi." This was one of the most virulent attacks on the Deep South to be found in any region's black press, and it clearly outlined the untenable situation of black Mississippians.[16]

Building on Hicks's themes, a *Call and Post* editorial argued: "Mississippi has no shame for the crime that was committed, nor any rapprochement for the twelve jurors whose ignorance and prejudice permitted them the joy of such a verdict." Complicit in the injustice were "the Mississippi churches," which produced no clergy condemning the Till lynching, "the Mississippi bar," which licensed an entire town of lawyers willing to defend murderers, and "a state" that consistently "has made a mockery of everything that is sacred in our Christian life, fair in our social philosophy or legal in our constitutional form of government." As a result, "the verdict of not guilty . . . is the greatest indictment of the white people of prejudice ridden Mississippi ever rendered."[17]

Midwestern black press outlets condemned all Mississippians as conspirators with Bryant and Milam, and the *Chicago Defender* publisher, John Sengstacke, used his paper as a forum to voice his anger over the verdict. Sengstacke rarely, if ever, hid behind the guise of objectivity. For the *Defender* publisher, the black press existed to "protect black people," a claim he defiantly issued in 1942 to Attorney General Francis Biddle when Biddle threatened to bring espionage charges against black newspaper publishers. Having heroically confronted the Department of Justice in the midst of wartime, Sengstacke had no qualms about challenging both Mississippi and federal inaction during the 1955 Till saga. "The acquittal of J. W. Milam and Roy Bryant and the miscarriage of justice in Sumner, Miss., is evidence that Negroes in Mississippi and the South have no rights that the white man will respect," he wrote. The *Defender* had always blamed the federal government for indifference to the unequal allocation of justice, and he used the Till case to continue his call for government intervention: "Since there is no justice in Mississippi, it is now up to President Eisenhower to overrule his attorney general who says Emmett Till's civil rights have not been violated." To that end, he wired the president, asking whether his office planned to do anything in response to Till's lynching, an event he called a "shocking act of lawlessness." Moreover, his visceral attachment to the case led him to allocate his paper franchises' most competent resources, the *Tri-State Defender* editor L. Alex Wilson and Moses Newson, an expert on southern race relations, to cover the southern end of the Till saga.[18]

For her part, Mamie Till-Mobley used her hometown *Defender* as a platform by remarking about the trial: "It's about the biggest farce I have ever seen. It is unbelievable and fantastic." Another entry from the same edition presented her direct accusations against Sheriff Strider: "The mother of Emmett Louis Till has accused Tallahatchie County Sheriff H. C. Strider of hiding two key witnesses; namely LeRoy (Too Tight) Collins and Henry Lee Loggins." This represented a forward approach, given 1950s gender conventions, which prevented women from confronting men, but, as is apparent from Sengstacke's comments, the *Chicago Defender* was determined to point up the saliency of this lynching by placing a premium on outrage over the trial outcome.[19]

Northeastern mainstream papers offered additional condemnation of the trial. The *New York Post* focused its attention on one of the accused: "Every time a stranger looked at J. W. Milam and wanted to hate him, there was always a little boy in the line of vision. That is the horror. For here was the man sitting in that place who was loved by his children and deserved their love and who is charged with killing a boy because he was black and didn't know his place." Unaffected by the children, Murray Kempton observed: "J. W. Milam is a violent man of bad reputation. The defense danced around his name yesterday because even though it knows its client will walk free sometime late this week, it is not proud of him." This would simply be another in a long line of legally sanctioned lynchings of African

Americans. One had only to look at the lack of prosecution in the Belzoni lynching of George Lee earlier that year, or the lack of indictment in the murder of Lamar Smith, to understand the nature of white supremacy in Mississippi. The only differences between those cases and Till's were that law enforcement officials actually arrested Bryant and Milam and a grand jury indicted them.[20]

In this turbulent climate, in which the *New York Times*'s John Popham argued that race relations were "extraordinarily touchy," popular northeastern press employees knew that this trial was a powder keg ready to explode. References to the hot, sticky weather in Mississippi and the potential for a tragic fire in the courtroom served as symbols of the heated nature of the trial and race relations in the state. In this tense environment, emotions ran high, and no one individual had more cause for emotion than Till's mother. While papers from across the country keyed in on her severe distress, the *New York Post* presented a thoughtful and intelligent portrait of her: "As the Till trial went on, [Till-Mobley] sat outside the court all by herself reading her paper; the ordinary Negroes of Tallahatchie County . . . not quite able to communicate with her; and she alone . . . seemed to understand the implications of this week."[21]

While they supported Mamie Till-Mobley, northeastern paper staffs failed to question the veracity of Carolyn Bryant's statements or her motives as she delivered testimony about Till's prank. According to Bryant, "this Negro man came into the store. . . . He caught my hand. . . . I removed my hand. . . . He said, 'How about a date, baby?'" As if this offense was not enough, the "Negro man" persisted: "I turned and started to the back of the store. He caught me at the cash register . . . and put both hands around my waist. He said, 'What's the matter, baby, can't you take it?'" The coverage left open the question of what it was that Carolyn Bryant could not take. Her statement primed traditional stereotypes of hypersexual black men at the very least and at the extreme thoughts of well-endowed African mandingos. The journalists did little to dispel these images and might have even subscribed to some or all of this stereotypical analysis. In fact, a *Pittsburgh Post-Gazette* journalist described the scene in the store using a suspiciously sexualized choice of words: "[Till] allegedly climaxed his visit with a wolf-whistle at the slender attractive brunette." That the visit "climaxed" further sexualized the incident and reinforced racist stereotypes of black men. This testimony was extremely condemning. By approaching a white woman, Emmett Till committed what to the southern white male mind was the ultimate crime. In America, one had only to whisper the word *rape,* and lynch mobs would form to enact vigilante justice on the accused.[22]

As Carolyn Bryant concluded her testimony amid this racial and sexual tension, she provided the trial attendees and those following the coverage in their local papers with yet another opportunity to let their minds wander, revealing: "The Negro then addressed her in terms too unprintable to relate, ending the sentence, 'I've been with a white woman before.'" No popular northeastern publication made any effort to verify Bryant's testimony. Perpetuating the age-old belief in the sanctity of white womanhood, Bryant was treated as if she were beyond reproach and, therefore, no further questioning of her was necessary. Concluding the feminine framing of Carolyn Bryant, the *Post-Gazette* added the pièce de résistance, an image of her resting her head on her husband's shoulder after her testimony.[23]

The *Pittsburgh Courier*'s James Boyack reported: "Men's souls [were throughout the trial] torn by fear . . . and hatred . . . and violence. Here, the atmosphere is depressing to the human spirit." The virulence of southern social norms was evident in the daily interactions and observances of black journalists. America was supposed to be a bastion of freedom, but to one reader the southern actions seemed "worse than anything the Chinese Communists have yet done." In the *New York Amsterdam News*'s estimation: "Representatives from newspapers, magazines and radio and television stations are here and photographers are swarming all over the little lawn [outside the Sumner courthouse] to get new angles on the age-old story of black oppression by white supremacists." For the New York black press, this farce of a trial was simply another chapter in the long annals of the oppression of African Americans.[24]

Many of the reports found in southeastern mainstream newspapers mirrored midwestern and northeastern attacks on the Mississippi proceedings. They challenged the segregated facilities, the lack of African Americans on the jury, and, most notably, the jury's deliberations. When asked about the verdict, the jury foreman acknowledged that the panel doubted that the nude and mutilated body dragged out of the Tallahatchie River on August 31 was that of Emmett Louis Till. According to articles in the Richmond, Charlotte, and Atlanta newspapers, Sheriff Strider's alleged doubt as to the identity of the body was bolstered when, "in summing up, Defense Lawyer John Whitten offered a theory that rabblerousers put a Negro body—dead some days—in the river, and falsely ballyhooed it as Till's." The *Washington Post* quipped: "The defense . . . suggested that young Till and his uncle, Moses Wright, . . . might have gotten in touch 'with some of the persons who were trying to create ill will among the whites and blacks' and arranged to put 'some deceased person' in the river wearing Till's ring." Strider's lie provided the jury with the perfect excuse for its support of white supremacy and murder. The panel expounded on the ludicrous allegations implicating not only sixty-four-year-old Moses Wright but also the slain fourteen-year-old boy. As was a customary part of white racism, these jurors developed convoluted stories and adapted their stereotypical views of African Americans to fit their needs instead of simply accepting the fact that white supremacist hatred led white people to abuse, brutalize, and kill African Americans.[25]

Of the verdict, the *Charlotte Observer* overtly charged: "If the trial of J. W. Milam and Roy Bryant proves anything, it proves that justice is all too often thwarted in many parts of the South—for whites and blacks alike—by incredibly inadequate law enforcement at the local level." Clearly, "a modern, professional criminal investigation would have closed the loopholes in the state's case. And so the defense was able to cast doubt on the identification of the body as that of Emmett Till." Thanks to the jury, "the verdict of public opinion will be that Mississippi has granted license to murder, if that is necessary to keep the black man in his place." However, "[the] thoughtful Southerner—and he is more numerous and more influential than residents of the non-South realize—is bitter and ashamed that an Emmett Louis Till could be murdered in this region without the murderers being found and brought to justice. But if he is a realist, he also knows that there may be other Tills in the South's future." Therefore, "his job is to fight with all his vigor against those who would take the law into their own hands, no matter what the provocation."[26]

Southeastern black press employees doubted that these right-minded white southerners would emerge, and they remained unconvinced that the state could put aside its racism and demonstrate that justice truly was color-blind in Mississippi. Hesitant to share fully his experiences covering the trial while he was still in Mississippi, James Hicks later chronicled his involvement in the Till saga through a four-installment article first printed in October 1955 in three black newspapers, the *Cleveland Call and Post,* the *Baltimore Afro-American,* and the *Atlanta Daily World.* Hicks experienced warrantless surveillance, verbal harassment, thinly veiled threats on his life, and false arrest during his time in Mississippi. Owing in no small part to his experiences covering the trial, this veteran journalist pointed up the saliency of this trial in the chronicles of American race relations: "The constitutional guarantees of 'life, liberty, and the pursuit of happiness' do not apply to the colored citizens of [Mississippi]." "Mississippi thus stands in the eyes of the nation today as a place where judgment and fair play have flown to the four winds and where men either have lost their reason or refuse to recognize it when they are faced by it," he further charged.[27]

James Hicks's allegations against the Deep South state were based squarely on the experiences he and his colleagues in the black press had while covering the Till trial, and his recollections, boldly printed in the pages of three black newspapers, memorialized the efforts of black press employees who risked their lives to expose Mississippi injustice. The day before the trial, Hicks attended a funeral at a black church, and a woman, who was hiding behind a car, informed him, "A boy named 'Too Tight' was on the truck the night of the murder. . . . [H]e had suddenly disappeared and no one knew where he was." When Hicks asked for more information, the woman told him to go to Glendora, Mississippi, and ask the black people in that town. She also warned: "Be careful and don't let the people know what you are looking for. Don't talk to any white people. . . . Don't . . . get caught down there after dark."[28]

Hicks heeded the woman's words and set off for Glendora. He found a local black dance hall, and he asked the bartender about "Too Tight": "The man stopped as if I had hit him in the face. I looked over to my right and some men seated at a table playing 'Georgia Skin' dropped their cards and turned to look at me." Clearly, even in this all-black establishment, the employees and clientele were hesitant to discuss the mysterious disappearance of one of their own. They feared that white racists had captured Collins in order to keep him from testifying at the trial. Hicks wanted to hear this information firsthand, so he pressed the issue. The bartender finally admitted in a whisper: "'Too Tight' is in jail." And he directed Hicks to a woman seated in the corner of the room.[29]

In his conversation with the woman, the reporter learned Collins lived with her and her partner, Henry Lee Loggins. She told Hicks: "[Both Collins and Loggins] worked for one of those white men who kidnapped that boy from Chicago and they came and got both of them." After this revelation, Hicks asked the woman whether she was willing to go with him to the jail and identify Collins and Loggins. She agreed to go; however, she would not go during the day: "The white for which she worked came around and whipped everyone who didn't go out into the cotton fields and pick his cotton. Even if they are sick he whips them." This statement, more than any other, showed that slavery was still alive and well in the Mississippi Delta. Extralegal violence, or threats of violence, haunted black residents and in many ways dictated their daily lives.[30]

Unfortunately for him, Hicks never made it back to Glendora, but when he returned to his motel in the all-black town of Mound Bayou, Mississippi, he learned even more from other black journalists. *Jet's* Simeon Booker and others told him that on the way from Money to Mound Bayou, they ran into a truckload of gun-toting white men. The reporters, who questioned why the men had guns, were told that they were deer hunting; however, deer-hunting season had not started yet. It was likely no coincidence that this encounter occurred on the same dirt road that Hicks used to get to Glendora, and this led him to speculate that the men in the truck were hunting for a "buck" named James Hicks.[31]

This frightening disclosure did not deter Hicks or his colleagues from their efforts to learn the facts behind the Till lynching. However, learning the facts and completing his job proved difficult endeavors in this racially charged environment. Hicks and his black colleagues heard from the Mississippian Dr. T. R. M. Howard that at least five additional black people could testify at the trial. The consummate journalist, Hicks wanted to inform his editors of this news, but Howard urged him to sit on the story, suggesting that "once a story got into the papers, their lives would not be worth a nickel" and warning that "the wires out of Mound Bayou are not safe." Even in this all-black town, white Mississippians monitored communications and attempted to maintain their control over black citizens.[32]

Efforts to maintain secrecy were thwarted when white reporters heard of the discovery and came to Mound Bayou to listen to Howard's story. The Mississippi doctor told the reporters, identified by Hicks as Clark Porteous of the *Memphis Press-Scimitar* and Jim Featherstone of the *Jackson Daily News*: "Till was not killed in Tallahatchie County but killed in Sunflower County . . . in the headquarters shed of the Clint Sheridan Plantation which is managed by Leslie Milam, brother of J. W. Milam." If it could be proved true, this information could have halted the trial in Sumner and led to a new trial by a new jury. It would also have taken investigative duties and law enforcement oversight out of the hands of the racist Sheriff Strider.[33]

The following evening, Hicks learned more about how black Mississippians circumvented the oppressive hand of white supremacy. He and his colleagues were to meet the witnesses in Cleveland, Mississippi. According to Hicks: "[On reaching the rendezvous point] a man . . . told me to park my car and get into his car. Then he drove me to a house which turned out to be the real meeting place." "I later learned that this is the way they do it down there. They announce one place as the site. But when you arrive there, it is really not the bona fide place. If you are the right person, you are taken from there to the meeting place. If you are not no one will admit knowing what you are talking about," the journalist concluded. Obviously, these African Americans were in tune with their environment. They knew how to survive and eke out a modicum of success within this oppressive culture. As much as they could, black Mississippians negotiated white racism and worked with their black neighbors to establish a survival code.[34]

That same evening, Hicks experienced firsthand just how untrustworthy Deep South whites were. When he reached the actual meeting location, he learned: "During the afternoon, the authorities, notified by the white reporters, had gone to the plantations ahead of them and questioned the prospective witnesses. This had scared them to death and they felt that we had gone back [on] our promise to get them out of there before telling the white people." As a result, "they refused to come to the meeting with us." Minutes after everyone had assembled, they learned that the *Press-Scimitar* journalist Clark Porteous was en route with "sheriffs from various counties, a special prosecutor sent by the Governor and other officials."[35]

From that point on, Hicks felt that the local whites knew everything that he reported to his editors before it reached the papers. He also noted a closer observation of his activities, recounting: "Those who could not get into the courtroom made it a habit to crowd around the open phones and the Western Union desk and listen to reporters call in their stories on special wires set up for them." It is not clear whether that was the case before the fateful night of the planned meeting with prospective witnesses, but it was certainly the case afterward. Hicks considered filing his story by way of the one black Sumner resident who owned a phone, but he decided against it when the man told him that whites listened in on everything he said over that phone line. No place was safe for blacks in this region, and this fact made the need for false rendezvous points and clandestine efforts even clearer.[36]

Hicks ran into additional trouble the following day. During the afternoon recess, he went to his rental car to get another notebook. Keys in hand, a pistol-packing white officer placed him under arrest. Despite numerous attempts on the part of Hicks, Jim Featherstone, and Sumner's mainstream daily publisher, W. M. Simpson, the sheriff's deputy refused to reveal the charges. It was not until a host of reporters, who had heard of the arrest, came to investigate that the deputy informed the crowd that Hicks had violated a traffic law that morning when he passed a "standing school bus." At that point, everyone voiced their outrage that Hicks was held on such a trumped-up charge. The justice of the peace who tried Hicks dismissed the charges, but the reporter admitted: "By this time . . . I was getting the general idea that perhaps I was a marked man for during his conversation with me the justice of the peace started telling where I was staying, what time I got to the trial in the morning, where I parked my car and who I was going to have lunch with that day." Interestingly, Hicks planned to eat lunch with Henry Lee Loggins's partner, but he changed his plans after his conversation with the justice of the peace.[37]

Hicks confessed: "All of these things gradually beat me down." In addition to the harrowing experiences surrounding the witness hunt, "a deputy threatened to knock Simeon Booker's head off because Booker held up his press card and asked the deputy to help him get through the crowd." Moreover, "a man who walked up to the press table and called all of us 'N——rs' was sworn in five minutes later as the bailiff." During courtroom recesses, white trial attendees "would come in and take the chairs from our table." Hicks recalled: "I stood up more than I sat down." Whites burned a cross outside the courthouse during the trial, an event that sparked no investigation. These and other such intimidations experienced by the black journalists who traveled to Sumner to cover the trial pointed up for readers the stifling nature of white supremacy in the Delta and the salience of the national battle to break down southern white hegemony.[38]

Although the *Afro-American* regarded these conditions as despicable, it realized that it was normal procedure in the South. In the paper's opinion, "if lynchers were properly punished as a matter of course, mobs [would] quickly disappear." Within the current racial climate, however, gang violence was on the rise, and the Baltimore black press identified Carolyn Bryant as an impetus for this mob ethos: "At first, Bryant said a Black boy whistled at her. But, as the trial approached, somehow the whistle magnified into a suggestion of sexual conduct. Bryant knew that this implicature would play well with whites, since white women could often get out of any difficulty by simply saying a black man attacked her."[39]

White women falsely accusing black men of impropriety was a storied tradition in the South. Of this age-old phenomenon, the *Afro-American* concluded: "There is nothing new in the Mississippi trial—victim kidnapped and lynched; woman concocts story of sex attack, mob members arrested, tried and freed." These false allegations resulted in a bloated record of over six thousand lynchings, as reported by the NACCP, and

Mississippi appeared most frequently as the location of the crime. Echoing similar sentiments, the *Daily World* asserted: "It is conclusively shown . . . that some local communities are unable or unwilling to effectively uphold justice; where interracial questions are involved."[40]

This intransigence with regard to race relations struck most acutely in the Deep South, and black papers from this region used the Till case to underscore a long legacy of racial oppression. The *Jackson (MS) Advocate* reinforced the importance of the case to black America, specifically indicating that the prominent Michigan congressman Charles Diggs dropped everything and traveled to Sumner to observe the trial. Diggs's attendance underlined the willingness of black Americans to speak out against this crime. His presence at the trial told the racists in Mississippi that their actions were a scourge on the entire country and that he did not have faith in the Mississippi justice system.[41]

Further highlighting the significance of the case to African Americans and their determination to see justice rendered, the *World* papers covered Moses Wright's courageous testimony at the Till trial. At obvious risk of violent reprisal, Wright, "an ordained minister in the Church of God in Christ," defied death threats to testify against the defendants. Moreover, Wright, "with dogged determination," vowed to remain in the state long enough to harvest his "bumper crop" of cotton.[42]

Deep South black newspapers also lauded Mamie Till-Mobley's decision to appear at the trial proceedings and testify that the body was, in fact, that of her son. Her appearance created a stir because Mississippians were not accustomed to such bravery on the part of black men, let alone a black woman. Rather than remaining in Chicago and watching the trial from the sidelines, Till-Mobley chose to travel to the heart of the Mississippi Delta and proclaim before the world that her son was the victim of the most egregious of crimes and that his murderers needed to be punished.[43]

At the time, whites in the Deep South could not see that with his death Emmett Till sowed the seeds of change that would sprout forth into the modern civil rights movement of the 1950s and 1960s. Even in the Mississippi Delta, his death served as a rallying point for blacks fed up with business as usual. Across the country, people united behind local efforts for justice, and these struggles coalesced into a national movement for equal rights and shared humanity. Regardless of race, Americans, galvanized by the brutal and insensate lynching of a fourteen-year-old boy, rallied around the cause of racial uplift, and these members of the Emmett Till generation would change the very nature of race relations in the United States.

6

Galvanizing the Emmett Till Generation

Even after the panel of all-white male jurors exonerated Roy Bryant and J. W. Milam of any culpability in his brutal lynching, Emmett Till's death lived on as a rallying point for a generation of civil rights activists. Some scholars, led by Clenora Hudson-Weems, argued that Emmett Till was the spark that ignited the flames of the modern civil rights movement. While much intellectual debate exists as to what actually was the seminal event that launched the movement, it is clear from activists' testimonies that Till's death resonated with and served as a driving force behind those who throughout the 1950s and 1960s fought for the rights of black Americans. These efforts were most intense in areas where civil rights were most egregiously violated, and, as evidenced by Till's lynching, the Deep South set the standard for racial oppression.[1]

In the face of growing criticism of the Deep South after the trial, white Mississippians stood behind Bryant's and Milam's acquittal, and some mainstream publications in the Deep South continued to use the case to defame black people and assuage white guilt. Partly in response to this entrenching of racial mores, Till's brutal murder galvanized a generation of activists (especially young people—see figure 6.1) who rejected Deep South racial rhetoric and thrust themselves into the fight against racial injustice. As the *Defender* franchise columnist Moses Newson put it, "a lot of the young people . . . began to . . . become more assertive and more active." The work of these activists continued to breathe life into the Till lynching and, in many ways, made necessary the outpouring of efforts to memorialize Till.[2]

After the Sumner jury reached its verdict, the defendants, as well as those whites connected to the trial locale, attempted a return to their pre-lynching lives; however, the unrelenting coverage in the national print media continued to focus a critical light on the Till saga and Sumner. As

Figure 6.1. Young people, both black and white, lining up to sign a petition calling on President Eisenhower to intercede in the Till saga. *Daily Worker* and *Daily World* Photograph Collection, Tamiment Library and Robert F. Wagner Labor Archives, New York University.

was the case with publications across the country, in the wake of the trial *Time* magazine used reader responses to lambaste the acquittal. For one married couple, the Till case underscored the true nature of white privilege, making them and their family realize how fortunate they were "to be born with white skin." As seen in countless letters, Till's death aroused a visceral response among white Americans, prodding them to join and help forward existing efforts promoting the cause of black uplift.[3]

In the early years of the modern civil rights movement, these battles for black equality focused on racial injustices in the American South, a region that even before the 1964 release of James Silver's epic *Mississippi* was framed by some as a "closed society." Predicting Silver's thesis, one *Time* reader argued: "The latest atrocity from behind the Grits and Gravy Curtain moves me to suggest that Mississippi, Georgia and Unoccupied Florida secede from the Union forthwith, all white Deep Southerners to receive free passage to another Union more in line with their philosophy— that of South Africa." Still others called on divine judgment to vindicate the slain youth. To the editors of *Life* magazine, James Mertz offered: "God will care for him [Till] and sooner or later God's infinite justice and sanctity [will] be vindicated."[4]

National outrage took many forms, from letters to the editors of national publications to the countless protest rallies that sprang up across the country. Always in tune with instances of dissent, the Communist *Daily Worker* announced protest meetings in New York, Massachusetts, Wisconsin, Illinois, California, Indiana, Connecticut, and Pennsylvania. Each rally boasted overflowing crowds, calls for political action, and palpable outrage.[5]

The massive outpouring of wrath over the acquittal was common in the national press; however, not everyone saw the verdict as unjust. Perhaps attempting to balance out the coverage, *Time* differed from its peers by printing responses from readers who defended the South and the verdict. One South Carolinian accused the magazine of overdramatizing the affair: "Whenever the [Cold War] is slack . . . the blasted editors of Time capitalize on such controversial articles as the Till case." In an even more scathing condemnation of the magazine, a native of Tallahatchie County argued that Till got what he deserved: "Any Negro or white from anywhere in the world knows it is wrong to roll his eyes, whistle lewdly, make obscene remarks, and sling an innocent lady around as if she were a barmaid." She questioned rhetorically: "Is it justice to make a hero of an immoral Negro?" In her estimation, the answer was no, and she challenged: "Time could at least have the decency to disapprove of his actions and sympathize with his victim."[6]

Without a doubt, there were many in the South, especially in the Deep South, who felt the need to calm racial angst. As evidenced in his personal communiqué to the Biloxi Chamber of Commerce member Anthony Ragusin, the *Delta Democrat Times* publisher, Hodding Carter, hoped to ameliorate Mississippi's growing racial tensions by submitting personal statements to national publications like *Life* and the *Saturday Evening*

Post. The latter fulfilled his request and printed an article in which he offered: "It is needful for the nation to know of the hardening of the hearts of white and black men in the Southern areas of greatest Negro density." This callousness was a result of what Carter saw as sensationalized coverage of the Till case, and he argued that Till died and his murders were acquitted because many white people in the South would not bring themselves to respect the life of any black. He felt that the ridicule of those from outside the South exacerbated an already tense situation in the wake of *Brown,* and he made the editorial decision to blame the rabid racists in the Deep South as well as outside agitators for creating an environment in which "matters are going to get more violent down this way before things take a turn for the better." Lamenting that he had "never felt quite as discouraged about racial relations and attitudes," Carter admitted that he would "rather be at the North Pole than in Mississippi."[7]

As Carter saw it, outside scrutiny only intensified southern white efforts to discredit and discount the validity of black life. National mainstream press coverage played up the symbolic determination of this closed society not to bend to the pressure for integration and increased racial equality. Mississippians' unflinching resistance to integration came across as *Time* quoted a surprisingly liberal response to the lynching found in an editorial from the *Jackson (MS) State Times:* "The case . . . wound up not on the solid ground of justice accomplished but . . . became a symbol of the white-hot determination of Mississippians to conduct their affairs as they pleased." As Mississippi's chosen symbol of the dangers of outside interference, Emmett Till became the battleground on which many waged a rhetorical war over the merits and the morality of racial segregation and racial equality. As was evident from the outrage, from 1955 to the present, over the lynching and the acquittal of Till's murderers, "the symbol was ill-chosen."[8]

Till was a poor rallying cry for states' rights or the ability of states to determine their own best practices even if their decisions defied federal legislation and court decisions. Arguments in favor of states' rights emboldened progressives to rally around his lynching as the impetus for racial equality. Equality was the key to differentiating the Western form of democracy from past and present versions of totalitarianism, and the national black press used the international stage to argue: "If America tolerates such a gross miscarriage of justice as to clear these two White men of the murder charge, then we [all Americans] can indeed be likened to the Gestapo of Hitler or the dreaded secret police of the Soviets."[9]

Keying in on such indignation, the NAACP sent letters to the White

Figure 6.2. On southern racial terror, President Eisenhower sees no evil, hears no evil, and speaks no evil. Political cartoon, February 11, 1957, Laura Gray Political Cartoons, Tamiment Library and Robert F. Wagner Labor Archives, New York University.

House. In these communiqués, NAACP leaders called on the federal government to intervene and stop the oppression and carnage that plagued the South and specifically the state of Mississippi. According to NAACP executive secretary Roy Wilkins, "this killing occurred in the midst of a reign of terror against Negro citizens of Mississippi involving various kinds of intimidation, threats of bodily injury, economic pressure as to employment, credit and homes, and murder." Despite the poignant plea, there is no indication that President Eisenhower addressed Wilkins's concerns. In fact, as depicted in a political cartoon from the Communist publication *The Militant* (see figure 6.2), when it came to southern racial terror, Dwight Eisenhower, and many others in Washington, became blind, deaf,

and mute. The lack of federal government intervention made more apparent the need for a strong and sustained national push for civil rights, for, in
the absence of decisive action to stamp out racial oppression, it appeared
that America was truly Mississippi writ large.[10]

Belying the national black press notions that guilt in the Emmett Till
case spread across the nation, staff at some midwestern publications felt
more comfortable focusing blame on the Deep South. Although the midwestern press in general provided little coverage of the posttrial reaction,
the *St. Louis Post-Dispatch* did focus on it and blasted the acquittal of
Bryant and Milam as a gross injustice. In a September 25, 1955, editorial,
the paper asserted:

> Much has been said of collective guilt on the part of this whole
> democracy of ours. Guilt, however, is individual and the effort
> to establish guilt through the trial at Sumner, Miss., was feeble
> at best. . . . Yet nobody had expressed doubt about identification
> when the body was found. The first doubt was started a week later
> by the Tallahatchie sheriff, who is still "looking" for Till. The
> prosecution struck at his testimony, but did not seek expert out-
> side medical opinion. . . . Thus in the course of the trial the body
> was made to appear that of somebody else. The "wolf whistle"
> incident which caused the kidnaping was made to appear a case
> of molestation. And in the end the trial of murder was turned into
> a trial of that Southern way of life. The jury obviously swallowed
> much of this. Justice would choke on it.[11]

Through letters to the editor, *Post-Dispatch* readers underscored their
belief that the southern justice system was a vice grip on the throat of
American democracy, asphyxiating any fledgling gasps of equal justice
under the law. It was an age-old story, and in the opinion of one reader,
"the acquittal of the Till case defendants was no surprise to people who
know Mississippi justice when Negroes are involved. If the men had confessed to the brutal slaying in open court, the verdict would have been
the same." Another reader added: "I hang my head in shame for my race,
and am amazed that there have not been volumes of mail in protest of this
grossly unjust trial." Mississippi justice was beyond the comprehension of
most Americans, and one letter pointedly asked: "Can there be a corner of
the world where Mississippi justice is not anathema?" Such abhorrent conditions existed because it was "almost impossible for those of the Negro

race to get a fair and honest decision below the Mason and Dixon Line." In an effort to prevent further injustices from occurring, one reader implored right-minded citizens: "Contribute generously to religious and charitable organizations aiding in the advancement of Negroes and other minority groups." In the coming decades, many would answer this clarion call, and the Emmett Till generation would change the very essence of the nation's disposition toward race relations.[12]

While the Emmett Till saga dominated the pages of the midwestern mainstream press before and during the trial of his murderers, these papers carried relatively little coverage after the court proceedings. Those in the region interested in extensive posttrial reaction had to find it in the midwestern black papers, which accentuated the fear that gripped blacks as they traveled to Sumner to bear witness to the defamation of American justice that was the Till trial. Surely, those who descended on Mississippi to observe the trial represented a temporary reverse migration of blacks from the North to the South. Among those migrants was Congressman Charles Diggs (D-MI) and the Deep South transplant Mamie Till-Mobley.

By November 1955, the latter found herself embroiled in a dispute with the NAACP. Ahead of her scheduled West Coast speaking tour under the auspices of the NAACP, Till-Mobley requested additional funding to help cover her mounting bills. Roy Wilkins denied this appeal and dropped her from the tour. It should come as no surprise that midwestern news outlets, and particularly the black press, offered their adopted daughter support in the face of increased condemnation from all sides. For example, the *Chicago Defender* challenged reports that Till-Mobley and the NAACP broke ties because the organization felt she was trying to profit from her son's death. Unlike many other black newspapers, the *Defender* did not take the NAACP's claim that it objected to Till-Mobley's new financial demands at face value. According to a statement released by Wilkins, which the *Defender* quoted, Mrs. Crocket, a "personal representative and secretary of" Till-Mobley, said that Till-Mobley would appear only if she were guaranteed "$5,000 for the 11 scheduled meetings or for a smaller guarantee plus one-third of collections plus all expenses." In response, Wilkins claimed, he dropped Till-Mobley from the tour and replaced her with NAACP southeastern regional secretary Ruby Hurley, "who attended the Till trial . . . and helped secure additional witnesses." And that was where the reporting ended in most papers. The *Defender,* however, dug deeper: "Mrs. Crockett said Mrs. Bradley wants it made clear that she is not engaged in a fight with the NAACP and had her bags packed when

Wilkins telegrammed her." However, "Mrs. Bradley had been going constantly for several weeks and had only received expenses from the NAACP and had to pay her own hospital bill when she suffered a nervous breakdown." Moreover, "[she] was being 'worn to a frazzle' by the schedule she had been following in behalf of the NAACP . . . [, and] friends advised her to inform officials of the organization that she could not make the western tour without adequate remuneration." The *Defender* was not the only paper to record the NAACP/Till-Mobley disagreement; however, it was the only one to seek out and use statements from Crockett. Some other papers similarly deflected blame from Till-Mobley, but they utilized statements only from her male advisers.[13]

The *Defender*'s support of Till-Mobley drew the ire of the NAACP; however, Wilkins acknowledged the organization knew that the decision to drop Till-Mobley would be controversial. He told Henry Moon, the NAACP director of public relations: "We knew when we cancelled the Bradley West Coast trip that there would be considerable discussion and probably some very inaccurate statements made by newspapers or by Mrs. Bradley's friends." Not wanting to reflect negatively on Till's mother, the NAACP leadership agreed not to challenge any of this negative press. However, one sentence in a *Chicago Defender* article forced the NAACP's hand. According to Wilkins: "The *Defender* story in the issue of November 19 contains the following statement: 'In addition, Mrs. Crocket told the *Defender* numerous checks that were given to Mrs. Bradley personally were signed over to the NAACP.'" With the NAACP's finances already under scrutiny by the IRS and the FBI, Wilkins felt he needed to act quickly to correct what he saw as errors in the *Defender* story. Both he and Moon dispatched letters to the *Defender* asking the paper to revisit its analysis of the dispute. Wilkins's curt letter requested: "We hope the *Defender* will correct the story because it is a serious charge reflecting on our honesty rather than our methods and procedures." Given the constant pressure placed on the NAACP by FBI director J. Edgar Hoover and other members of the Department of Justice, it seems likely that the effort to combat the *Defender*'s copy was more about deflecting the condemnation of the racist leadership of the FBI than it was about open conflict with either Till-Mobley or the *Defender*.[14]

Coverage in the *Defender* throughout November 1955 clearly showed that the paper held no ill will toward the NAACP. *Defender* staff downplayed the disagreement between Till-Mobley and the NAACP and, attempting to mediate the situation, in a November 26, 1955, article informed readers: "Both she [Till-Mobley] and NAACP officials are willing to concede now that faulty communications was [*sic*] responsible for the apparent break between her and the organization." The *Defender* felt that it was crucial to highlight the fact that there had been a misunderstanding and that neither side was guilty because "there is a growing feeling in Chicago, if nowhere else, that recent events have conspired to give a wrong picture of this woman." The cause of this poor picture? "Some newsmen have complained that she has changed from a simple grief-stricken mother to an arrogant celebrity full of her own importance. Others have charged that she has become greedy and anxious to 'cash in' on the misfortune that befell her son." In the face of the negative images of Till-Mobley that began to surface after the initial break with the NAACP, the *Defender* supported her: "There has been some deliberate misrepresentation of Mrs. Bradley, especially by the southern white press which apparently feels that by discrediting her they are removing themselves from blame in the case."[15]

As it did throughout the coverage, the *Chicago Defender* made efforts to validate Mamie Till-Mobley's actions and defend her character. No other paper went to such lengths. It is likely that these efforts were a result of Till-Mobley's close ties with the paper. Whatever the reason, the paper defended her in the face of accusations in southern papers and sparse coverage elsewhere.[16]

The vitally important efforts to defend Till-Mobley were a hallmark of midwestern black press coverage of the Till saga, and that region's analysis of the Emmett Till lynching presented a unique story. In addition to supporting the mother of the slain boy, the midwestern black papers provided readers with countless attacks on Mississippi and clear justification for the migration of black people from that state. They condemned Bryant and Milam, but the articles, editorials, and letters to the editor found in them also indicted elected officials in Mississippi. These papers continually addressed black people's inability to obtain justice in the Deep South state. Unlike any other region's press, the midwestern black press accused everyone, including the prosecuting attorneys, of participating in a white supremacist conspiracy. In poignant and unrivaled attacks, these black newspapers led the call for federal intervention and went so far as lobbying for the expulsion of Mississippi from the Union.

Taking a somewhat different yet equally critical angle on the Till saga, northeastern mainstream papers chose to focus their attention on the peculiar and foreign set of racial norms that dictated Deep South views of justice. Particularly prescient in their reports was the identification of whites' fear of outside incursion, fear that the 1954 *Brown v. Board of Education* decision exacerbated. As the northeastern mainstream press saw it, through the Bryant and Milam acquittal, the jurors, the town, and the state told the justices of the High Court that more legally sanctioned lynching would occur with increased contact between the races. Truly, Emmett Till must have seemed to Deep South whites a picture of what integration would bring. If they did not fight for segregation, black men would feel free to approach white women, and white men would again have to rise up and stamp down these offenses. Thus, "on the sanctity of white womanhood, a Mississippi jury is only a vehicle for expressing the mass fear and hatred of the Negro. . . . The poison of racism had eaten so deeply into the Milams, and the Bryants, and the lawyers, and the people who cheered the verdict, that it has made them immune to a sense of truth or even of reality." Emmett Till, as an outsider, carried his integrationist thinking to this violently segregated region and, with his death, brought the progressive integrationist eyes of the country down on this region.[17]

Southerners did not understand that, the more they promoted segregation, the more those outside the region challenged the entire South. To that end, a *New York Times* journalist proclaimed: "Sumner, Mississippi . . . the county seat of Tallahatchie County, is the epitome of the way of life, the mores, the racial attitudes and the racial tensions that are summoned up by the words 'deep South.'" Similarly, one reader invoked the closed society metaphor thusly: "Just the fact that the boy was a Negro would have been enough to justify this terrible act, according to the state of Mississippi." Another letter to the editor went so far as to call racism a sickness: "What happened in Mississippi is a cruel example of a moral disease that eats at our national vitals, saps our strength and makes hypocrites out of Americans. . . . By his death Emmett Louis Till took racism out of the textbooks and editorials and showed it to the world in it's [*sic*] true dimensions." These "true dimensions" conflicted with the image of American democracy that northeasterners trumpeted during the Cold War era: "The slaughter of Emmet[t] Till . . . is a blot on our democracy. It spreads like a whirlpool touching the shores of every land."[18]

The only exception to this otherwise blanket condemnation of the South came in a *Pittsburgh Post-Gazette* plea for rational behavior that warned readers to temper their attacks on the South in the aftermath of the Till lynching and trial. Andrew Bernhard, the *Post-Gazette*'s white editor, claimed that this obvious injustice was "a faltering advance of sorts towards equal justice in the Deep South." His rationale? "We can remember, not so many years back, when the white men in a case such as this would never have been indicted." He continued: "Underlying the whole case . . . is the fact that there are no registered Negro voters in Tallahatchie County. . . . If only two Negroes had been on the jury panel, the proceedings would have looked much better to a critical world." While most white-on-black crimes were, indeed, swept under the carpet by the southern judicial system, that Bryant and Milam were indicted and tried was hardly a "faltering advance"; it was injustice by other means and, thus, simply business as usual.[19]

Six days after its appeal for a tempered interpretation of the verdict, the *Post-Gazette* printed two responses that spoke to the obvious partiality of the trial. The first challenged: "The enemies of the United States do not have to concoct lies to discredit this Government in the eyes of the world . . . [because] the state of Mississippi used the courts as an instrument to support and encourage adherents of white supremacy as well as to protect and perpetuate a tradition which boasts that no white man has ever been executed for killing a Negro." The second spoke directly to Bernhard: "You want justice, but you give no direction. . . . [Y]ou object to Federal troops being stationed in Mississippi to assure these rights. . . . If your objection to Federal troops is a defense of states' rights, then you are allying yourself with the worst of Southern elements—people who believe that their very lives depend on depriving the Negro of his. . . . I hope you will speak out more clearly on this. You owe it to yourself and your readers." This latter reader was so incensed that she not only condemned Mississippi but also accused her local newspaper editor of "allying" himself with the southern racist element.[20]

Such letters made it clear that most people were tired of business as usual when it came to cases of racial violence. The climate was ripe for progress on extending civil rights, and readers wanted to see critical analysis of American race relations in the pages of their newspapers. Pittsburgh readers in particular challenged Bernhard's idea that Mississippi was making fledgling steps toward achieving justice for all and instead called for decisive action. When the only solution to the problem that the *Post-Gazette* could propose was remaining calm, they called the paper out for its lack of vision. These responses did have an effect. The *Post-Gazette* made no further effort to defend the Deep South or minimize the impact of the Till lynching.

Other *Post-Gazette* readers simply ignored the Bernhard editorial and instead proposed their own solutions to the southern problem. One letter stated: "I think the Federal courts should enter into the picture to do away with these outrages in the South: the Ku Klux Klan, segregation, and all the other tripe." Another said: "We are all guilty just as long as we keep one group of our nation in the status of second-class citizen." The Till lynching and trial prompted people to take a stand once and for all; it was a clarion call for a generation of activists, some of whom went so far as to envision a renewed federal occupation of the South.[21]

At least one person deemed such an occupation necessary owing to the lack of religious values in Mississippi: "God created all men equal. But a jury in Mississippi does not believe in God's teaching. . . . It makes you think of all the money we spend sending missionaries to foreign countries. We could send them South to teach the Ten Commandments." While the pious North had been spending its hard-earned money trying to convert foreigners, the Deep South state remained a backward, racist, closed society espousing the false doctrine of white supremacy.[22]

White supremacist ideology included embedded views of black male hypersexuality, black female immorality, and white female chastity. Deconstructing these preconceived notions through letters to the editor, readers voiced their opinions and protested the Till lynching and trial. However, in the pages of northeastern papers, no one raised any concern about either Mamie Till-Mobley or Carolyn Bryant. The only reference to masculinity or femininity came in the letters about the male actors. Readers were particularly expressive about Emmett Till's father, Louis Till. The senior Till died while stationed in Italy during World War II. Once the public learned this fact, it began to compare his actions serving his country with the cowardly acts of Bryant and Milam. Both Bryant and Milam served in the military, but the northeastern mainstream press readers chose to focus on the patriotism of Louis Till. Given the Cold War desire to see America as the upholder of liberty and freedom, it is not surprising that people gravitated to Till's military service. Conversely, given the brutal and heinous nature of Emmett Till's murder, neither is it surprising that people ignored Bryant's and Milam's service. In the minds of many, Louis Till paid the ultimate price. As one reader reflected, "the father of the Till boy . . . was a real defender of justice when he gave his life on the field of battle in a foreign land that all Americans, regardless of their nationality, might live a quiet and peaceful life free of hatred, prejudice and fear."[23]

Another northeastern press devotee lauded: "During World War II, this boy's father died protecting not only his own race, but all people, including these two [men]." However, it was revealed after the Till trial that Louis Till was convicted by a military tribunal of raping and murdering three white women while stationed in Italy and subsequently executed. The files on the senior Till, which had been sealed since the execution, were uncovered and given to the Mississippi press by Mississippi senator James Eastland. The mainstream northeastern press did not print anything about this incident, evidently content to allow the public to see the senior Till as a war hero. It made a better story, and it allowed them to avoid dealing with the racial and sexual implications of Louis Till's conviction.[24]

Ignoring the distraction of Louis Till's conviction and execution, the mainstream northeastern press focused on the backward and racist culture found in the Deep South. Early reports dismissed the lynching as a regional phenomenon, but, starting with the trial coverage, the northeastern popular press increasingly criticized the Deep South as an American problem. Chief among the sins of this regional pariah was the fact that, in protecting their friends and neighbors, these particular southerners reinscribed doctrines of states' rights and white supremacy that were foreign and subversive. As was the case in midwestern papers, Deep South residents became the other, the bad seed, but it was the northeastern black press that most adequately placed Deep South racism within the context of Cold War efforts to promote American democracy.

Illuminating historic indifference toward brutality against black people, a letter to the editor of the *Pittsburgh Courier* challenged: "If the United States can send its armed forces 6,000 miles across the seas to Korea to fight Korean and Chinese Communists, in the interest of world democracy, it would appear that the Federal Government should use its vast powers to stop the lynching of Negro citizens by Mississippi racists in the interest of American democracy." This argument held great importance because, in every instance from the Revolutionary War to the Korean War, African Americans chose to battle enemies of the United States while still living their lives under racist and oppressive conditions. Surely, as depicted in a 1956 Laura Gray political cartoon of Senator Eastland (see figure 6.3), a long line of Mississippi elected officials fostered an environment in which it seemed normal to fight intolerance abroad while maintaining racial oppression at home.[25]

Journalists for, editors of, and readers of the northeastern black press continually framed the Deep South as the antithesis of American democracy. Another description read: "The 'cracker' hoodlums . . . were set free by an all-white jury of Mississippi farmers, who apparently don't know

SAVE THE COUNTRY
FROM RED FORCE
AND VIOLENCE !

EASTLAND

MISSISSIPPI
TERRORISM

Figure 6.3. *The Hypocrite from Mississippi*. Political cartoon, January 16, 1956, Laura Gray Political Cartoons, Tamiment Library and Robert F. Wagner Labor Archives, New York University.

the meaning of the word justice." On returning to Michigan, Congressman Charles Diggs exclaimed that "he was delighted to breathe the 'clean fresh air of Michigan' after returning from 'the jungles of Mississippi.'"[26]

Readers found additional descriptions of Mississippi as a "purgatory of racial tension," a "'hell-hole' of American democracy, 1955 style!" Every chance it had, the northern black press condemned the social norms that sanctioned Emmett Till's lynching. Its readers were confronted with information about the persistence of racism and white supremacy in the Deep South. As James Boyack of the *Pittsburgh Courier* saw it, "Americans who have never visited Mississippi . . . who have never been subjected to the 'fear complex' . . . can't possibly understand what happens to a Negro in this state." The "fear complex" was the key to white control of the region, and Boyack claimed that Till's murder showed Mississippi was "still living in a civilization 100 years removed from 1955." The editors of the *New York Amsterdam News* added to this historical framing: "During the past 69 years, 536 Negroes have been lynched [in Mississippi]." Of course, these were only the reported lynchings: "Only God knows the number of colored men, women and children that have been murdered by white mobs down there without the outside world knowing about it." Exacerbating the problem, "in all of these years of brutal killings, no white man has ever had to pay the penalty for these savage and bloody deeds." Thus, "there is a definite pattern behind all of these recent lynch murders in Mississippi. They are aimed at keeping the Negro in his place." However, one did not have to be a victim of lynching to understand a black person's place in Mississippi. Clearly, many northeastern black journalists who attended the trial quickly learned, as Boyack did, that "a 'nigra's' life is not important . . . not in Mississippi." Such reports from northerners provided readers with real and personal accounts of southern white supremacy that moved far beyond the unemotional coverage in the northeastern mainstream press.[27]

When describing Mississippi and the Till trial, some articles in northeastern black newspapers focused on the racist treatment of Mamie Till-Mobley. They discussed her courage in the face of white Mississippians, but, as with the pretrial coverage, she was feminized. That is, even though her presence at the trial put her in a powerful position, they focused on her physical appearance instead of on what she said or did, thus trivializing her. None of the male actors in the Till saga were treated in this way, because their appearance did not matter. They were men battling over serious issues in a tense environment. Till-Mobley was simply an object of interest and not a player to be taken seriously.

The exoneration of the defendants marked the final slap in the face of northeastern African Americans. The framing of Mississippi found in the reports covering the acquittal can be summed up in one statement by James Boyack: "Nobody loves her ways; not even Mississippians!" The *Pittsburgh Courier*'s Robert Ratcliffe elaborated on Boyack's claims, relating how white and black reporters had very different experiences covering the trial in Sumner. During the daily lunch break, the white journalists enjoyed the café across the street from the courthouse, while the black journalists "trekked to a back street and dined at Jessie Griffin's Place, a combination café and pool hall." Ratcliffe similarly recounted: "Negro reporters . . . had to be satisfied with an old card table set outside of the rail on the far right of the room." Meanwhile, the white reporters and specta- tors were provided the prime seats in the courtroom. Truly, the African Americans who traveled to Sumner to cover the trial had to endure longer commutes to the courthouse, fatigue from less agreeable living conditions, limited sustenance because they could eat only in one overtaxed estab- lishment, and more difficulty reporting on the events because of and their poor listening and viewing location and the limited seating. Everywhere they turned, the black reporters from the Northeast were reminded of the racial segregation that existed in the South. It is no wonder that there were so many differences between the coverage of the popular press and that of the black press. Doubtlessly, Deep South racism added fuel to black press reports. With countless examples to draw on, trial attendees filled north- eastern black newspapers with poignant personal accounts of life under white supremacy.[28]

Reports from prominent black officials were condemnatory. For exam- ple, U.S. congressman Charles Diggs of Michigan noted: "[Southerners were] engaging in the prostitution of every American concept of democ- racy and dignity of man under God." He went on: "I went to Mississippi because the danger that democratic principles face in that state is a risk to our nation's principle of freedom." Diggs's words showed the saliency of this lynching and the depth of concern black Americans felt about the outcome of the trial and what the trial meant for black people's access to democracy. All the black attendees faced a climate in which, in Diggs's words, the "pistol-packing white men were milling around the courthouse, itching for the chance to shoot any Negro who did not accord them proper respect." "One could see hatred oozing from pistol-packing, red-necked Mississippians who crowded around the streets and steps leading up to the courtroom," Diggs explained. Every day the blacks had to run a gauntlet of southerners to enter the courtroom. Their observations showed the harsh realities of black life in the Deep South, and their words allowed readers to see the region as a land devoid of democracy and justice.[29]

Black journalists, editors, and readers understood that this case was more than a simple murder trial. The verdict would serve as a commen- tary on the state of democracy in the country. For the black journalists, this case was a natural extension of *Brown v. Board of Education* and, as such, a yardstick against which to measure the progress of integration and equal rights in the United States. If white men could be convicted of

Figure 6.4. *Bipartisan Policy.* Political cartoon, November 17, 1955, Laura Gray Political Cartoons, Tamiment Library and Robert F. Wagner Labor Archives, New York University.

a crime against a black boy, then the country would be one step closer to a true democracy. But of course Mississippi failed the test. The media spotlight that this trial brought caused white residents to reaffirm their dedication to states' rights and the protection of white supremacy at any cost. Sadly, as depicted in another Laura Gray political cartoon (figure 6.4), many Republicans and Democrats in Washington chose to ignore this southern retrenchment and, even as movements for civil rights mounted in the wake of the Till lynching, disregarded protests calling for antilynching and civil rights legislation.

Diggs was not the only prominent African American to have his reflections memorialized in the *Courier.* This paper also printed the words of the black Mississippian and integration champion Dr. T. R. M. Howard, who explained: "The thing that disgusted me the most was that these two white men, being tried for murder, came into the courthouse unaccompanied by either the sheriff or his deputies, . . . that they walked about during recess periods, shaking hands, talking and laughing with their friends and when it was necessary for them to go to the rest rooms, they went into the judge's private chambers, and no deputy nor anyone else went along with them."[30]

Given Mississippi whites' blatant refusal to put on even a show of seeking justice, the *New York Amsterdam News* charged all black people with the task of bringing democracy to the race. In the paper's estimation: "Long after the vocal indignation over the Emmett Louis Till lynching has subsided, Negro women will still be raped and colored adults will be kept away from ballot boxes and little boys will be murdered if they displease their white neighbors because all of these deplorable conditions are a part of life in Mississippi." Summarily rejecting this untenable situation, the paper staff argued: "A persistent, frontal attack, backed by a relentless campaign must be aimed at the system and not at hoodlum Bryant and his half-brother, hoodlum Milam, because they are just the tools of the system. They are the pitiful little men who have been taught to hate everything black and exalt everything white as a deeply rooted way of life." What to do in the face of this deep-rooted system of racial oppression? "There is no short cut to changing these conditions. Getting 'fighting mad' in a barber shop in Harlem won't help. Giving advice about what Southern Negroes should do won't change the system either." Indeed, "[the system] will remain intact and become more vicious all the time unless Negroes can be guaranteed the right to vote, and the right to learn, and the right to work like their white neighbors in Mississippi." This was the time for all African Americans to stand up and fight for the rights of the race, to fight for equality, justice, and democracy. Over the next decade, countless individuals—the Emmett Till generation—would heed this call as local activism coalesced into broader national and international movements.[31]

The NAACP took the lead in many of these endeavors for racial justice; however, it sidestepped the gender issues that were surfacing in the 1950s and 1960s. A good example of its stance on gender issues is its relationship with Mamie Till-Mobley. As we have seen, early in the Till saga it had partnered with her in her antilynching crusade, but by November 1955—the relationship having become strained—it cut its ties with her. The rift came despite the fact that her speaking engagements consistently sold out and she raised a substantial amount of money for the NAACP. In fact, one person was so moved by one of her speeches that he suggested they be taperecorded so that more people could hear her inspirational words.[32]

So what really caused the rift? Put simply, when Mamie Till-Mobley asked for more money to cover her expenses—expenses that were generated largely in service of the NAACP and that, without more money, she could not pay because she could not work while she was traveling the country—she crossed a gender line. She had overestimated a (black) woman's worth in 1950s America, and she was being too forward (read: unfeminine) in bringing her financial problems to the attention of the public.

The press blamed Till-Mobley's predicament on her advisers. According to the *Pittsburgh Courier,* "poor" Till-Mobley was a "'confused woman' as opposing factions stage [a] 'tug of war.'" The paper continued: "It was the opinion of observers that Mrs. Bradley had been poorly counseled by short-sighted advisors." Another report described her as "bitter about being 'dropped' by the NAACP": "[She] was nonetheless hopeful of a conference with NAACP officials and anxious to resume her speaking tour under their sponsorship." In this estimation, Till-Mobley wanted peace, but those around her, including her father, John Carthan, were advising her to the contrary. The report continued: "[Till-Mobley's] father, John Carter [*sic*], who is accompanying her [on] her current tour, was vehement in his condemnation of the NAACP. 'I believe the NAACP is using Emmett Till for its own use,' he declared. 'It seems to me that as long as my daughter can be useful to them, everything's all right, but the minute she asks for something it's a different matter.'"[33]

Through it all, Till-Mobley was framed by the black press as typically feminine—passive and subject to the whims of those surrounding her. The northeastern black press in particular focused on the men who counseled her. This strong male presence was especially important to emphasize because, as the *Courier* pointed out, Till-Mobley was at the time a single woman.[34]

The arrest of Rosa Parks in the beginning of December 1955 provided the NAACP with the opportunity to attack a new issue with a more socially acceptable figure. Parks was a lighter-skinned, middle-class, married seamstress and NAACP worker whose lifestyle did not raise the questions of family, morality, sexuality, and promiscuity that Till-Mobley did. Her case also did not raise the more worrisome question of miscegenation.

The question of miscegenation was, however, front and center in the Till saga. Not surprisingly, many letters to the editor published in the southeastern mainstream press blamed Till's murder on the lad's attitude and behavior. Writing to the *Charlotte (NC) Observer,* R. C. Bolen asserted: "This letter is not any attempt to justify the killing of Emmett

Till, but there is an angle to this unfortunate affair that seems overlooked. That is the personal rights of Mrs. Bryant." Bolen claimed: "Mrs. Bryant has a perfect right to conduct her affairs without any offensive suggestions or 'Wolf Whistles' from either a Negro or a white person." However, implicit in this statement is the notion that black males in particular who behaved in this way were lacking in respect and violating the sanctity of southern white womanhood. Apparently, this was the crime that Till committed when he allegedly wolf-whistled at Carolyn Bryant. Did he deserve to lose his life for this? Bolen did not think so. Nevertheless, "if this boy wanted to accept the hospitality of the State of Mississippi he should conform himself to the customs and laws of that state. If he had done so he probably would be alive now." According to Bolen, by stepping out of his place and (supposedly) making overtures to Bryant, Till had created a firestorm, his behavior striking at the heart of the age-old myth that black men desired sexual relations with white women. His fate was, therefore, sealed. Laying the blame for the lynching squarely at the feet, not just of Till himself, but of all black people, another letter writer, Chalmers Davidson, proclaimed: "Teach the negro to respect his own race and color—they are God-given—and the South may live in peace."[35]

In the opinion of still many other readers of the *Observer* and *Atlanta Constitution,* Bryant and Milam were innocent, and others had no right to judge the legal process in Mississippi. Alton Ogbern wrote: "In reply to letters of Rev. Joe A. Rabun and Ernest Hinson of Oct. 4 issue, I have this to say: They seem to feel that the jury in the Emmet[t] Till trial was not justified in acquitting the defendants, Roy Bryant and John W. Milam. Since neither they nor I were at the trial to hear the evidence, we cannot judge as to the innocence of the men. And they have no right to pass judgment on Mississippi justice." R. L. Ponder added: "Several letters to the Pulse of the Public, including one even from a preacher, indicate some people can be very bloodthirsty in wanting other people condemned to death, without evidence, as in the case of the Mississippi trial." But even more infuriating to Ponder than this was the fact that some even had "condemned the State of Mississippi because the jury acquitted the defendants." Ponder was unmoved by the suggestion that the acquittals of Bryant and Milam would invite criticism of the United States from people in Russia or China: "Naturally they will, for in those countries accusation is proof of guilt. But in this good country of America we have held to that good old Anglo-Saxon doctrine that no man can be convicted, whether of murder or illegal parking, without evidence."[36]

Tom Adams also perceived a lack of evidence in the case, so much so that for him it was clear that Bryant and Milam were innocent. Miming the defense's argument that the body taken out of the Tallahatchie River was not Emmett Till's, Adams concluded by placing the blame on blacks for creating a climate of racial hatred in the South and maintaining that trouble between the races would end "if the colored people would stop flirting with our white women and stop trying to mix with the white people." As evidenced in reports from other publications, specifically those in the Midwest and Northeast, Adams completely ignored a long history of white violence against black people by the numerous white supremacist groups and neglected to take into consideration the fact that few black men would dare make social advances toward white women. Historically, most of the social intermingling of the races both consensual and forced involved white men and black women, and the large numbers of biracial babies born to southern black women served as a testament to this fact.[37]

The realities of mixed-race births notwithstanding, in an effort to embarrass and humiliate Mamie Till-Mobley and to take attention away from the brutal lynching of Till and the ensuing mockery of a trial, the *Charlotte Observer* played up the "black brute" stereotype—according to which black men were focused only on the sexual conquest of white women—by reprinting a story initially published by the *Jackson (MS) Daily News.* The *Daily News,* Mississippi's most racially divisive paper, broke the story that Till's father had died not a war hero but a convicted rapist and murderer. Till-Mobley and her supporters quickly switched to damage-control mode. In the pages of the *Observer,* Till-Mobley indicated that she never learned any details pertaining to her husband's death, despite having made several inquiries. "I wrote the commanding officer, to the chaplain, and to (the late) President Roosevelt, but received no satisfaction," she was quoted as saying.[38]

Was Louis Till really guilty of rape and murder? The question remains unanswered. However, the vitriolic white racism, racial discrimination, and segregation that existed in the U.S. military during the Second World War made it highly unlikely that, whatever the circumstance, Till could have had a fair trial. No doubt many blacks were indicted and convicted of crimes they did not commit. In response to growing inquiries into the life and death of Louis Till, Mamie Till-Mobley's attorney William Henry Huff responded: "[The information] may be true, but it has no bearing upon the case pending [the Emmett Till kidnapping and lynching]."[39]

While many southeastern mainstream press readers recorded their support of the Mississippi trial outcome and of Bryant and Milam, still more attacked what they perceived as a gross injustice in Mississippi. Responding to an editorial run in the *Charlotte Observer* entitled "A Drama Plays Out, but Its Full Meaning May Be Missed," Edmund Hyde wrote: "Your editorial on the Emmett Till murder trial was magnificent. I hope every person involved in this pitiful travesty of justice and every resident of Mississippi will read it. This case, coming as it did at the close of Constitution Week, provided a note of bitter irony. Mississippi has proved to us that the Constitution is but a worthless document unless those who act by its authority are enlightened enough to honor their Constitution, with all its sacred implications, above the popular appeasement of the masses." Similarly, L. W. McKinley argued: "I am sure all right-thinking people applaud your stand on integration and the ones who criticized your editorial are a very small minority. . . . My advice to them is to move to the state founded and maintained by bigots—Mississippi, where murder is legal." Robert Clark wrote: "I wish to congratulate you on the very fine editorial that appeared in your paper on September 25th. . . . The meaning of this drama will not be missed by me. According to newspaper accounts, many wealthy white planters in the Mississippi Delta are using their influence to get these murderers off free. I consider it a disgrace to the whole State of Mississippi." Like the editorial, these letters placed the onus on the state of Mississippi and vindicated Emmett Till. Fully embracing the image of Mississippi as the center of the closed society, McKinley even requested that the few people outside Mississippi who supported the verdict should simply move to that state.[40]

Still other letters to the *Charlotte Observer* and the *Atlanta Constitution* focused their criticism on what they considered a farce of a trial, defended Mamie Till-Mobley's actions in the saga, and labeled the whole affair as a black eye in the face of America. These readers aimed their rhetorical bullets at the incomprehensible notion advanced by the defense, and swallowed hook, line, and sinker by the all-white jury, that the body pulled out of the Tallahatchie River was not that of Emmett Till. Leading the charge, Laverne Gordon wrote: "Statements have been made that the body was not the body of Emmett Till and that the NAACP planted it." And she posed the question, "What mother wouldn't know the body of her own son?" In her opinion, of course, Till-Mobley had positively identified the body of her son. Additionally, Ernest Hinson asserted: "I wonder how the mother feels to have someone who has never seen her boy tell her she didn't know her own son. How can the jury account for the fact that the son has never shown up, and that no one else has been reported missing?" Gordon, Hinson, and the Reverend Joe Rabun all concerned themselves with how the international community would view the acquittal. Gordon noted: "I wonder if we can call ourselves Christians and true American citizens?" Apparently, she had some doubts: "The Communists are laughing at us." Hinson observed: "As long as things like this still happen I think we had better quit bragging to the rest of the world about the American way of life." Indeed, such worries were real, for by the 1950s the United States was firmly entrenched in the Cold War. Communist nations such as China and the Soviet Union consistently pointed to the hypocrisy of America holding itself up as the beacon of democracy and highlighting human rights violations abroad while at the same time, and particularly in the South, perpetuating a system of white racism, discrimination, and violence against its African American citizens.[41]

Gordon, Hinson, and Rabun were all southern whites, and their words had a soothing and reassuring effect on at least one African American, H. H. Strong. As he wrote to the *Constitution,* he had nearly lost faith in southern whites as a result of the Till case, as he "had been watching the paper since the verdict was first announced, wondering if there were not some good white people in the South who had the courage and the interest to condemn this sort of thing through the public press." Fortunately for Strong, some did summon the courage, and Strong acknowledged particularly Hinson and Rabun. As he rightly pointed out, even in the Southeast there were racially conscious whites who internalized the saliency of the Till lynching and felt compelled to speak out against this injustice. These outspoken white voices helped fuel the burgeoning Emmett Till generation, and southeastern black press employees welcomed the opportunity for real interracial collaboration for civil rights.[42]

Buoyed as H. H. Strong was by some racially progressive white voices in the South, southeastern black newspapers continued their relentless attack on the racial injustices perpetrated and supported by many southern whites. The *Norfolk (VA) Journal and Guide* left no doubt where it stood on the matter: "Frankly, we believe from all the available evidence that the youth, handicapped by polio and forced to stutter, was guilty only of walking into the store and failing to be suitably servile. It is a terrible offense not to remove one's hat and say 'Yes, Maam' in Mississippi. But even if he 'laid hands on' the woman, the court could have weighed his offense. There was no excuse for killing him." In this estimation, his killers were far guiltier than he since they committed society's most heinous crimes, kidnapping and murder.[43]

Calling attention to the hypocrisy of American democracy, the *Journal and Guide* noted that the picture of American justice that the verdict gave the world was a sorry one. However, it saved its most penetrating criticism for H. C. Strider, a supposedly expert witness for the defense, whom it described as "the non-medically-trained Sheriff of the county": "Who was he to expertly determine that it was not the body of three-day missing Till, but instead that of somebody dead about two weeks? Who was he to question the mother's grief-stricken identification of her own flesh and blood? And, who was he to contradict the clear evidence presented by the ring still worn by the boy when found, a family gift to him?" Agreeing with the NAACP, the *Journal and Guide* also argued: "The jurors who returned the acquittal verdict deserve a medal from the Kremlin in Moscow." Furthermore, "the blood of this boy is on the souls of the ruling white people of Mississippi and especially on the promoters of the White Citizens Council which has staged a campaign of terrorism and intimidation and created the climate for bestial brutality and blood-letting in resentment against the desegregation of public schools." The desegregation of public schools, which many southern whites saw as the federal court's enforcement of racial and social equality, may not have been entirely to blame, but it certainly did not lessen racial tensions.[44]

Numerous letters to the editors of southeastern black newspapers further highlighted anger over the Till verdict. M. E. Lee, for example, told the *Journal and Guide:* "The lynching of young Till was horrible. I couldn't harm a dog that way. How can anyone be so cruel? I have all the sympathy in the world for his mother. This could have happened to any mother, regardless of color. . . . To the wonderful mother of that slain boy: There's little one can say or do, but may you know that heartfelt prayers go out to you in sympathy." In attacking the white notion that blacks are savage and heathens, Lee asserted: "I guess the killers in Mississippi don't think the Negroes are human; they sure didn't show it toward Emmett Till. Those murderers were turned loose with the verdict of 'not guilty' but deep in their hearts they know they are. I guess they just don't care. I'd like to be the judge of this." She ended by calling on divine judgment: "The final verdict isn't in. I'm one who will be glad to see God take over and say 'guilty' on that glorious Judgment Day."[45]

Additionally, a heart-wrenching letter published in the *Journal and Guide* spoke indirectly to the grave of Emmett Till and forecasted a new day when his murder would be avenged: "As I pondered the cold murder of Emmett Till, I was impelled to pen these lines which follow: Emmett, you will be avenged. Poor, poor little fellow, lying there in a cold, silent grave. How often have you wondered what you could possibly [have] done to bring this horrible climax to your innocent, young precious life?" Moreover, in alluding to the incomprehensible notion that the body pulled from the Tallahatchie River was not that of Emmett Till, the writer prophesied that, when the new day arrived, identification would not be a problem. The day of justice might be a long time coming. Still, "we are still fighting, and will go down fighting, too. And this time, we are not fighting by ourselves. The rest of the world is on our side. . . . So, rest in peace Emmett. There will soon be another Emmett Till's day in court but in heaven this time, and you'll be avenged." Indeed, this letter represented the most touching of all responses to the Till murder and underscored the depth of religious belief held by many black southerners. Despite all the trials and tribulations on earth, heaven promised to be divinely rewarding.[46]

Quite naturally, Mamie Till-Mobley's life was greatly affected by the ordeal of her son's lynching and the acquittal of his killers. As a consequence, she was determined to expend a significant amount of time and effort to raise awareness of her son's brutal murder. Thus, in spite of her grief, she agreed to numerous speaking engagements under the auspices of the NAACP. The *Baltimore Afro-American* covered one of these engagements, reporting: "Mrs. Mamie Till Bradley, leading a whirlwind life since the Mississippi slaying of her son, Emmett Till, came to Washington Sunday, with three companions and told a reporter in a clear controlled voice: 'when I can find the time, I'll cry.' She said: 'Emmett's dead, and I cannot bring him back, but his death has changed my entire way of thinking. The things that happened to him must not happen to anyone else. I feel compelled, almost driven, to do everything in my power to prevent it.'" And, indeed, she did. She became an activist in the civil rights movement, but she expanded her fight to seek freedom, justice, and equality for all Americans, regardless of their race or ethnicity.[47]

On the heels of their reporting on an NAACP rally headlined by Till-Mobley, southeastern black newspaper staffs chose to add to the growing coverage of the rift between her and the NAACP. In addition to offering many of the same details found in press reports in other regions, the *Afro-American* provided a platform for Till-Mobley to assert that "the NAACP has 'used the case of Emmett Till to its own gain.'" In her opinion, the case should not have serve the specific needs of the NAACP; the overall objective should have been the prosecution of those involved in her son's murder: "What I really wanted was for them to work out a civil suit against J. W. Milam and Mrs. Roy Bryant." She also maintained that the money offered her by the NAACP failed to cover her expenses. Despite the disagreement and her father saying flatly that he would rather leave the NAACP out of things, she hoped to work out a compromise since she shared the organization's goals. And, as the *Afro-American* reported, she wrote the NAACP directly:

The objectives of the NAACP are of much greater concern to me than my pocketbook. I set out to trade the blood of my child for the betterment of my race; and I do not now wish to deviate from such course. I feel very bad that the opportunity to talk for the Association would be taken from me. I know that you have tried very hard and sincerely to see to my day-to-day financial needs. It is unfair and untrue for anyone to say otherwise. If the NAACP is willing to continue to do what is [*sic*] has to defray my travel and living expenses, that should suffice. Please let me go forward for NAACP. It is a duty. I would not want it said that I did anything to shirk it. Very sincerely yours, Mamie Bradley.[48]

In sharp contrast to the extensive and nuanced posttrial reactions found in the midwestern, northeastern, and southeastern press, western mainstream newspapers continued their sparse reporting and, true to their earlier form, continued to defend southern advancement. Several pieces recounted reports from the prosegregationist *Jackson (MS) Daily News*. The Deep South was condemned only when Till-Mobley's statements were reproduced. Like those in other regions of the country, after the trial western newspapers too began printing reactions from their readers. Overwhelmingly, these letters defended the Deep South or urged the South to "continue" progressive reforms. A few also condemned the western mainstream newspapers for spending so much time on the Till trial while "more important news," like Mississippi senator Eastland's claim that the leaders of the integration movement were supported by the Communist Party, received scant attention.

As expected, Mamie Till-Mobley lashed out at white Mississippi officials for making a mockery of the judicial system by acquitting Bryant and Milam in the face of substantial evidence. Indeed, in her opinion the two certainly were guilty. Both the *San Francisco Examiner* and the *Denver*

Post recorded her comments on this issue. The *Examiner* asserted: "Mrs. Mamie Bradley contended today that 'no effort was made to find an eye witness' to testify in the trial of the two men accused of murdering her son. . . . She added she believed two important witnesses were being held in Charleston, Miss., jail to prevent them from testifying." Additionally, "Mrs. Mamie Bradley . . . said the trial at Sumner, Miss., was a comedy. 'What I saw of the trial was a shame before God and man,' she said." Similarly, in reference to reports that Emmett Till was still alive and that his death was staged, the *Denver Post* told readers: "At Detroit, Mrs. Mamie Bradley . . . called the rumors a 'cruel hoax,' and said she was willing to have the body exhumed for an examination." The *Examiner* highlighted Till-Mobley's outrage over the acquittal and showed that she felt the trial was a joke. As in previous reports, the *Examiner* took a neutral stance, allowing its readers to draw their own conclusions about the fairness of the trial and the accuracy of Till-Mobley's accusations. Because it failed to communicate the salience of the event to their readers, those readers in turn failed to demand more incisive coverage. Emmett Till proved to be of little or no importance to them.[49]

The *Post* told readers that the controversy over the identity of the body stemmed from comments by Sheriff Strider and reports in the *Jackson Daily News;* however, it did not remind them that Strider had consistently displayed a contempt for both the trial itself and the black people attending the trial, nor did it inform them that the *Daily News* was vehement in its prosegregationist rhetoric. Without the aid of editorialization and critical analysis, readers could easily believe the *Daily News* and Sheriff Strider over Mamie Till-Mobley, something they seemingly wanted to do.

Western dailies did consistently question the acquittal of Bryant and Milam; however, they continued to praise the efforts of some "better" Mississippians. In the view of the *Denver Post*, "when the Till boy's body was first found, the reaction in the white community of Mississippi was described as 'sincere and vehement . . . outrage.'" This erroneous impression was based on the fact that "newspapers denounced the killing and warned that the people of that state could defend their theories of separation of the races only if the law enforcement machinery assured equal justice for both races." Despite the perceived "laudable" efforts on the part of Mississippi newspapers, "the recent actions of Mississippi white leaders, undertaking a desperate fight to preserve the dual race system from effects of court decisions ordering desegregation, produced a backlash in the Till case." Naturally, the western dailies blamed African Americans for sparking this backlash. Specifically, the *Post* accused: "When the NAACP and other 'outsiders' and 'political shysters' from the north got into the act, the righteous indignation of the white people of Mississippi against the boy's killers cooled down." Thus, in the presence of this outside interference, "the murder of a Negro boy, under provocation of an 'insulting' act, may still be sanctioned in the minds of white people who are clinging to a crumbling supremacy." The editorial ended: "The people of Mississippi should be aggrieved and ashamed, as we imagine many of them are." The *Post* attacked Mississippi residents for "sanction[ing]" a boy's murder, but the attack was tempered by the belief that the state would have earned a conviction if not for the battle over integration and the interference of groups like the NAACP. In short, if left to their own devices, the people of Mississippi were moral enough to punish whites for brutalizing blacks.[50]

Given the fact that white Mississippians were cognizant of the potentially devastating effect the Till case could have on their state's image, some tried to counter this likelihood by lying about the state of race relations in Mississippi. Unlike dailies elsewhere in the country, which chose to ignore these outlandish claims or frame them as absurd, the western press reserved space for them. According to Gladys Vied, who wrote to the *San Francisco Examiner:* "The South is undergoing a great change; but one has to live there to understand how much it is misrepresented by vigorous and fanatical propaganda. Sound reasoning would cause the average American citizen to disregard rumors that tend to weaken our Government. Does it not seem logical that if all the articles published regarding segregation and politics in the South were true, that there would be a mass migration, that not a single poor misunderstood Negro person would be left below the Mason-Dixon line?" She not only argued that the South was misunderstood but also called reports of racial oppression *propaganda.* In her opinion, if the South were as bad as many reports claimed, all the African Americans would leave. These comments ignored the fact that the twentieth century saw an unprecedented migration of black people from southern states. She did not consider how racial oppression drastically limited the socioeconomic prospects of black people in the South and how poverty often made relocation impossible. Moreover, she refused to acknowledge the fact that, as bad as the situation was for blacks, the South was still their home. It is not clear whether Vied's comments were representative of the majority of western mainstream newspaper readers, but that the *Examiner* printed this letter without any editorial response lends credence to the notion that the paper's leadership shared her opinions.[51]

Subsequent letters printed in the *Examiner* lent further proof that the paper's readers were southern apologists who felt no connection to the struggle for black equality even after the Till murder. Richard Haase maintained: "The question is not how self-respecting is the Negro, as an individual, but how self-respecting is the white individual behind the scenes, who are these civil rights manipulators." In an effort to buttress his case, Haase referenced the notoriously vehement racist James Eastland: "Senator Eastland dropped a bombshell in the United States Senate on May 26, which may have repercussions for years to come. The Senator publicly disclosed the Commie front documents of the psychologists and social scientists which the High Court cited as its authority in [the] desegregation decision." Here we have a 1950s iteration of the racist argument that blacks did not deserve equality because they were incapable of effective leadership and were forced to rely on Communist support to accomplish their goals. Furthermore, Haase attacked the Supreme Court for relying on arguments generated by Communists and praised Eastland for exposing the truth.[52]

A letter that appeared the day after Haase's put forward the same argument but accused the *Examiner* of ignoring Eastland's key revelation:

> Your comparative coverage of two recent southern States stories is impressive, if not confusing. 1—The murder trial going on in an obscure village in the deep South, Sumner, given columns of space, pictures and everything. 2—Senator Eastland's speech in the United States Senate dealing with the citations of authorities on psychology by our Supreme Court in its school desegregation decision. Obviously, when our Supreme Court drops its law books for the vagaries of K. B. Clark, Theodore Brameld, E. Franklin Frazier, Gunnar Myrdal, etc., it is news, . . . but I fail to find any coverage of that astounding development in your valued paper.

In other words, the *Examiner* was spending too much time on an anomalous event that affected no one outside the "obscure village" of Sumner and all but ignoring the vastly more important story of the Supreme Court favoring Communist ideology over the American tradition of law in outlawing desegregation.[53]

Some of the letters printed in the western dailies did, however, see through the Mississippi lies and expressed outrage over the Till case. For instance, one letter to the *Seattle Times* mocked the notion that the body identified as Till's could not have been his: "I have sent the original of the following letter to the governor of Mississippi: 'Dear Governor: Now that a Mississippi court has decided that it had no proof of the murder of Emmett Till, are you not under some obligation to the moral sense of the nation to see that the live Emmett Till is returned safely to his mother?' I hope the governor of Mississippi receives many such letters." This pointed jab called on Mississippi to continue to investigate the Till case. And the tone of the letter showed that the writer felt that Bryant and Milam had gotten away with murder and that it was imperative for others to press Mississippi officials to ensure that justice would eventually prevail. This reader also called on others to write Mississippi and call for action in the Till case. Judging by the letters printed in their respective newspapers, it is not clear how many readers held similar views. But a survey of the western region's papers suggests that readers in Seattle and Denver were somewhat sympathetic to the Till family, while readers in San Francisco were largely disinterested in the Till case.[54]

A letter published in the *Denver Post* was even more condemnatory of Mississippi and other Deep South states. Bernice Johnston wrote: "It is difficult in the western portion of the United States to conceive of such a miscarriage of justice in the southern states. Perhaps these men are innocent. . . . Then where has he [Till] gone?" Obviously, this reader knew the answer to her rhetorical question. The body was in fact Till's, and it was buried in Illinois. That point settled, she continued: "It is horrifying to think of these two full grown men with their strong racial prejudice kidnaping a 14-year-old boy, and what must have ensued." Hammering home the point that events like the lynching of Emmett Till damaged America's image abroad, she related: "In the two years my husband and I spent abroad we were continually reading and negating to our French friends literature they had concerning America and the status of the Negro. One sentence in particular stated, 'The American Negro when he passes a white man on the street shrinks against the wall in fear.'" While Johnston acknowledged that "much of this literature is Communist inspired," she lamented: "It fills me with remorse to see it actually happening in the town of Sumner, Miss." Hopeful for change, she noted: "However dismal the case appears at the present time, I feel that in the long run this will be a memorable verdict in that the majority of people are aware of a great miscarriage of justice, and we have not read or heard the last of the 'Till Case.'" Unfortunately, few western readers seemed to agree with her.[55]

In the face of such press coverage and reader response, the western black press called into question information found in the region's mainstream newspapers. Sympathizing with a disappointed Mamie Till-Mobley after the verdict was given, the *Los Angeles Sentinel* highlighted that she was not in the courtroom when the verdict was read because she did not want to see the initial celebration of those she knew were responsible for the murder of her son. Instead, she vented her dissatisfaction with the trial and the acquittal in the pages of the *Sentinel:* "[She asserted that] no effort was made to find an eyewitness to testify in the trial. She called the acquittal 'a shame before God and man.'" Armed with overwhelming evidence proving Bryant and Milam's guilt, the jury turned a blind eye and freed the "good ole boys." The murder investigation not only failed to convict the perpetrators; the testimony for the prosecution of some brave African Americans brought repercussions. Refusing to let those who risked their lives to testify on the side of right and justice slip into obscurity, the *Sentinel* detailed, for example: "Willie Reed left last Friday night enroute to Detroit with Congressman Charles Diggs to find a new life in Michigan. He was spirited out of the State [of Mississippi] after his testimony for fear of reprisal from the families of those against whom he testified." By standing up for the slain Till, Reed risked the same fate that Till had met; however, his courage led to him receiving a one-way ticket out of the badlands.[56]

The balance of the reports dealt with Mamie Till-Mobley's disagreement with the NAACP and involved some final reflections on the acquittal. The two articles dealing with the conflict between Till's mother and the civil rights organization did not introduce much information that differed from that reported by other regions' black newspapers; however, they did emphasize Till-Mobley's importance. Given that the *Sentinel* was the largest black newspaper in this region, readers might expect a detailed account of why the NAACP dropped Till-Mobley from the tour; however, the paper did not provide such detail, nor did it recount statements made by Till-Mobley or the NACCP in the aftermath of the disagreement.[57]

The *Sentinel* did report, however, that, after Till-Mobley was dropped, western-region NAACP officials considered canceling the speaking engagements because they felt that she was key to the tour. The paper reported that national NAACP officials had told western offices to continue with the tour but that there was still speculation that it would be canceled. After much dialogue, most of the engagements proceeded as planned, with Moses Wright replacing Till-Mobley as the chief speaker.[58]

The only meeting that did not occur as planned was the Los Angeles rally. Representatives from the Los Angeles NAACP chapter first tried to book Till-Mobley without the approval of the national office. According to a telegram from Lester Bailey to Roy Wilkins, "[Tom Neusom of the LA chapter] says he can ge[t] Bradley free for LA NAACP leadership meeting." Wilkins responded by instructing the branch not to circumvent the national office. He was "greatly disturbed by information Los Angeles Branch plans to use Mrs. Bradley," and he saw this move as a "grave error." Eventually, the scheduled rally was simply canceled. Nevertheless, the remaining stops of the West Coast tour were a tremendous success. As Frank Barnes (part of the NAACP West Coast region leadership team in charge of southern California) wired Roy Wilkins, for example: "Seattle meeting smashing success. Hurly [*sic*] and Wright terrific team. $1300.00 cash 1,000 pledges."[59]

Notwithstanding this incident between the NAACP and Mamie Till-Mobley, the Till murder trial had many positive effects. Till-Mobley entered the national spotlight as a bold and determined civil rights activist, the barbarism of white Mississippians was laid plain, and Americans learned of the bravery of black Mississippians. Furthermore, the *Los Angeles Sentinel* reported: "The kidnap slaying . . . in Mississippi last month has brought a deluge of telephone calls and letters into NAACP headquarters from persons of both races." Emboldened by these victories, the *Sentinel* continued to hammer away at the acquittal of Bryant and Milam, which it regarded as a farce and an insult to human decency. Underscoring its sentiment on the acquittal was an editorial that included the text of a letter from an angry American veteran to Mississippi governor Hugh White: "I suggest the State of Mississippi immediately secede not only from the United States of America, but from the human race. The white population of your State should immigrate to Red China where they would be at liberty to torture and kill innocent people. For shame, I am only sorry that your State was a part of the great nation that I fought for." In conclusion, the *Sentinel* declared: "This telegram fired at Gov. Hugh White of Mississippi by a former American Legion commander pretty well sums up our feelings."[60]

Regardless of the fact that the *Sentinel* deplored the verdict in the Till case, the outcome, it felt, was a foregone conclusion: "The trial, held in dusty Sumner, Miss., followed its expected course—complete with trumped-up evidence, lying defense witnesses, weak prosecution, conniving officials, and an ignorant, irresponsible all-white jury." The attack continued: "The defense battery added to a coup de grace to a shabbily prosecuted case with the 'brilliant' summation that a rotted body dressed in Till's clothing had been tossed into the river by unidentified agitators." This line of argument was incomprehensible, and the *Sentinel* posed the question, "Whose body?" "Dead bodies cannot be picked up like pebbles on a beach," it explained. "It took the jury 65 minutes to arrive at its decision. It could have done it in two minutes." The *Sentinel,* however, fired its most powerful salvo at the prosecution, which "either by accident or design supported the defense by admitting the case against Bryant and Milam was 'highly circumstantial,' and failed to offer any 'expert' testimony (which was available) on their own."[61]

Notwithstanding its perception of the trial as a grave injustice, the *Sentinel* chose to place the proceedings in a broader context: "On trial, to our mind, was a lot more than just two murder suspects. The State of Mississippi—its woeful decadence and arrogant stupidity its pitiful people and Dark Ages system; its legacy of white supremacy handed down from father to son—were the real defendants. Mississippi, for its part flunked its opportunity to join the ranks of decency, magna cum laude."[62]

In light of this unprecedented scrutiny and criticism directed at their legal system from all corners of the country, Deep South mainstream papers felt it necessary to defend the legal process. Even liberals like the *Delta Democrat-Times*'s Hodding Carter were unwilling or unable to reject the region's historically institutionalized racism, and the coverage in these mainstream papers presented the traditional Mississippi-as-scapegoat metaphor, which argued that whites in the region were the paternalistic protectors of African Americans.

Whenever there were instances of assertiveness on the part of blacks in their interactions with white people, the Deep South mainstream press blamed them on the northern liberal incursion spearheaded by the NAACP, charging that the civil rights organization created an atmosphere in which black people eagerly sought revenge against white people for the Till murder. According to the *Democrat-Times*, "in the past week four Memphis blacks ravished a white woman." The paper noted that this type of behavior was not uncommon, although generally it did not comment on it. However, "the thing that sets this beastly crime apart is that they attempted to justify themselves by referring to the Emmett Till 'wolf whistle' murder case." The paper also argued: "Since the NAACP was so ready to blame all of Mississippi and all white Mississippians with the slaying of the Chicago Negro who was impolite to a Money, Miss. white woman, we wonder if the NAACP is ready to take the blame for inciting these four young

Negroes to commit rape?" It concluded: "It is certainly as logical. The atmosphere of hatred created by the NAACP against white people could very well have precipitated this crime in Memphis." What most white southerners saw as the NAACP stirring up black hatred of white people was in reality the civil rights organization leading a vibrant and potent campaign for black equality. No doubt the efforts of the NAACP helped politicize African Americans and led to more assertive behavior, but the organization would never condone rape.[63]

In addition to the NAACP, the Deep South mainstream press also attacked what it saw as the hypocrisy of northerners and the northern press, taking aim at several pieces about the Till murder that exposed the system of white supremacy in the South and cast doubt on the likelihood of a conviction. At the same time, it noted that similar crimes were common in the North but ignored by the region's press, which focused extensively on the Till case. This was further proof that its northern counterparts were engaged in a vendetta against the entire American South. This "us against the world" theme pervaded the Deep South mainstream coverage and was the driving force behind posttrial reactions, reactions that served as fodder for Joseph Crespino's metaphor of Mississippi as scapegoat. Surely, racism, segregation, and racial oppression existed throughout the nation. It would be naive to think otherwise. However, these abominable traits were clearly more overt in the Deep South and specifically in the Mississippi Delta region.[64]

Coverage after the trial took a confrontational stance toward the North while maintaining a racist and paternalistic tone. After the acquittal, Sheriff Strider boasted: "Well I hope the Chicago niggers and the NAACP are satisfied." The *Memphis Commercial Appeal* had a more circumspect yet equally racist reaction: "It seemed to us that evidence necessary for convicting on a murder charge was lacking." Given the propensity of the editor of the paper, Frank Ahlgren, to ingratiate himself with his readership by proving that he could match their bigotry, a practice that earned him praise from the race-baiting politician Walter Sillers Jr., the tone of coverage in the Memphis paper was not surprising to the readers. Furthering its argument, the *Appeal* maintained, "We believe that if the jury hearing this circumstantial evidence had agreed on conviction, the decision would have been reversed by any appeals court in the land, including Mississippi, Illinois and New York." Similarly, the *Jackson Daily News* surmised, "The cold fact concerning the acquittal in Tallahatchie county of the two alleged slayers of a Negro youth from Chicago is that the prosecution failed to prove its case." As the *Daily News* saw it, "there was no lack of vigor in the prosecution." Therefore, since Mississippians acted honorably, the paper argued, "the NAACP cannot truthfully contend that a Mississippi court was guilty of 'an atrocious miscarriage of justice,' as its loud-mouthed leaders are shouting. . . . They took no part in the case but the NAACP atmosphere they brought with them surely must have had an adverse effect on the state's case." Similarly, the *Democrat-Times* added: "We must . . . give due condemnation to the NAACP spokesmen for their part in the case."[65]

Not even Mamie Till-Mobley avoided the critical eye of the Deep South mainstream newspapers. One letter to the editor of the *Commercial Appeal* accused: "Who doubts Mamie Bradley's role in the NAACP? She exhibited the body of her son (at least she said it was her son) in Chicago for days to arouse hate against Mississippi, and to enrich the treasury of the NAACP. Does anyone believe a true and a loving mother would do that to her son?" Furthermore, "I wonder, if true facts were known, just who is behind the NAACP, and why are they making a three-ring circus out of the Till case? I think the Government should investigate the leaders of this organization and find out exactly why they are trying to stir up racial hatred."[66]

Given the alleged interference and the propaganda campaign waged by Mamie Till-Mobley and the NAACP, Deep South press employees urged people to forget about the Till case. Quoting an editorial from the *Tupelo (MS) Journal,* the *Democrat-Times* asserted in an October 30, 1955, editorial: "The time seems to have come for Mississippi to shelve the Till murder case and all the many ramifications resulting from it. . . . The sensible course for Mississippi, therefore, is to ignore as nearly as possible all further exploitation of the Till murder by northern organizations." Since whites in the region felt "kindly and sympathetically towards [poor and inferior] colored people," and since Mississippians did more for African Americans than anyone else, it was time for them to forget about Till. In reality, what Mississippi white people did was use racist ideology to keep black people in permanent servitude. They allowed their dedication to agriculture, and their fear of integration and the improved state for African Americans that industrialization would produce, to perpetuate Deep South poverty.[67]

The balance of the coverage after this editorial focused on the *Jackson Daily News* investigations of Louis Till. Although the *Daily News* broke the story about Till's court-martial, the most extensive article appeared in the *Memphis Commercial-Appeal,* which reported: "Pvt. Till was court-martialed and hanged for the premeditated murder of Anna Zanchi and the rape of Benni Lucretzia and Frieda Marl records showed. . . . More than a year elapsed between the crime and the execution, indicating the case was given extended consideration by Army authorities." Additionally, "the revelation of the Negro soldier's heinous crimes and disgraceful demised added a strange new turn to the efforts of radical pressure groups to exploit the 'Emmett Louis Till Case.'" Then the attention turned to Mamie Till-Mobley: "In Chicago . . . the youth's mother insisted she didn't know how her former husband died. . . . 'I have heard rumors, and I have tried to find out what actually happened. . . . I wrote to the commanding officer, to the chaplain, and to President Roosevelt, but received no satisfaction.' She apparently forgot that President Roosevelt died April 12, 1945 and was succeeded by President Truman." In case they were wondering, readers also learned: "The offices of Mississippi's two senators, James O. Eastland and John Stennis, assisted reporters by obtaining most of the important facts from the Army and urging the release of additional details." Instead of focusing on their jobs, elected officials tasked their staffs with the chores of lynching Emmett Till's family lineage. It was not enough that Bryant and Milam robbed him of his life; Mississippi's senators saw fit to attack his parents' legacy as well.[68]

Deep South mainstream papers ended their coverage of the Till saga by reporting on reactions to the lack of indictment on kidnapping charges. John Herbers noted in a United Press newswire story picked up by the *Democrat-Times:* "The Greenwood Morning Star defended the grand jurors as 'men who know justice and are capable of making the right decision. . . . Till attempted to molest Mrs. Bryant, grabbed her and made indecent proposals,' Editor Virgil Adams wrote. 'Where is there a husband worthy of the name who would not protect his wife?'"[69]

In the end, however, the supposedly liberal *Democrat-Times* presented one of the few progressive assessments of the situation: "A Leflore County grand jury has told the world that white men in Mississippi may remove Negroes from their homes against their will to punish them or worse, without fear of punishment for themselves. . . . The records of our courts reveal a shocking number of related incidents. . . . A curse lies on our state. . . . Most of what is happening in Mississippi has nothing to do with segregation. . . . [T]his is naked racially-inspired terror." The acquittal in the murder trial was acceptable since Sheriff Strider provided the prosecution with a weak case; however, the failure to indict Bryant and Milam in the face of overwhelming proof that they kidnapped Till was inexcusable. Hodding Carter stepped forward and blasted his neighbors for their blind devotion to white supremacy and, for the first time during the coverage, labeled Mississippi white supremacist activity as "naked racially-inspired terror."[70]

This terror was a fact of everyday life for blacks in the Deep South, and the region's black press offered sufficient, if guarded, condemnation of the verdict in the Till trial. The *Jackson (MS) Advocate*'s Percy Green produced an editorial about the Till lynching and foreign opinion. At first glance, he seemed to be defending the Mississippi verdict: "There appears to be enough in the case to justify the verdict in the eyes of those who would apply the strict letter of the law in such cases." However, the *Advocate* cautioned: "In the forum of world opinion . . . there must be times when the strict letter and interpretation of the law must give way to the demands of the higher virtues of justice, morality, right, and Christianity."[71]

The *Birmingham World* employed a similar tactic when a staff writer discussed reports in Paris and London papers. In all accounts it was argued that the Till case damaged America's image abroad. Additionally, the international press condemned the state of Mississippi and its justice system for conducting a farce of a trial. And it was business as usual, as another *World* staff writer pointed out: "Since before the turn of the twentieth century, no white man has been given the death penalty for killing a Negro." Why should anything change as a result of the Till lynching?[72]

In the *Birmingham World,* readers were informed that over one thousand people attended a Paris rally "protesting the acquittal of Roy Bryant and J. W. Milam." Turning attention to events closer to home, the *Memphis World* carried an article entitled "Public Protest Mounts on Emmett Till Case" in which it was reported: "Mass protest meetings on the Mississippi trial verdict . . . drew huge crowds here [New York], in Detroit, in Youngstown, and in Dotham, Ala." Clearly, despite efforts by Deep South mainstream papers to move past the Till case, the international arena disagreed vehemently with the position that the case should be forgotten and undoubtedly continued to show solidarity with those voices bemoaning the trial verdict. People wanted to lend any support they could to the fight for racial equality, and, as the *Memphis World* reported, "NAACP headquarters has been deluged with telephone calls and letters offering financial and other assistance to the organization in its fight to end . . . a 'reign of terror' in Mississippi." Despite the best efforts of the Deep South mainstream press, articles like this one proved that the Till case was a national and international rather than a local issue and that much of the population wanted to remember rather than forget the Till lynching. As one *Tri-State Defender* editorialist noted, "if Mississippi thinks the Emmett Till case is dead, the people of that parochial state are badly mistaken. . . . Public reaction in Africa and Europe . . . was swift, violent and universal and did much to damage United States prestige abroad."[73]

Even when Deep South mainstream newspapers attempted to discredit the prosecution witnesses and present the role of the NAACP in the Till trial in a negative light, such reports were clearly fantasies. For example, when the racist *Jackson Daily News* sent its reporter Bill Spell to Chicago to interview Willie Reed and Amanda Bradley, he claimed that the two Till trial witnesses were being held captive in that city by the NAACP. But, as Spell reported, when asked whether she was indeed being held captive, Bradley responded: "That's the most fantastic thing I ever heard. Nobody is keeping me here. I wanted to come, and I did paying my own way." Asked whether he too was being held captive, Moses Wright quipped: "I guess I have now heard everything. I not only came to Chicago of my own free will, but I brought my wife, and our three children." Furthermore, Reed's mother was quoted as saying: "The more I hear about what's supposed to be happening to us, the more fantastic it gets."[74]

Spell's narrative was quickly shot down by the Deep South black newspapers. He traveled to Chicago and gained access to the witnesses by arriving in a Mississippi National Guard airplane and impersonating a Mississippi state official. Clearly, he had the blessing of not only his newspaper's management but also Governor White. Through Spell's report and others, white Mississippians launched a racist counterattack against the accurate and sensible reports found in the Deep South black papers. Prepared for such tactics, and armed with years of experience dealing with virulent racism, the black papers flanked their overconfident enemies and presented a narrative of the Till lynching, trial, and aftermath that openly condemned the crime, highlighted black activism in the fight for justice, and furthered the legacy of Emmett Till, a legacy that would take full form over the next decade and become the driving force behind the push for civil rights.[75]

7

In Remembrance of Emmett Till

The national narrative constructed around the legacy of Emmett Till is shaped by individual and collective memories of the events, memories that developed out of reactions to the regional stories and racial dispositions found in the print media. Since memories are often embellished and distorted over time, and since print media narratives of the Till saga varied in scope, detail, and emphasis, many conflicting accounts of key events have developed. According to some, particularly Carolyn Bryant and her family, Emmett Till physically and verbally assaulted Bryant as she tended the family store; others maintain that Till simply whistled at the former beauty queen. Some called the whistle a response to a bet, while others believe he whistled to stop himself from stuttering.[1] Similar debates exist, or have existed, over the location of the murder, the number of people who participated in the kidnapping, and the number of people present when J. W. Milam shot Emmett Till in the back of the head. Till's relatives, historians, reporters, literary scholars, documentarians, and civil rights activists have clamored to find the truth behind the Till lynching. While the growing body of investigative works and first-person testimonials brings us closer to the facts of the case, this book focuses more on how individually and collectively we remember the life, death, and legacy of the Chicago boy. Emmett Till's memory is an aggregation of shared ideas, shared responses, shared experiences, and shared visions of what his death meant for the past, the present, and the future of race relations in American society. With his death, Till shone the light on the awful state of oppression that existed in Mississippi and much of the Deep South with respect to the black condition.

In the immediate wake of the trial and acquittal, journalists, civil rights activists, and the general public reacted by attempting to make sense out of the senseless. From Mississippi, cries of foul play and accusations of an NAACP conspiracy blared from the pages of even the most liberal of

regional papers. Across much of the rest of the nation, outrage and condemnation of the Deep South abounded. Spurred on by persistent coverage of the lynching in the local and national press, civil rights–minded
organizations and individuals collected en masse at countless rallies to
protest the verdict and the culture of oppression in Mississippi that made
such injustices possible. Once they reached a safer space than Mississippi
offered, black journalists who attended the trial documented the vitriolic
racism that they confronted head-on, thus memorializing their experiences
in the Delta. Under the auspices of, first, the NAACP and, later, labor and
similar organizations, Mamie Till-Mobley persisted in her claim that the
body was that of her son, and she continued to call for justice.

These short-term efforts ensured that Till's death continued to figure
prominently in public discourse and, thereby, influence the way in which
people responded to the American narratives of post–World War II race
relations. Certainly, throughout the rest of the 1950s, and across the 1960s
and 1970s, activists in the civil rights and black power movements would
continue to invoke Till's death as a rallying cry in their efforts to strike
down segregation and all vestiges of Jim Crow white supremacy. With his
death, Emmett Till inspired a generation.

Reflecting on their work within the movement, civil rights champions from across all the most highly publicized clashes in the movement
pointed to Till as an impetus for their refusal to accept business as usual
when it came to race relations. Rosa Parks famously noted that he was on
her mind when she refused to give up her seat on the Montgomery bus. An
active member of the Montgomery chapter of the NAACP, Parks doubtless followed the Till saga through the pages of local and national press
outlets. She would have seen in Montgomery's NAACP office, and likely
too in her home, issues of *The Crisis* in which were detailed the horrors
that befell the fourteen-year-old boy as well as Mississippi's intransigence
in the face of mounting criticism of its racial mores. For Rosa Parks, and
for many other blacks in the South, coverage in national publications like
Jet and accounts in local editions of the *Defender* and the *Daily World*
publications proved impossible to ignore.[2]

Highlighting the singular effect of the incident, Myrlie Evers-Williams,
the civil rights activist and widow of Medgar Evers, said of the Till lynching: "This one somehow struck a spark of indignation that ignited protests around the world." These worldwide protests occurred because, with
his death, Till showed everyone "that even youth was no defense against
the ultimate terror, that lynching was still the final means by which white

supremacy would be upheld, that whites could still murder Negroes with impunity, and that upper- and middle-class white people of the state would uphold such killings through their police and newspapers and courts of law." As Evers-Williams saw it, in a very real way Till's death, and the acquittal of his murderers, "was proof, if proof were needed, that there would be no real change in Mississippi until the rest of the country decided that change there must be and then forced it." Thus, "young Emmett became in death what he could never have been in life: a rallying cry and a cause."[3]

As many scholars have underscored, with his death Emmett Till changed the face of American race relations. Charles Payne noted that the volumes of response to the Till lynching showed that Americans outside Mississippi were increasingly concerned with how race relations in that Deep South state cast the entire nation in a negative light. Certainly, the throngs of journalists who descended on Tallahatchie County to cover the trial and the large crowds of local blacks who showed up in protest of this injustice proved to the Mississippi establishment that times were changing and southern blacks were increasingly standing up against racial oppression.[4]

No group internalized the saliency of the Till saga more than the young black men and women who were coming of age during this turbulent era. Across the country, the Till lynching had a profound effect on black youths, the discourse around Till and the graphic images of his broken body printed in *Jet* magazine influencing their racial dispositions as they came of age in the midst of the civil rights movement. Chronicling the rise of prominent civil rights activists of the 1960s and 1970s like Stokely Carmichael, Julian Bond, and Diane Nash, Andrew Lewis pointed out: "For young African Americans . . . Emmett Till overshadowed everything else that happened during the 1950s. It scared them, erasing the distance between the violence of Jim Crow and their lives. . . . The murder hung over the rest of their youth, a bad memory that would not go away."[5]

When asked in a 2010 interview for MSNBC what event impressed on her the gravity of racial prejudice, Minnijean Brown Trickey, one of the Little Rock Nine (the nine black students who, in 1957, amid massive protests, integrated Central High School in Little Rock, Arkansas), noted that it was the Till lynching. His death resonated with Trickey because, had he lived, Till too would have been entering the eleventh grade in 1957. Also born the same year as Emmett Till and Minnijean Brown Trickey was Jibreel Khazan, who, under his birth name, Ezell Blair Jr., on February

1, 1960, joined his Agricultural and Technical College of North Carolina (now North Carolina Agricultural and Technical University) classmates in an effort to integrate the Woolworth's lunch counter in Greensboro, North Carolina. This highly publicized protest ushered in an era of widespread nonviolent direct action sit-in movements that swept across the country. As Khazan noted: "Emmett Till showed us what could happen if we broke the code. . . . If we spoke out of turn we could die."[6]

Along with Parks, Trickey, and Khazan, countless civil rights champions pointed to Till's death as the impetus for their activism, and scholars have underscored the fourteen-year-old boy's effect on the Emmett Till generation. With her 1994 monograph on Till, Clenora Hudson-Weems resurrected the study of Emmett Till, incorporating in her work poignant testimonials about Till's effect on their lives from a diverse body of activists, including the black studies scholar Molefi Asante and the civil rights attorney Alvin Chambliss Jr.[7]

Emmett Till's lynching raised America's conscience, and because of his death, many people intensified their efforts in the battle for civil rights. To that end, as noted by Christopher Metress, the congressman and civil rights activist John Lewis proclaimed: "[Till's lynching] galvanized the country. A lot of us young black students in the South later on, we weren't sitting in just for ourselves—we were sitting in for Emmett Till. We went on Freedom Rides for Emmett Till."[8]

Without a doubt, this enormous effect is due in large part to the fact that the print media kept the nation informed throughout the affair. As Evers-Williams pointed out perceptively, change in Mississippi, and really in the entire country, required a unified effort on the part of a large number of Americans. And, after Till's lynching, many did join the struggle. Throughout the next decade, black and white Americans fought for continued school integration, the integration of public facilities and public transportation, the registration of black voters, workers' rights, civil rights and voting rights acts, antilynching legislation, the end of housing discrimination, and the rights of all citizens. As America marched through the turbulent 1960s, the media followed the modern civil rights movement and highlighted activists like Dr. Martin Luther King Jr., Roy Wilkins, Rosa Parks, Medgar Evers, Gloria Richardson, Bayard Rustin, and A. Philip Randolph, to name a few. While focusing on these other issues and individuals, local and national publications continued to update their readers on the Till lynching. In this way, they kept the Till saga alive long after 1955.

Till updates came in many forms. For instance, in January 1956, Roy Bryant and J. W. Milam sold their confession to William Bradford Huie and *Look* magazine. Countering journalistic conventions (which at that time did not condone paying people to tell their stories), Huie paid Bryant and Milam $3,500. Obviously, Bryant and Milam did not mind taking money. Giving Huie his money's worth, they recounted their version of the wolf-whistle, kidnapping, lynching, and disposal of the body. Of course, their version of the events defied nearly every account found in the print media coverage of the Till lynching. The *Look* article described the wolf-whistle incident as follows: "He [Till] entered the store, alone, and stopped at the candy case. Carolyn [Bryant] was behind the counter; Bobo [Till] in front. He asked for two cents' worth of bubble gum. She handed it to him. He squeezed her hand and said: 'How about a date, baby?' Allegedly, she jerked away and started for Juanita Milam [who was in the back of the store]. At the break in the counters, Bobo jumped in front of her . . . and said: 'You needn't be afraid o' me, Baby. I been with white girls before.'"[9]

Clearly, this account was a rehashing of Carolyn Bryant's fabricated testimony at the murder trial. The Reverend Wheeler Parker and Simeon Wright, Till's cousins who were at the store, maintained that Emmett Till neither touched Bryant nor spoke of being with a white woman. Correspondingly, Mamie Till-Mobley had pointed out that her son had never had a white girlfriend. She speculated that, in the unlikely event that he was bragging about a white woman, he was referring to a picture of Hedy Lamarr that came in the wallet she had bought him. Furthermore, there were no white girls in his school, so there would have been little or no opportunity for him to get a picture of a white girl. However, despite the fact that Bryant and Milam were clearly lying, Huie allowed them to continue. In his refusal to challenge their tall tale, Huie ignored two key elements. First, he had already circumvented journalistic convention when he paid Bryant and Milam for their account; at the very least he should have ensured that he bought an accurate portrayal of the events. Second, and more importantly, the publication of these lies in *Look* created a new and lasting story of Till that adversely affected the memory of the youth and the murder. Of note is the fact that Bryant and Milam claimed that they were the only perpetrators; thus, on their account Till's death could not be considered a lynching, which requires three or more people. More importantly, by reinforcing Carolyn Bryant's testimony, Bryant and Milam damaged Emmett Till's character and continued to prime stereotypes of hypersexual black men who needed white men to put them in their place.[10]

As the Huie article continued, readers learned that Bryant and Milam took on the "white man's burden" and dealt with Till in the "only acceptable manner." Proclaiming that Till drove them to murder him, Bryant and Milam argued that their "initial thought was 'just to whip him . . . and scare some sense into him.'" However, Till would not stop insisting that he was their equal, no matter what they did: "We were never able to scare him. They [northerners] has just filled him so full of that poison that he was hopeless." Apparently, Bryant and Milam, following the racist traditions of the patriarchy, felt justified in determining whether a black male was beyond hope, and Huie, a fellow southerner, did not question this logic. Instead, he allowed Bryant and Milam to put words in Till's mouth. Specifically, they reported that, as they were beating him across the face and body with their ".45 Colt automatic pistols," Till supposedly still had the fortitude to yell: "You bastards, I'm not afraid of you. I'm as good as you are. I've 'had' white women." As if this was not inconceivable enough, once the two had decided that they had to kill Till, they drove to "Progressive Ginning Company" and "stood aside" while Till, seemingly still energized, loaded the "74 pound" cotton gin fan into Milam's pickup truck. With the fan in place, they allegedly drove to the Tallahatchie River. Pistol whipped nearly unrecognizably, an eyeball hanging out of its socket, and doubtlessly bleeding from every part of his body, Till supposedly carried the seventy-four-pound gin fan another thirty yards to the river, stripped off his clothes, and again told Bryant and Milam that he was their equal and that he had been with white women. Finally, at the end of his patience, and no longer able to control his "righteous" anger, Milam found that "that big .45 jumped in [his] hand" and "the youth turned to catch that big, expanding bullet at his right ear." With that, Emmett Till died. The level of mendacity in this account defies belief, but more disturbing is the fact that Huie, *Look,* and publications like the *Saturday Evening Post* that reprinted this interview chose to publish this rendition of the lynching without editorial commentary.[11]

As was the case throughout the mainstream coverage of the saga and throughout the history of black journalism in general, the black community refused to remain silent in the face of this blatant propaganda emanating from Mississippi. Civil rights organizations like the NAACP went on the offensive, with Executive Secretary Roy Wilkins charging: "*Look*'s story of the Till murder in Mississippi carries the material covering the alleged remarks and acts of the dead boy as 'fact.' . . . Who stands behind these 'facts'?" The *Chicago Defender,* the *Baltimore Afro-American,* and the *Atlanta Daily World* all commented on the article; however, the most poignant reply came in the pages of the *California Eagle* (Los Angeles). The *Eagle*'s five-installment correction to the *Look* article was published under the pseudonym Amos Dixon. Dixon stated that he covered the Till trial and that he had talked with those who knew what happened. (His biographical revelations have been confirmed by scholars like David and Linda Beito to have come from the black Mississippi doctor and civil rights champion Dr. T. R. M. Howard.) In these articles, Dixon corrected inaccuracies in Bryant and Milam's testimonial. He began: "Milam is pretty well satisfied with the [*Look*] article" because it tells the story of the Till lynching from the "Mississippi viewpoint." With Bryant and Milam's Mississippi bias clearly stated, Dixon noted: "The 'Mississippi viewpoint' that pleased Milam so much was that the story told Milam's version of how Emmett molested Roy Bryant's wife and of how Till boasted about the white women he had 'had.' Moreover, the story shielded others who had taken part in the murder. That suits J. W. Milam just fine. But that isn't the truth."[12]

Instead of the blatant molestation described by the white Mississippians, what actually happened, according to Dixon, was that "when he [Till] left the store he turned to Carolyn Bryant and stuttered out a 'g-g-good bye.'" "Carolyn Bryant didn't like that," he continued, speculating that she had taken offense because "she's a poor white with little education, married at 17, living in the rear of a store with no TV to keep her company, no car to give her status." Despite her abject poverty, however, Bryant felt so emboldened by the vitriolic racism in her state that she refused to tolerate a black boy, especially one who had reached middle-class status, speaking to her.[13]

In the face of such an affront to her white womanhood, it was up to the white men around Carolyn Bryant to defend her honor: "J. W. Milam at once laid out a plan to take Emmett Till out early Sunday morning and give him a good 'pistol whipping.' That plan also included participation by two other Milam brothers, Leslie who lives in the town of Drew in Sunflower county, and another brother who has never been completely identified." According to plan, "about 2 o'clock Sunday morning, Aug. 28, . . . a Chevrolet truck belonging to J. W. Milam drew up in front of Mose Wright's farm. J. W. Milam, Roy Bryant, Leslie Milam and the unidentified Milam brother were riding in the cab of the truck. There was another man on that truck, too. That other man was a Negro, Henry Lee Loggins, . . . [who] has worked for J. W. for 12 years and whatever J. W. says is gospel as far as Loggins is concerned." Now that they had Till, the group drove to the plantation where Leslie Milam worked, and they proceeded to beat him to the point where the passersby Willie Reed and Mandy Bradley could hear. As was the case with most African Americans, the *Eagle* reporter did not subscribe to Milam's assertion in *Look* that there was no choice other than to kill Emmett Till: "J. W. Milam has painted himself as a hero, upholding a way of life approved by every government official in his state." However, "J. W. Milam made that statement as an after thought, when he was trying to depict himself as a hero in the cause of White Supremacy. The statement throws a great deal of light on the thinking and believing of four men turned into beasts who were willing to beat a 14 year-old boy to death but the fact remains that it is only the boasting of a bully. It's an excuse, an attempt to make a horrible crime palatable to his neighbors by an appeal to their prejudices."[14]

Unwilling to allow Milam's sanitizing of the story to go unchallenged, Dixon continued: "Their frantic effort to hide the body to destroy the evidence, discredits J. W. Milam's boasts in *Look* magazine in which he tried to make the crime appear as a heroic act, born out of a deliberate determination that Emmett Till had to be killed because he refused to knuckle under and deny that he had 'had' white women or admit that he wasn't as good as his tormentors." It was not heroism, he noted: "It was a senseless, wanton killing perpetrated in rage and frustration in an alcoholic haze. When it was done, the murderers wanted to hide their crime because they knew that even hardened Mississippians wouldn't approve of it." He concluded: "Figure it all up, add it up any way you will, and the result is always the same. Emmett Till was the victim of the system of race relations in Mississippi. There will be more Till cases as long as that system prevails." As it had in the past, the black press once again set the record straight and exposed the crime for what it was, a cold-blooded slaying.[15]

Likely because of the outrage expressed in papers like the *California Eagle,* in 1957 Huie again wrote a piece dealing with the Till lynching. This *Look* article, "What Happened to the Emmett Till Killers?" highlighted the repercussions of that fateful day in August 1955. Milam told Huie that Till's death had haunted the family. Specifically, "they [the Bryant-Milam family] have been disappointed. They have suffered disillusionment, ingratitude, resentment, misfortune. For years before the slaying, the numerous Milam-Bryant clan had operated a chain of small stores in the Delta, stores dependent on Negro trade. . . . Now, all these stores have been closed or sold. The Negroes boycotted them and ruined them." Compounding matters, "Milam, too, at that time [before the lynching], employed Negroes to operate his cotton pickers. He was reputed to be expert in 'working niggers.' Now, many Negroes won't work for him, and he has to employ white men at higher pay." Clearly, infuriated by the brutal slaying of Emmett Till, black Mississippians took a stand against these racist business owners.[16]

The *Look* article noted that, despite the family hardships, "Milam obviously isn't sorry he killed Bobo—to him, he had no choice—but it was an unlucky event for him." He felt that he still could rely on support from his white neighbors; however, the family learned that even white Mississippians wanted to distance themselves from the Till legacy. For that reason, "when Bryant's store was closed, he had trouble getting a job." Similarly, Milam "was shocked when landowners who had contributed to his defense declined to rent to him."[17]

Exacerbating the problem, "in all of Tallahatchie County—the county which had 'swarmed' to his defense—he couldn't rent land. The Bank of Charleston, largest in the county, refused him a loan." Of these hardships, Milam lamented: "I had a lot of friends a year ago . . . [who] contributed money to my defense fund." Apparently, this money disappeared, for, as Milam told Huie: "We never got half of what they say was contributed. I don't know what happened to it, but we never got it." "Since then, some of those friends have been making excuses," Milam said. He claimed to be a confused man: "[Last year] I got letters from all over the country congratulating me on my 'fine Americanism'; but I don't get that kind of letters any more." Instead: "Everything's gone against me—even the dry weather, which has hurt my cotton. I'm living in a share-crop with no water in it. My wife and kids are having it hard." Unlike the first Huie article, this piece did not draw a public response. Given the sad state of the Bryant-Milam family, it is likely that many readers, especially those from the African American community, felt that the racist killers and their families were receiving their just desserts. Many would argue that, after the unconscionable crime and the shamefaced acquittal, these men were lucky that God did not strike them down where they stood. As Huie saw it, "Milam and Bryant will not be tried again; but as landless white men in the Mississippi Delta, and bearing the mark of Cain, they will come to regard the dark morning of August 28, 1955, as the most unfortunate of their lives."[18]

Fate continued to punish these "sons of Cain." It is not clear, but it seems likely that the stress of the Till legacy affected both Bryant's and Milam's marriages. Both Carolyn Bryant and Juanita Milam, who had stood with them throughout the ordeal, eventually left their husbands. Abandoned, both men slipped into obscurity. However, in the early 1990s, Roy Bryant had one more encounter with Mamie Till-Mobley, an encounter that also played itself out in the media. During a radio interview that she had granted, the talk show host asked Till-Mobley whether she wanted to listen in while he called Roy Bryant. The host had done some research and found Bryant's home telephone number. After some hesitation, Till-Mobley agreed. As she recounted in her book, Bryant had the audacity to complain that "Emmett Till has ruined his life" and lament, "Emmett Till is dead. . . . I don't know why he can't just stay dead." Naturally, Till-Mobley was incensed, and she recalled: "It was all I could do to keep my breathing steady and not make a noise." However, always the picture of composure, she remained quiet. She allowed Roy Bryant to continue with his tirade, thus giving Americans another image of African American resolve in the face of senseless white racism. By the time of this encounter, Milam was already dead, having succumbed to cancer in 1981. Bryant outlived his brother by thirteen years, although he spent many of those years in near darkness because a welding accident left him legally blind. He died on September 1, 1994, thirty-nine years and one day after Till's lifeless body was pulled from the Tallahatchie River.[19]

When asked about her feelings toward her son's murderers, Till-Mobley told the independent researcher Devery Anderson: "Mercifully, the Lord just erased them out of my mind, out of my sight, with no conscious feelings towards them." Nevertheless, she did remain informed about their lives. She said of their fates: "They became friendless, family-less, home-less, jobless. I mean, they lost it all. And at least I have gained a world of friends. I have a home. I had a job. I had something to look forward to because I work with children constantly. Our lives just went in opposite directions. I became a benefactor to society, they became a scourge to society." Thus, Till-Mobley, laudably without malice, painted a realistic picture of the divergent paths of the principals in the Till case.[20]

Unlike Bryant and Milam, Mamie Till-Mobley became a national figure who continued to garner attention, largely in the print media. Dedicating a special series to her memories of the Till saga, in 1956 the *Chicago Defender* continued to update its readers on the Till case. As was the norm throughout its 1955 accounts, the paper framed Till-Mobley as a take-charge individual. Recounting the events of August and September 1955 in her own words, Till-Mobley recalled that, after hearing about her son's kidnapping, she had had her boyfriend, Gene Mobley, drive her to her mother's house, but not fast enough. Till-Mobley related to the *Defender*'s Ethyl Payne: "In my state of anxiety, I thought he was going too slow. At 63rd and Halsted, I asked him to pull over to the curb. I slid under the wheel and stepped on the accelerator as hard as I could. I guess I broke all speed records and went through every red light."[21]

Till-Mobley took charge, refusing to allow anything to stand in her way. She admitted to Clenora Hudson-Weems that her goal in going to her mother's house was to lay her sorrows on her mother, However: "As God would have it, when I walked in her door, I found out that she was in worse shape than I was." Confronted with her mother's grief, it was Till-Mobley who made the decision to contact the NAACP and to use the local press as the medium through which she memorialized her son. Expressly, she recalled: "On Monday I visited the N.A.A.C.P. office and called the *Chicago Tribune.*" As a result of these efforts, she was able to transfer the saliency of the lynching to the general public as "the story of Bo's disappearance began to break in the papers," and she retained "the NAACP . . . Atty. William Huff . . . considered an authority on . . . civil rights cases." While Till-Mobley retained Huff's services, it was actually her coordinated effort with Crosby Smith, a Mississippi relative, that led to the return of Till's remains to Chicago. Again, she told Ethyl Payne: "I learned from Uncle Crosby that they were trying to bury Bo in Mississippi and I told him to stop the burial at any cost and bring my baby—what was left of him—out of Mississippi." Answering the call, Smith assured her that "he would get the body which had not been embalmed and bring it to Chicago if he had to get a truck and fill it full of ice and drive it himself." As Till-Mobley explained, the entire family understood the saliency of the event, and all were dedicated to seeing justice in the case and ensuring that Emmett Till's final resting place would not lie within the borders of a racist state like Mississippi; however, it was her quick action and clear decision-making that led to her son's return.[22]

Immediately after the conversation with Crosby Smith, Till-Mobley decided to lie down and try to rest. This was a taxing time, and she was having difficulty coming to grips with the horrible tragedy. This religiously devout woman told the *Chicago Defender*'s Ethel Payne: "I was angry with God that He had let Bo be kidnapped and slain so brutally and aloud I demanded, 'Why did You do this[?] Why are You so cruel that You would let this happen? Why do You allow this kind of persecution?'" These concerns quickly subsided when a "presence" answered her thusly: "Mamie, it was ordained from the beginning of time that Emmett Louis Till would die a violent death." Therefore, "you should be grateful to be the mother of a boy who died blameless like Christ." Most importantly, the presence told her: "Have courage and faith that in the end there will be redemption for the suffering of your people and you are the instrument of this purpose. Work unceasingly to tell the story so that the truth will arouse men's conscience and right can at last prevail." Of course, this vision had a profound effect on Till-Mobley. It was the reason why she was able to ease her mind after the death of her son. As she recounted to Payne and, later, the radio talk-show legend and author Studs Terkel, she slept easily after this revelation because she had been told, "the Lord will fight your battles." She also told Payne that, on another occasion, the Lord told her, "Your heart will be encased in glass and no arrows can pierce it." With God's barrier protecting her, Till-Mobley answered the divine call to tell her story. Of course, one of the first venues in which she recounted her story was the trial of her son's killers. In an interview with the Emmett Till researcher Devery Anderson, she recalled: "I knew that for me to attend the trial did not mean that I was going to get back alive." Undeterred, she went anyway: "I made the decision that I had business in Mississippi, and my coming back dead or alive was of less importance than my being there on the scene alive as long as I could maintain life. . . . I had to go to Mississippi."[23]

As she told Payne, Till-Mobley astutely realized that it was key to spread the word because "the large class of decent people in this country are guilty of the sins of omission when they fail to speak out for the right and take a stand against injustice." She refused to be one of those people who chose not to speak out and, instead, boldly proclaimed: "That's why I am telling the story of my life and Bo's." She told Payne: "There is work for me to do [after Emmett's death] and I am thinking of the future. . . . At 33, I should have some useful years left and I think I would enjoy working with children." As presaged in her 1956 *Chicago Defender* interviews, she did, in fact, spend the coming decades caring for and educating children as well as continuing to speak out for civil rights.[24]

Till-Mobley always wanted to be a teacher, but the lack of African American instructors as role models made her feel that this goal was unobtainable. *Defender* readers learned that she confronted these doubts head-on when, in the fall of 1956, she enrolled in Chicago Teachers College. Three and one half years later, she graduated cum laude, fifth in her class.

In her interview with Studs Terkel, she reinforced: "The thing that has come out of Emmett's death, is to push education to the limit. I mean learn all that you can learn." She tackled her education with the same determination she brought to the honoring of her son's memory and the prosecution of his murderers.[25]

Armed with her teaching degree, Till-Mobley embarked on the task of educating tomorrow's leaders at Carter Elementary School in Chicago. In fact, even her work as a teacher displayed the grassroots community activism that was a hallmark of the modern civil rights movement. In her memoir, she admitted: "One of the most important lessons a black child can learn is how to work together with others as a community." That is, she saw the classroom as more than tests, homework, and grades; it was where students learned life skills: "This was about developing an approach to life. That was important to me. So many students I would meet over the years had never been given that kind of guidance. It was my duty to provide it, to show them that they should let nothing stand in the way of their success."[26]

Already a skilled teacher, in 1973 Till-Mobley earned a master's degree in administration and supervision from Loyola University. Coincidentally, that same year she organized a school assembly for Black History Month that led to the creation of the Emmett Till Players. Again, she detailed this event in her autobiography: "It was a huge undertaking and I wasn't sure at first what I would do." Of her dedication to her task, she wrote: "My mission was to teach, so anything I was involved in had to involve some kind of learning." Consequently, "in developing a concept for the school assembly, I was able to find that lesson. I found it through my own experience, all the parts of my life coming together. I conceived a program built around speeches by Dr. Martin Luther King, Jr., linked by a narrative that showed the kids the significance of it all." The idea came about through a great deal of hard work. In fact, Till-Mobley remembered the night the plan came together. She spent the evening at home listening to three records full of Dr. King's speeches. She told Devery Anderson: "I became so engrossed with what Dr. King was saying, until when I went to school the next morning, I had not been to bed. I had put those records on cassette tapes, and then I transcribed them on the typewriter. . . . I think I finished up about 5:30 that morning, and got myself ready for school." As she did with all her tasks, she threw her whole self into planning the assembly and sacrificed at least one night of sleep to ensure it was a success. That successful program evolved into the Emmett Till Players. At that time, Till-Mobley also established the Emmett Till Foundation. This nonprofit organization, designed to support the Emmett Till Players, had the purpose of "teaching boys and girls to become responsible American citizens and serious scholars as well as becoming well-versed in Christian living."[27]

Under the constant guidance and tutelage of Till-Mobley, who until her death was the president of the Emmett Till Foundation, the Emmett Till Players presented their work to countless thousands across the country. Till-Mobley wrote in her memoir: "I would work with students from my school and with members of my church. We would travel across the country over the coming years, performing before family members of Dr. Martin Luther King, Jr., in Atlanta, and even folks in Mississippi." However, the most memorable performance came in Denver in 1976 when the city unveiled a monument "dedicated in honor of Dr. King and Emmett." "So many family members and church members and, of course, Emmett Till Players went with us to share in this joyous event," Till-Mobley remembered. The monument pictured Dr. King looking forward with his hand on the shoulder of young Till. While the two never met, the fact that the artist chose to put these two figures together showed that he viewed Emmett Till as the inspiration behind the modern civil rights movement. (Since its dedication, the monument has been moved, and it now resides at its permanent home in front of the Dr. Martin Luther King Jr. Culture Center in Pueblo, Colorado.)[28]

The unveiling of the monument was a glorious day for the legacy of Emmett Till, and it no doubt drove Till-Mobley to continue her work. She recounted: "Following my retirement from teaching in 1983, I was able to step up my work with my church and with the Emmett Till Players." She continued to speak out against atrocities, and African Americans continued to relate racial killings to the death of her son. For example, as the *Chicago Defender* reported, the Reverend Jesse Jackson Sr. called on the memory of Till when he denounced the June 1998 lynching of James Byrd Jr. in Jasper, Texas, calling the event "the most heinous race crime since the Emmett Till lynching." The *Defender* also reported the facts of the matter: "[Byrd] was given a ride and then beaten, chained to the back of a pickup truck and dragged until his body was torn to pieces. . . . Byrd's head, arm and neck were severed and strewn along a two-mile stretch of country road. . . . They also found his dentures and almost 75 pieces of his flesh along the road." Like Till, James Byrd became a rallying cry for civil rights.[29]

By the turn of the twenty-first century, Till's legacy was completely secured. In 1992, Chicago mayor Richard M. Daley proclaimed July 25 Emmett Till Day. Not surprisingly, the *Chicago Defender* covered the event, pointing out: "The proclamation comes exactly one year after 71st Street between South Kedzie Avenue and Lake Michigan was renamed in the slain teen's honor." Of course, Mamie Till-Mobley was at the heart of both celebrations: "In honor of her only child, [Till-]Mobley will present five scholarships at an awards program Sunday at the Evangelistic Crusaders Church of God in Christ. . . . All of the recipients, members of the Emmett Till Players, . . . will be entering college in the fall." By all accounts, participation in the group and the tutelage of Till-Mobley helped drive these youths to get a college education. Again, the *Defender* noted: "One Emmett Till Player who was thought to be retarded until the eighth grade when he joined the organization learned a King speech and recited it tirelessly on any occasion. After learning that speech, he was no longer withdrawn and began to make the honor roll in school." Thus, Till-Mobley armed these students with the confidence they needed to succeed in life. As evidenced by the essays many group members wrote for a contest sponsored by Till-Mobley: "The players stated that they learned to be leaders instead of followers as a result of Mobley's guidance. Players also say that they now have patience and the incentive to learn." Doubtlessly, Till-Mobley's life's work positively affected countless people.[30]

While committed to education and civil rights, Till-Mobley also proclaimed continually the salience of her son's death. Despite the wealth of material already written about Emmett, she felt compelled to pen her own version of the story. As she said in her memoir: "I wanted to tell the story myself. I had come close. But only close. I had cooperated with scholar Clenora Hudson-Weems. . . . Still, I wanted to do my own book, my own story." To that end, she teamed with the Chicago-based lawyer and writer Christopher Benson, and *Death of Innocence* was published by Random House in 2003.[31]

Sadly, Mamie Till-Mobley did not live to see her book hit the shelves. On January 6, 2003, at the age of eighty-one, she died at Jackson Park Hospital. Of her memorial service, the *Chicago Sun-Times* wrote: "Attended by more than 500 people, the homegoing service celebrated the life of a woman who, ever since her son was killed at the hands of Mississippi racists in 1955, was a force in the civil rights movement." *Ebony* added: "Mamie Till Mobley . . . fueled outrage that was an emotional spark of the

Movement. Mobley, a woman of grace, dignity and courage, continued as a crusader for civil rights, keeping the tragedy of her son's murder on the public's consciousness until she died." Clearly, through their eulogies, the print media acknowledged Till-Mobley's key role in the civil rights movement, and, in remembrance of Emmett Till, they continued to update their readers on her remarkable life.[32]

After her death, the memorials continued. That year, Stanley Nelson's critically acclaimed documentary *The Murder of Emmett Till* aired on the Public Broadcasting Network. It won numerous awards, including the Sundance Film Festival Special Jury Award. It used striking images from Mississippi and video footage of the Till funeral as well as extensive interviews with Mamie Till-Mobley to provide one of the clearest stories of the Till lynching ever produced. The Reverend Wheeler Parker said of the film that it was the most accurate version of the facts behind the Till case. In it, Nelson laid out the events at the Bryants' store. In his estimation, Till's greatest offense, if any, was a whistle; however, as Till-Mobley maintained, Emmett was taught to whistle when he stuttered. Apparently, the whistling helped him gain his composure and speak clearly. Following this line of argument, Nelson offered that, on that fateful day in Money, Till was simply whistling to stop himself from stuttering. Nelson also reintroduced the possibility of more than two murderers.[33]

The question of the number of murderers, which was crucial to the lynching accusation, was a main subject of Keith Beauchamp's documentary *The Untold Story of Emmett Till.* Beauchamp, a first-time documentary producer, spent his own money and ten years researching and creating this groundbreaking film. His investigation of the Till case was spurred by 1955 newspaper accounts, as well as the *California Eagle* series from 1956, that talked about additional perpetrators in the Till lynching. Following these leads, Beauchamp used newspaper articles, FBI documents, and interviews with people like the Reverend Wheeler Parker to dig deeper into the Till case. He speculated that there were up to fourteen murderers, clearly making it a lynching. His documentary received critical acclaim from mainstream media film critics, and it led the Justice Department to reopen the Till murder case.

The 2005 exhumation and DNA analysis of Till's remains attempted to prove the identity of the body, check for bullet fragments, and see whether the murderers left any usable DNA evidence. As a result of these efforts, the body was proved to be that of Emmett Till, and possible bullet fragments were collected, but there was not enough evidence for the Leflore County grand jury to issue an indictment.[34]

Although the reinvestigation did not lead to any indictments or convictions, the FBI scrutiny did again raise the Till lynching to a state of national prominence, and a new generation was able to learn about the past and follow a new Till saga in the local and national press. As a direct result of this reexamination, the U.S. Senate drafted a resolution in which the country finally apologized for the "more than 4,700 people" who were lynched "from 1882 to 1968." Specifically, as the *Washington Post* reported, the Senate apologized for the historic lack of effort in passing antilynching legislation. Thus, this body was effectively apologizing for allowing southern racists like Theodore Bilbo, Strom Thurmond, John Stennis, James Eastland, James Davis, Fred Vinson, Orval Faubus, Herman Talmadge, and Olin Johnston to filibuster and otherwise thwart much-needed strong antilynching legislation that would facilitate the prosecution of the perpetrators of these hate crimes. Still, with America's storied history of vitriolic racism, thirteen senators went on record against this monumental resolution: Lamar Alexander (R-TN), Robert Bennett (R-UT), Michael Enzi (R-WY), Craig Thomas (R-WY), Judd Gregg (R-NH), John Sununu (R-NH), Richard Shelby (R-AL), Jon Kyl (R-AZ), Gordon Smith (R-OR), John Cornyn (R-TX), Kay Bailey Hutchinson (R-TX), Thad Cochran (R-MS), and Trent Lott (R-MS). These thirteen represented the sad fact that racism still permeates the highest echelons of government in the United States.[35]

In spite of these shortsighted individuals, the Senate also, according to the *New York Times*, "approved a measure that would create a Justice Department office to investigate and prosecute 'cold case' killings from the civil rights era." The report continued: "The bill was inspired by efforts to reopen the case of Emmett Till." Outside the nation's capital, people continued to memorialize the death of innocence. In 1984, the city of Chicago joined Mamie Till-Mobley and Rosa Parks in dedicating Emmett Till Road (see figure 7.1). Eleven years later, a Chicago bridge that crosses the Dan Ryan Expressway was renamed the Emmett Till Memorial Bridge. This bridge links to Emmett Till Road, thus, as the *Defender* noted, "complet[ing] an uninterrupted memorial to the young man who was killed." In a similar vein, there was in that same year an effort to have the church where Till's rites were held named a landmark. The *Chicago Defender* pointed out later that "Roberts Temple Church of God in Christ" should be "a chapter in American history." In the words of Jonathan Fine,

Figure 7.1. Dedication of Emmett Till Road (n.d.). *Daily Worker* and *Daily World* Photograph Collection, Tamiment Library and Robert F. Wagner Labor Archives, New York University.

president of Preservation Chicago: "This is part of the civil rights trail. . . . The civil rights trail begins in Chicago and it began in this church." In March 2006, the city agreed and named the iconic church a city landmark. Furthering the memorial efforts, in 2005 the park at 6404 South Ellis Avenue in Chicago was renamed Mamie Till-Mobley Park. Similarly, Chicago's McCosh Elementary School was renamed the Emmett Till Math and Science Academy in 2006. In the words of the *Chicago Defender:* "Current students at the school can tell you that Till attended McCosh before two Mississippi white men decided the 14-year-old should die for whistling at a white woman. His 1955 murder was among the most significant events that led to the modern day Civil Rights Movement."[36]

The state of Mississippi has in recent years attempted to heal some of the scars left by the lynching. On July 2, 2005, it renamed a portion of Highway 49 East the Emmett Till Memorial Highway. This section runs through or near towns that were key during the Till lynching saga. One of these towns, Glendora, whose mayor, Johnny B. Thomas, is the son of Henry Lee Loggins, one of the black sharecroppers suspected of witnessing the Till lynching, has established an Emmett Till Museum as part of an effort to restore the Tallahatchie County courthouse where Bryant and Milam escaped justice. The Emmett Till Memorial Commission of Tallahatchie County successfully lobbied to have the county issue a formal apology to the Till family. The apology reads: "We the citizens of Tallahatchie County recognize that the Emmett Till case was a terrible miscarriage of justice. We state candidly and with deep regret the failure to effectively pursue justice."[37]

So much of the ongoing memorialization of Emmett Till has played out through the press. It was the print media, spurred on by the efforts of Mamie Till-Mobley, that originally introduced the public to Till's death. It was the print media from across the country, and the black press in particular, that continued to underscore the salience of the lynching within the context of post–World War II global politics. In articles and editorials, print media outlets framed the lynching in ways that spoke to their regional dispositions toward post-*Brown* race relations. Through the ongoing dialogue around Till, observed through letters to the editor and internal editorial discourse about how to report on this tragic event, racial dispositions solidified and transformed for countless Americans. Emmett Till's death remains a lens through which we view the vulgar legacy of white supremacy in America. Even long after his death, media sources continued to update us on the actors in this saga, and the media continued to use Till as a barometer against which we can measure other racial atrocities, particularly those committed against young people. Since the 1955 lynching, this media coverage—which inspired a generation of civil rights activists—has shaped memories of and invoked responses to the too short life and violent death of a fourteen-year-old Chicago boy, Emmett Louis Till.

Acknowledgments

I am grateful that I was first introduced to the Emmett Till lynching, and the print media coverage of the event, in an undergraduate speech communications class taught by Deborah Atwater. I was intrigued by the case, and I always thought I wanted to know more about it. Little did I know that my undergraduate curiosity would lead to this book. This manuscript represents the culmination of years of preliminary research, outlining, drafting, revising, and refining efforts. Each keystroke was made possible by the support of family, friends, colleagues, mentors, foundations, librarians, and archivists who saw fit to lend their expertise to my endeavor. Every triumph in this text is due to the efforts of my support network, and every flaw is my own.

Much of the continued research for and the refining of this manuscript was funded by the generous support of the Christian R. and Mary F. Lindback Foundation's Minority Junior Faculty Grant, Cabrini College's Faculty Summer Grants, and the 1976 Foundation Faculty Fellows Grants. As part of this funding, I was able to employ undergraduate research assistants, and Ashley Marie Rivera offered so much to my conceptualizing of the print media's influence on this case. Ashley brought rays of sunshine and excitement to this research at times when I had doubts, and she helped me elucidate the critical roles that black journalists like James Hicks played in the trial coverage. Thank you, Sunshine. Thanks too to Allison Clark, who eagerly took on the unenviable role of the preliminary editing of this manuscript. Allison, yours was a tough job, but you leaped into the fray and forwarded the cause. I wish to thank the phenomenal staff at the University Press of Kentucky, namely, Anne Dean Dotson, Bailey Johnson, and Stephen Wrinn, and the peer reviewers who vetted my manuscript drafts.

Over the years, I have been blessed with a host of people who have supported this manuscript from the early stages of research through the finished work you read today. I must thank my mentors at Temple University—Susan Klepp, Kenneth Kusmer, James Hilty, Herbert Ershkowitz, Richard Immerman, Gregory Urwin, and Petra Goedde—for their instruction during the nascent stages of my research. Wilbert Jenkins, Bettye Collier-Thomas, Bryant Simon, Teshale Tibebu, and Nathaniel Norment guided the development of that research. Concurrently, Patricia Melzer and Joyce Joyce armed me with the tools necessary to deconstruct gender and sexuality. My time with them in the Women's Studies Graduate Certificate Program was invaluable and has made me a more well-rounded and conscious scholar. And thank you to my Temple crew—Darius Eschevaria, Anthony Q. Hazard, Craig Stutman, Jay Wyatt, Richard Grippaldi, Smadar Shtuhl, Dianna Reinhard, Dianna DiIllio, Uta Kresse-Raina, Ginger Davis, Bob Wintermute, Phil Gibbon, John Devoti, and Laura Szemanski-Steel—for support and commiseration.

I also need to acknowledge the fact that Joseph Fitzgerald's influence is all over this book and beyond. Joe, I have told you this many times before, but your friendship and our talks have kept me sane through this entire process. You continue to recharge my battery each time we talk. You have been a devoted confidant, dedicated colleague, and dear friend. Thank you for reading and commenting on drafts of this work, for coaxing me to strengthen my gender analysis, for the laughs you provide, and for always being willing to bring me back to reality when I get too far afield. Thank you for making me be a better, more conscious me.

Numerous archivists and librarians have offered so much of themselves toward the completion of the manuscript. I thank the wonderful people at Temple's Paley Library and especially Justin Hill, who worked tirelessly ordering microfilm for me through interlibrary loan. Thank you too to the staff at Temple's Charles L. Blockson Collection for sharing your rich archives.

Most recently, the staff at Cabrini College's Holy Spirit Library, namely, Lawral Wornek and Anne Schwelm, have supported the final stages of research necessary to bring this manuscript to print. They have gone above and beyond the call of duty. Their efforts uncovered skilled contacts at the archives holding the Abbott-Sengstacke Family Papers, the Dorothy Schiff Papers (Susan Malsbury), the C. A. McKnight Papers Special Collections (Marilyn Schuster), the Field Foundation Archives, the American Folklife Center's Civil Rights History Project (Jennifer Cutting and Kate Stewart), the Hodding II and Betty Werlein Carter Papers (Mattie Abraham), and the Walter Sillers Jr. Papers. I owe a tremendous amount of gratitude to all these archivists, as I do to Erika Gottfried and Kate Donovan at the Tamiment Library and Robert F. Wagner Labor Archives and Terrie Albano at the Communist Party USA.

Since coming to Cabrini College in 2005, I have met nothing but open arms and eager encouragement. Thank you to Antionette Iadarola, Jonnie Guerra, and Charlie McCormick for taking a chance and hiring me. Thank you to Jolyon Girard and Courtney Smith for embracing me. My eternal gratitude goes out to James Hedtke for welcoming me like a son. Jim, your friendship, guidance, and support have meant the world to me. To my current Cabrini colleagues and friends, I extend my appreciation. I hope this work helps forward our shared mission in pursuit of social justice and the common good.

Too few know how much caring and support Lisa Ratmansky and Dawn Oliver lend to scholarly efforts at Cabrini College. They have created a learning commons par excellence, and their labors in support of faculty scholarship are legendary. To my dear friend Nancy Watterson, I owe an eternal debt of gratitude. Before I even knew her, I watched how she shaped the fledgling master's thesis of my then girlfriend, Nikki Guy, into a solid contribution to the study of urban medical anthropology. Since joining the faculty at Cabrini College (talk about small worlds), Nicholas Rademacher and I have benefited greatly as together we encourage and shape young scholars in our Voices of Justice Living and Learning Community. And, at the end of a year of revisions (revisions in which Nancy played an indispensable role), I can only say that her comments on the drafts of my manuscript have made me a better writer, a better academic, and a better interdisciplinarian. I thank her for always asking the tough questions about my research and for asking them with kindness.

To my mother dearest, Jacqueline Mace, and my dear sister, Tracy Renee Mace, your insatiable thirst for knowledge is infectious, and I have tried as best I can to mirror your passions. This desire to learn has led me to this point, and you have been with me every step of the way. Thank you for inspiring me to dig deeper. James Guy, Nadine Taylor, Natalie Guy, Rodney Taylor, Lauryn Taylor, and Lexi Taylor, thank you for being supportive and for welcoming a poor starving Ph.D. student into your family. Mr. Guy, I wonder if you ever thought all your daughters and sons-in-law would hold either a master's or a doctoral degree. I bet you "the mother" did.

To the love of my life, Nikki Karyn Mace. Nikki, on countless evenings and weekends, you have sacrificed a husband, a companion, and a friend. You have supported my dreams. You have been the ever-present voice of reason and encouragement, but you have never stopped short of telling me when I was wrong. You have blessed me with your love and with the joy of our two sons, James Samuel Mace III and Christopher Moore Trotter Mace. You have read countless drafts, and I think you know as much about Emmett Till as I do.

To my Mom Mom, Elizabeth Beasley Trotter, I love history because my fondest memories of my childhood are of you telling me stories. When we were together—which was often since you lived down the street from me—you never failed to relate stories from Petersburg, or Bethlehem, or Philadelphia. Your stories helped frame my visions of the Great Migration, World War II, Jim Crow segregation, the civil rights movement, the black press, and the American South. You told those stories with such interest and such passion, and you always had a captive audience in me. I write this book about regional stories and racial dispositions because you first showed me the power of stories.

Finally, and most importantly, I want to acknowledge those who helped me and continue to help me through my journey but did not live to see its end. Rest assured, as I am certain, that the love you showed me continues to breathe life into every word of this manuscript. Pop Williams (Thomas Moore Williams Jr.), Grand Pop (James Samuel Mace Jr.), Grand Mom (Dorothy Lee Mace), Pop Pop (George L. Trotter), "The Mother" (Makeela Elease Guy), and My Hero and Father (Ronald James Mace), I love you all and miss you all dearly. This work is temporal, but your souls and spirits are eternal. May God in his eternal grace reunite us in heaven.

Notes

Preface

1. It was common during this period for northern African Americans to visit southern relatives over the summer. Black migrants maintained ties with family members who remained in the South even after the Great Black Migration. This was the case with Emmett Till's family, his mother having moved to Illinois with her parents when she was two years old. The 1995 trip was for Emmett Till his first to the South; however, he was familiar with some of his Mississippi relatives because they had visited Chicago.

2. While generally thought of as an act of mob violence ending in a black man hanging from a noose, lynching—as the act is understood by the Tuskegee Institute—covers any violent murder of an individual by three or more people acting under the guise of justice. See Christopher Waldrep, *African Americans Confront Lynching: Strategies of Resistance from the Civil War to the Civil Rights Era* (Lanham, MD: Rowman & Littlefield, 2009), 169.

3. The fact that Bryant and Milam chose to weigh Till's body down suggests that they had some concern for repercussions; however, the confidence they displayed in jail and during the trial suggests that they felt assured their peers would acquit them. This confidence made sense because few, if any, white men were ever convicted of killing a black man in Mississippi.

4. This was an obvious attempt to cover up the murder. Sheriff Strider had Bryant and Milam behind bars on kidnapping charges, but he would rather spill Till's body into an unmarked grave than charge the two men with murder. Interestingly, no one ever challenged his tampering with evidence and attempted concealment of a capital crime, likely because, like Strider, state and federal officials preferred that the crime not gain national exposure, the former fearing it would be fodder for integrationists, and the latter worrying that it would draw the ire of international community.

Introduction

1. From here on, when I use the phrase *Emmett Till incident, Emmett Till saga,* or *lynching of Emmett Till,* I am referring to the events occurring from August through December 1955.

2. Howard W. Odum and Harry Estill Moore, *American Regionalism: A Cultural-Historical Approach to National Integration* (New York: Holt, 1930), 39, 620.

3. Michael Bradshaw, *Regions and Regionalism in the United States* (London: Macmillan, 1988), 9, 106; John K. Roth, ed., *American Diversity, American Identity: The Lives and Works of 145 Writers Who Define the American Experience* (New York: Holt, 1995); Jack Temple Kirby, "Bioregionalism: Landscape and Culture in the South Atlantic," in *The New Regionalism,* ed. Charles Reagan Wilson (Jackson: University Press of Mississippi, 1998), 19–44.

4. *Textual analysis* is a communications term that connotes a qualitative rather than a quantitative analysis of a source. I will analyze how the inclusion/exclusion of information led to differing stories of the Emmett Till incident.

5. By *mainstream newspapers,* I mean those newspapers that would not be distinguished by racial or ethnic classifications. I use the term *mainstream* rather than *white* because, while these newspapers are largely owned and operated by white people, their readership includes people from a variety of racial and ethnic backgrounds. Black newspapers are owned and operated by black people and serve a largely black audience.

6. Roland Edgar Wolseley, *The Black Press, U.S.A.* (Ames: Iowa State University Press, 1990), xiv (quote), 24; and William G. Jordan, *Black Newspapers and America's War for Democracy, 1914–1920* (Chapel Hill: University of North Carolina Press, 2001), 1.

7. This process of claiming regional superiority is similar to efforts to assert racial/gender superiority, and it is an extension of Jean-Paul Sartre's idea of "othering." See Jean-Paul Sartre, *Existentialism and Human Emotions* (New York: Wisdom Library, 1957).

8. Stuart Hall, "Ideology and Communication Theory," in *Paradigm Issues,* vol. 1 of *Rethinking Communication,* ed. Brenda Dervin, Larry Grossberg, Barbara J. O'Keefe, and Ellen A. Wartella (Newbury Park: Sage, 1989), 40–52, 52 (first quote); Maxwell McCombs, "News Influence on Our Picture of the World," in *Media Effects: Advances in Theory and Research,* ed. Jennings Bryant and Dolf Zillmann (Hillsdale, NJ: Erlbaum, 1994), 1–16, 4 (second quote); Maxwell McCombs and Tamara Bell, "The Agenda-Setting Role of Mass Communication," in *An Integrated Approach to Communication Theory and Research,* ed. Michael Salwen and Donald Stack (Hillsdale, NJ: Erlbaum, 1996), 93–110, 106–7 (remaining quotes).

9. See Howard Smeed, *Blood Justice: The Lynching of Mack Charles Parker* (New York: Oxford University Press, 1996); Willie Morris, *The Ghosts of Medgar Evers: A Tale of Race, Murder, Mississippi, and Hollywood* (New York: Random House, 1998); and Civil Rights Historical Sites, "Reverend George Lee," 2005, *Bluejean's Place,* http://www.bluejeansplace.com/civil-rights-historical-sites/rev-george-lee.html.

10. Joseph Crespino, "Mississippi as Metaphor: Civil Rights, the South, and the Nation in the Historical Imagination," in *The Myth of Southern Exceptionalism,* ed. Matthew D. Lassiter and Joseph Crespino (Oxford: Oxford University Press, 2010), 99–120.

11. James W. Silver, *Mississippi: The Closed Society* (1964; reprint, New York: Harcourt, Brace & World, 1966), 6 (first quote); Crespino, "Mississippi as Metaphor" (2010), 100 (second quote); John Ray Skates, *Mississippi: A History* (New York: Norton, 1979), 13 (third quote); James C. Cobb, *The Most Southern Place on Earth: The Mississippi Delta and the Roots of Regional Identity* (New York: Oxford University Press, 1992), vii (fourth quote). See also Joseph Crespino, "Mississippi as Metaphor: State, Region, and Nation in the Historical Imagination" (paper presented at the conference "The End of Southern History," Emory University, Atlanta, March 23–24, 2006).

12. Crespino, "Mississippi as Metaphor" (2006).

13. See Crespino, "Mississippi as Metaphor" (2006), and "Mississippi as Metaphor" (2010).

14. See chapter 4, n. 1, below.

15. See chapter 7, n. 9, below.

1. Emmett Till's America

1. Studs Terkel, interview with Mamie Mobley, November 30, 1999, *The Studs Terkel Program,* WFMT-FM, http://www.studsterkel.org/results .php?keywords=mobley. See also Clenora Hudson-Weems, *Emmett Till: Sacrificial Lamb of the Civil Rights Movement* (Troy, MI: Bedford, 1994), 232.

2. Mamie Bradley, "Mamie Bradley's Untold Story, Installment VIII, As Told by Ethel Payne," *Chicago Defender,* June 9, 1956, 5.

3. Summit lies twelve miles southwest of the Chicago Loop—Chicago's business district. The locale has a long history of racial and ethnic diversity. In 1911, Summit expanded its boundaries by annexing an area that included the Corn Products Refining Co. corn-milling plant, which locals called Argo in honor of one of the company's best-known products. John D. Schroeder, "Summit, IL," 2005, *Encyclopedia of Chicago,* http://www.encyclopedia.chicagohistory.org.

4. Mamie Till-Mobley and Christopher Benson, *Death of Innocence: The Story of the Hate Crime That Changed America* (New York: Random House, 2003), 19.

5. "Twenty-Six Lynchings in 1923 as against 61 in 1922," *Broad Axe* (Chicago), December 29, 1923, 2.

6. Michael W. Fitzgerald, "'We Have Found a Moses': Theodore Bilbo, Black Nationalism, and the Greater Liberia Bill of 1939," *Journal of Southern History* 63 (1997): 293–320; Vincent Arthur Giroux Jr., "Theodore G. Bilbo: Progressive to Public Racist" (Ph.D. diss., Indiana University, 1984).

7. Michael J. Klarman, "The White Primary Rulings: A Case Study in the Consequences of Supreme Court Decision Making," *Florida State University Law Review* 29 (2001): 55–102; P. L. Harden, "Tennessee Attorney Attacks Bilbo on Negro Colonization in Liberia," *Kansas City (KS) Plain Dealer,* March 18, 1938.

8. Fitzgerald, "'We Have Found a Moses'"; Giroux, "Theodore Bilbo," 95–96; Klarman, "The White Primary Rulings," 93. On the press campaign against Bilbo, see issues of the *Kansas City (KS) Plain Dealer,* the *Arkansas State Press* (Little Rock), and the *Negro Star* (Wichita, KS) from December 1946.

9. Giroux, "Theodore Bilbo," 10–11; Gary W. Gallagher, introduction to *The Myth of the Lost Cause and Civil War History,* ed. Gary W. Gallagher and Alan T. Nolan (Urbana: Illinois University of Illinois Press, 2010), 1–10.

10. Michael Siegel, "Principal States of Origin of the Migrants, 1910–1930," 2005, *In Motion: The African American Migration Experience,* Schomburg Center for Research in Black Culture, New York Public Library, http://www.inmotionaame.org; Kenneth L. Kusmer, *A Ghetto Takes Shape: Black Cleveland, 1870–1930* (Urbana: University of Illinois Press, 1976), 157; Wisconsin Legislative Reference Bureau, *Wisconsin Blue Book, 2011–2012* (Madison, WI: Joint Committee on Legislative Organization, 2011), 789.

11. E. Marvin Goodwin, *Black Migration in America from 1915 to 1960: An Uneasy Exodus* (Lewiston, NY: Edwin Mellen, 1990), 12; Charles A. Simmons, *The African-American Press: A History of News Coverage during National Crises, with Special Reference to Four Newspapers, 1827–1965* (Jefferson, NC: McFarland, 1998), 29–41; Wolseley, *The Black Press,* 53–55. For detailed discussions of Chicago labor, housing, and political issues, see Rick Halpern, *Down on the Killing Floor: Black and White Workers in Chicago's Packing Houses, 1904–1954* (Urbana: University of Illinois Press, 1997); Arnold Hirsch, *Making the Second Ghetto: Race and Housing in Chicago, 1940–1960* (Chicago: University of Chicago Press, 1998); and Paul Kleppner, *Chicago Divided: The Making of a Black Mayor* (DeKalb: Northern Illinois University Press, 1985). For a discussion of Milwaukee, see Joe William Trotter, *Black Milwaukee: The Making of an Industrial Proletariat, 1915–1945* (Urbana: University of Illinois Press, 1985); and Thomas J. Sugrue, *The Origins of the Urban Crisis: Race and Inequality in Postwar Detroit* (Princeton, NJ: Princeton University Press, 1996).

12. Mamie Bradley, "Mamie Bradley's Untold Story, Installment I, As Told by Ethel Payne," *Chicago Defender,* April 21, 1956, 5; Terkel, interview with Mamie Mobley.

13. Till-Mobley and Benson, *Death of Innocence,* 19, 34.

14. "After-War Migration," *Savannah (GA) Tribune,* October 25, 1919, 4. For an analysis of Ford Motors's hiring policy, see August Meier and Elliott Rudwick, *Black Detroit and the Rise of the UAW* (New York: Oxford University Press, 1979), 5.

15. Robert A. Crump, "Negro Workers Lose $86,000 Daily in Ford Strike," *Kansas City (KS) Plain Dealer,* April 18, 1941, 2; Sugrue, *Origins of the Urban Crisis,* 101, 130, 132, 146–47. See also Meier and Rudwick, *Black Detroit,* 4–6.

16. For city-specific analyses of these conditions, see Trotter, *Black Milwaukee;* Kusmer, *A Ghetto Takes Shape;* Meier and Rudwick, *Black Detroit;* Sugrue, *Origins of the Urban Crisis;* Halpern, *Down on the Killing Floor;* Hirsch, *Making the Second Ghetto;* and *Race: The Power of an Illusion,* episode 3, *The House We Live In,* dir. Llewellyn M. Smith (San Francisco: California Newsreel, 2003), videocassette.

17. Roberta Senechal, *The Sociogenesis of a Race Riot: Springfield, Illinois in 1908* (Urbana: University of Illinois Press, 1990). On the Chicago race riots, see William Tuttle, *Race Riot: Chicago in the Red Summer of 1919* (New York: Atheneum, 1970). St. Louis had a race riot in 1917, and Detroit endured riots in both 1943 and 1967. Also notable were the 1917 St. Louis race riot and the 1943 and 1967 Detroit race riots. On these, see Malcolm McLaughlin, *Power, Community, and Racial Killing in East St. Louis* (New York: Palgrave Macmillan, 2005); and Sugrue, *Origins of the Urban Crisis,* 79, 191.

18. On miscegenation, see Alex Lubin, *Romance and Rights: The Politics of Interracial Intimacy, 1945–1954* (Jackson: University Press of Mississippi, 2005); Elsie Virginia Lemire, *"Miscegenation": Making Race in America* (Philadelphia: University of Pennsylvania Press, 2002); and Charles F. Robinson, *Dangerous Liaisons: Sex and Love in the Segregated South* (Fayetteville: University of Arkansas Press, 2003). For the argument that white men historically viewed black men as the embodiment of the bestial, the violent, the penis-as-weapon, and the hypermasculine and that white-controlled advertising served only to perpetuate this stereotype, see bell hooks, *Black Looks: Race and Representation* (Boston: South End, 1992), and *We Real Cool: Black Men and Masculinity* (New York: Routledge, 2004). For the resurgence of such views in the late nineteenth century and the early twentieth, see Thomas Dixon, *Clansman: An Historical Romance of the Ku Klux Klan* (1905; reprint, Lexington: University Press of Kentucky, 1970); *The Birth of a Nation* (1915), dir. D. W. Griffith (Image Entertainment, 1998), DVD; William Archibald Dunning, *Essays on the Civil War and Reconstruction and Related Topics* (New York: Macmillan, 1898); and Ulrich B. Phillips, *American Negro Slavery: A Survey of the Supply, Employment, and Control of Negro Labor as Determined by the Plantation Regime* (1918; reprint, Baton Rouge: Louisiana State University Press, 1960).

19. See Smeed, *Blood Justice;* Morris, *The Ghosts of Medgar Evers;* and "Reverend George Lee."

20. Pete Daniel, *Lost Revolutions: The South in the 1950s* (Chapel Hill: University of North Carolina Press, 2000), 1–2, 27; James C. Cobb, *Away Down South: A History of Southern Identity* (New York: Oxford University Press, 2005), 4–8 (quote 5).

21. Paul Hendrickson, *Sons of Mississippi: A Story of Race and Its Legacy* (New York: Knopf, 2003), 162; Grace Elizabeth Hale, *Making Whiteness: The Culture of Segregation in the South, 1890–1940* (1998; reprint, New York: Vintage, 1999), 232–33.

22. Dewey Grantham, "Conceptualizing the History of Modern Southern Politics," *History Teacher* 17, no. 1 (1983): 9–31, 9–10 (first quote); Lewis M. Killian, "Consensus in the Changing South," *Phylon* 18, no. 2 (1957): 107–17, 115 (second quote).

23. Odum and Moore, *American Regionalism,* 39 (first two quotes); Bradshaw, *Regions and Regionalism in the United States,* 8 (third quote). The American South is obviously the most ready manifestation of regionalism. However, as Bradshaw argues: "'Regionalism' involves the belief that a regional solution may be found for a social, economic or political problem, and often results from a community of interest or embattled position in time of economic hardship or political stress." Similarly, Jack Kirby argues: "Postwar 'revolutions' in human rights and on the landscape, in fact, encouraged a vigorous new regionalism that bears striking resemblance to the old—especially in the morphology of right-left factions." Kirby, "Bioregionalism," 19. See also Odum and Moore, *American Regionalism,* 8, 9; and James R. Shortbridge, "Persistence of Regional Labels in the United States," in Wilson, *The New Regionalism,* 45–70, 47.

24. On the similarity of asserting racial/gender superiority to Sartre's idea of othering, see n. 7, introduction, above.

2. August Nights

1. Mary L. Dudziak, *Cold War Civil Rights: Race and the Image of American Democracy* (2000; reprint, Princeton, NJ: Princeton University Press, 2002), 6.

2. Ibid., 96, 15; Silver, *Mississippi;* Matthew D. Lassiter and Joseph Crespino, "Introduction: The End of Southern History," in Lassiter and Crespino, *The Myth of Southern Exceptionalism,* 3–23, 15; Crespino, "Mississippi as Metaphor" (2010), 101.

3. Frank Newport, David W. Moore, and Lydia Saad, "The Most Important Events of the Century from the Viewpoint of the People," December 6, 1999, Gallup News Service, http://www.gallup.com; "Timeline of Polling History: Events That Shaped the United States, and the World," n.d., Gallup News Service, http://www.gallup.com.

4. "The Shape of Things," *The Nation,* September 17, 1955, 234–35; Roy Wilkins to Department of Justice, September 7, 1955, microfilm reel 13, *Papers of the NAACP: Part 18: Special Subjects, 1940–1955: Series C: General Office Files* (Bethesda, MD: University Publications of America, 1995).

5. "A Boy Goes Home," *Newsweek,* September 12, 1955, 32; "Chicago Boy, 14, Kidnaped by Miss. Whites," *Jet,* September 8, 1955, 4; Joseph Mosnier, inter-

view with Simeon Booker and Moses J. Newson, July 13, 2011, Civil Rights History Project Collection, Archive of Folk Culture, American Folklife Center, Library of Congress, Washington, DC.

6. Mosnier, interview with Booker and Newson.

7. "Find Kidnaped Chicago Boy's Body in River," *Chicago Tribune,* September 1, 1955, sec. 1, p. 1; "Chicago Boy Found Slain in Dixie," *Chicago Sun-Times,* September 1, 1955, sec. 1, pp. 1, 4; "Two Governors Demand Inquiry in Race Killing," *St. Louis Post-Dispatch,* September 2, 1955, A12; Mosnier, interview with Booker and Newson.

8. "South Pushes Murder Trial," *Philadelphia Evening Bulletin,* September 1, 1955, sec. 1, p. 44 (quote). Examples of similar coverage include "Two Indicted in the South for Boy's Death," *Pittsburgh Post-Gazette,* September 7, 1955, A1; "Mississippi Nabs 2 in Death of Boy," *Philadelphia Inquirer,* September 1, 1955; "Protest Killing of Negro Boy," *Milwaukee Journal,* September 1, 1955, sec. 1, p. 9; and "Chicago Boy Found Slain in Dixie." For more information, see Dudziak, *Cold War Civil Rights,* 67.

9. "Nation Horrified by Murder of Kidnaped Chicago Youth," *Jet,* September 8, 1955, 6; Roy Wilkins to Hugh White, memorandum, August 31 1955, microfilm reel 14, *Papers of the NAACP: Part 18 . . . Series C: General Office Files.*

10. "Ask Ike to Act in Dixie Death of Chicago Boy," *Chicago Tribune,* September 2, 1955, sec. 1, p. 2.

11. "Ask Mississippi Governor to Denounce Killing of Boy," *Chicago Tribune,* September 1, 1955, sec. 1, p. 2; "Protest Killing of Negro Boy." William Henry Huff was a prominent African American intellectual. He was born and raised in Georgia and boasted degrees in the fields of pharmacology and law. He was accepted into both the Illinois and the Indiana Bars. He also published several collections of poetry. See M. Marie Booth Foster, *Southern Black Creative Writers, 1829–1953* (Westport, CT: Greenwood, 1988), 39.

12. "Protest Killing of Negro Boy"; "Chicago Boy Found Slain in Dixie" (quote).

13. Will Muller, "New 'Klan in Tuxedos' Fights Desegregation," *Detroit News,* September 1, 1955, A49.

14. Ibid.

15. "'Murder,' White Says; Promises Prosecution," *Chicago Defender,* September 10, 1955, National, A1 (first quote); "Blood on Their Hands," *Chicago Defender,* September 10, 1955, National, A1 (subsequent quotes). In this battle between states' rights and national intervention, each side accused the other of being "rabble-rousers." This showed the disdain each side felt for its opponent.

16. *Congressional Record,* 75th Cong., 3rd sess. (1938), 83:873; Robert L. Fleegler, "Theodore Bilbo and the Decline of Public Racism, 1938–1947," *Journal of Mississippi History* 68, no. 1 (Spring 2006): 1–27, 9.

17. Bilbo quoted in "Prince of the Peckerwoods," *Time,* July 1, 1946, 23. See also Fleegler, "Theodore Bilbo and the Decline of Public Racism," 1.

18. Mattie Smith Colin, "Mother's Tears Greet Son Who Died a Martyr," *Chicago Defender,* September 10, 1955, National, A1–A2; "No. Three in Reign of Terror," *Cleveland Call and Post,* September 10, 1955, A1; Abel Meeropol, "Bitter Fruit," *New York Teacher,* January 1937. See also Harold Heft, "'Strange' Evolution of Legendary Song: Jewish Composer Penned Tune Made Famous by Billie Holiday," *Jewish Daily Forward,* March 30, 2012, online.

19. "Negro Youth's Killing Probed," *Pittsburgh Post-Gazette,* September 2, 1955, A1–A2; "Abducted Boy Found Slain," *Evening Bulletin,* August 31, 1955, sec. 1, p. 1; "2 Held for Trial in Slaying of Boy," *New York Times,* September 7, 1955, A19; Joseph R. Daughen, "A Personal Odyssey," in *Nearly Everybody Read It,* ed. Peter Binze (Philadelphia: Camino, 1998), 111–26, 111.

20. McCombs and Bell, "The Agenda-Setting Role of Mass Communication"; "Mississippi Nabs 2 in Death of Boy"; "South Pushes Murder Trial"; "Two Indicted in the South for Boy's Death."

21. "Housing Target of Urban League," *New York Times,* September 6, 1955, A39, A52. (It should be noted that the *Times* did not note Dunaway's race in its article.) The National Urban League was founded in 1910 and focused its attention on securing the prosperity of African Americans who moved to northern cities from the South. The league got its start with the 1910 meeting of the Committee on Urban Conditions among Negroes. For detailed information, see Jesse Thomas Moore Jr., *A Search for Equality: The National Urban League, 1910–1961* (University Park: Pennsylvania State University Press, 1981).

22. John Popham to Turner Catledge, October 29, 1955, and Turner Catledge to John Popham, November 2, 1955, quoted in Gene Roberts and Hank Klibanoff, *The Race Beat: The Press, the Civil Rights Struggle, and the Awakening of a Nation* (New York: Knopf, 2006), 106, 107 (see also 108).

23. "Negro Boy," *New York Post,* September 1, 1955.

24. "Lynching Resumed," *Philadelphia Tribune,* September 3, 1955, A4; "Murder in Mississippi," *New York Amsterdam News,* September 10, 1955, A14; Theodore Coleman, "Latest Atrocity in Mississippi Arouses Nation," *Pittsburgh Courier,* September 10, 1955, A1, A4; Nina Simone, vocal performance of "Mississippi Goddam" on *Nina Simone in Concert,* Philips Records, 1964, ISRC GBAWA0652908; Stanley Nelson, dir., *The Black Press: Soldiers without Swords* (San Francisco: California Newsreel, 2000), DVD. For an extensive look at George Schuyler, see esp., among his many works, George S. Schuyler, *Black No More: Being an Account of the Strange and Wonderful Workings of Science in the Land of the Free, A.D. 1933–1940* (College Park, MD: McGrath, 1969). See also Michael W. Peplow, *George S. Schuyler* (Boston: Twayne, 1980).

25. Roberts and Klibanoff, *The Race Beat,* 12–13.

26. "The Seeds of Terror Are Planted," *Charlotte (NC) Observer,* September 8,

1955, B2. See also Harry Ashmore, *Hearts and Minds: A Personal Chronicle of Race in America* (Cabin John, MD: Seven Locks, 1988), 218–19.

27. "Kidnaped Boy," *Richmond (VA) Times-Dispatch,* September 1, 1955, A12; "Negro 14, Called Insulter," *Atlanta Constitution,* September 1, 1955, A1; "Kidnaped Negro," *Charlotte (NC) Observer,* September 1, 1955.

28. "Mississippi Will Probe Boy's Slaying," *Richmond (VA) Times-Dispatch,* September 2, 1955, A10; "Virginius Dabney, Pulitzer Winner, Dies as Historian, Author, Richmond Editor, He Challenged Views on Race and History," *Virginian-Pilot* (Norfolk, VA), December 29, 1995, A9; Ashmore, *Hearts and Minds,* 218–19; Edward Wyatt, "D. Tennant Bryan, 92, Chief of Newspaper and TV Empire," *New York Times,* December 12, 1998, online.

29. "Boy's Slaying Brings Wrath of Governor," *Charlotte (NC) Observer,* September 2, 1955, A2; James L. Knight to C. A. McKnight, February 13, 1958, folders 17–19, box 1, C. A. McKnight Papers, Special Collections, J. Murrey Atkins Library, University of North Carolina at Charlotte.

30. "Gov. White Orders Trial in Boy's Kidnap-Slaying," *Atlanta Constitution,* September 2, 1955, A2. See also Roberts and Klibanoff, *The Race Beat,* 91.

31. "Sheriff Says Body Found May Not Be Chicago Boy," *Richmond (VA) Times-Dispatch,* September 4, 1955, A7; "Doubts Body That of Till," *Charlotte (NC) Observer,* September 4, 1955, A16; "Thousands Pass Bier of Slain Negro Boy," *Washington Post,* September 4, 1955, A3.

32. "Fourth Race Victim in Mississippi; State Attempting to Shift Blame; Hundreds View Boy's Remains," *Norfolk (VA) Journal and Guide,* September 10, 1955, sec. 1, pp. 1–2.

33. "Two Held in Connection with Chicago Lad's Death," *Atlanta Daily World,* September 1, 1955, A1; "The Mississippi Lynch-Murder," *Atlanta Daily World,* September 2, 1955, A4.

34. William Gordon, "The Sins of Mississippi," *Atlanta Daily World,* September 4, 1955, A4.

35. Ibid. See also Maria E. Odum-Hinmon, "The Cautious Crusader: How the *Atlanta Daily World* Covered the Struggle for African American Rights from 1945 to 1985" (Ph.D. diss., University of Maryland, 2005), 88–91 (interview with C. A. Scott), 150–64.

36. "Mississippi's Governor Orders Probe of Killing," *Daily Oklahoman* (Oklahoma City), September 2, 1955, A18; "Abducted Boy Found Dead; Two Men Held," *Seattle Times,* August 31, 1955, Night Sports final, sec. 3, p. 48.

37. "Governor Orders Probe of Negro's Slaying," *Seattle Times,* September 1, 1955, Night Sports final, sec. 1, p. 16; "Governor Acts in Slaying of Boy, 15," *Los Angeles Times,* September 2, 1955, sec. 1, p. 14. See also "Overview of the Seattle Times," n.d., *Seattle Times,* http://www.seattletimescompany.com/communication/overview.htm; and *Inventing LA: The Chandlers and Their Times,* dir. Peter Jones (Peter Jones Productions, 2009), DVD.

38. "Painful Progress," *Denver Post,* September 6, 1955, A16; "Governor Orders Probe of Negro's Slaying."

39. "Painful Progress" (first two quotes); "Negro Youth, 14, Slain; Two White Men Jailed," *Denver Post,* September 1, 1955, A8 (third quote); "Governor Orders Probe of Negro's Slaying."

40. "An Investigation, Then What?" *Los Angeles Sentinel,* September 8, 1955, A9. This editorial likely came from the *Sentinel* founder, owner, and editor, Leon H. Washington Jr. Hugh Lawson White was the wealthiest man to hold the office of governor in Mississippi's modern history. For more information, see Richard A. McLemore, *A History of Mississippi,* 2 vols. (Jackson: University Press of Mississippi, 1973–81), 2:110–19, 145–57.

41. "An Investigation, Then What?"

42. "Law Moves Ahead," *Memphis Commercial Appeal,* September 7, 1955, sec. 1, p. 6; "A Brutal Slaying," *Delta Democrat-Times* (Greenville, MS), September 2, 1955, Red Streak final, A4; "Newspapers over State Blast Murder of Negro," *Jackson (MS) Daily News,* September 3, 1955, Home final, sec. 1, p. 1.

43. William Sorrels, "Murder Indictment to Be Asked of Slain Negro Boy," *Memphis Commercial Appeal,* September 2, 1955, final, A1 (first three quotes); William Street, "Murder Trial Publicity Irks Placid Town," *Memphis Commercial Appeal,* September 18, 1955, final, sec. 5, p. 10 (last two quotes); "More Fitting Commentary," *Delta Democrat-Times,* September 12, 1955, Red Streak final, A:4.

44. "T. M. Hederman, 73; A Longtime Editor in Southern Capital." *New York Times,* January 8, 1985, B6; "*Jackson News* Is Sold: Passes to *Clarion-Ledger* After Long Control Battle," *New York Times,* August 8, 1954, 84; Walter Sillers Jr. to Major Frederick Sullens, May 25, 1945, folder 12, box 6, Walter Sillers Jr. Papers, Delta State University Archives and Museum, Delta State University, West Cleveland, MS, http://collections.msdiglib.org; Cobb, *The Most Southern Place on Earth,* 212.

45. Phil Stroupe, "Delta Residents Expected Indictments and Want Justice Done in Till Case but Outside Interference Resented," *Jackson (MS) Daily News,* September 7, 1955, Home final, sec. 2, p. 3; "Claims Mississippi Has Executed White for Negro Murder," *Delta Democrat-Times* (Greenville, MS), September 23, 1955, Red Streak final, A1.

46. "Impose Equal Justice," *Jackson (MS) Daily News,* September 19, 1955, Home final, sec. 1, p. 10.

47. "National Indignation Seen as Nationwide Editorial Comment Condemns Slaying of 14-Year-Old Negro Boy in Wolf-Whistle Incident at Money, Mississippi," *Jackson (MS) Advocate,* September 10, 1955, A1–A2; "Battered Body of Boy, 14, Found in River in Miss.," *Birmingham World,* September 2, 1955, sec. 1, pp. 1, 8; "Battered Body of Boy, 14, Found in River in Miss.," *Memphis World,* February 2, 1955, sec. 1, pp. 1, 8.

48. "The Mississippi Lynch-Murder," *Memphis World,* September 2, 1955, sec. 1, p. 8; "The Mississippi Lynch-Murder," *Birmingham World,* September 9, 1955, sec. 1, p. 6; "It Now Becomes All Our Business," *Memphis World,* September 2, 1955, sec. 1, p. 8.

3. Home Going

1. Stephen F. Lawson, "Long Origins of the Short Civil Rights Movement, 1954–1968," in *Freedom Rights: New Perspectives on the Civil Rights Movement,* ed. Danielle L. McGuire and John Dittmer (Lexington: University Press of Kentucky, 2011), 16. For more on Scottsboro, see Dan T. Carter, *Scottsboro: A Tragedy of the American South* (1969; reprint, Baton Rouge: Louisiana State University Press, 1979); and James E. Goodman, *Stories of Scottsboro* (New York: Pantheon, 1994).

2. Lawson, "Long Origins of the Short Civil Rights Movement," 17.

3. "A Boy Goes Home"; "The Shape of Things"; "Nation Horrified by Murder of Kidnaped Chicago Youth."

4. "The Shape of Things"; "A Boy Goes Home."

5. "Mayor Daley Protests Slaying of Chicagoan," *Chicago Sun-Times,* September 2, 1955, sec. 1, p. 3 (first quote); "Slain-Boy's Body Arrives Here; Sets Off Emotional Scene at Depot," *Chicago Sun-Times,* September 3, 1955, sec. 1, p. 4 (subsequent quotes); "Biographical Note," n.d., "A Guide to the Field Foundation Archives, Pt. 1," Field Foundation Archives, Briscoe Center for American History, University of Texas at Austin, http://www.lib.utexas.edu/taro/utcah/00091/00091-P.html.

6. "Kidnaped Boy Whistled at Woman: Friend," *Chicago Tribune,* August 30, 1955, sec. 1, p. 2; "Kin Tell How Murdered Boy Was Abducted," *Chicago Tribune,* September 3, 1955, sec. 1, p. 11.

7. "Slain-Boy's Body Arrives Here."

8. Ibid.; David Jackson, "Image of Emmett Till," *Jet,* September 17, 1955, 8–9.

9. "Slain-Boy's Body Arrives Here."

10. "Kin Tell How Murdered Boy Was Abducted"; "2,500 at Rites Here for Boy, 14, Slain in South," *Chicago Tribune,* September 4, 1955, sec. 1, p. 2; Clay Gowran, "Urban League Asks Action in Till Case," *Chicago Tribune,* September 6, 1955, sec. 1, p. 8.

11. "Statement of National Committee Communist Party on the Murder of Emmett Louis Till," September 9, 1955, microfilm reel 14, *Papers of the NAACP: Part 18 . . . Series C: General Office Files.*

12. "Kin Tell How Murdered Boy Was Abducted"; "Urge Tolerance at Till Boy's Rites," *Chicago Sun-Times,* September 4, 1955, sec. 1, pp. 1, 3.

13. "Urge Tolerance at Till Boy's Rites."

14. "Thousands Crowd into Church to See Body of Slain Boy," *Milwaukee Journal,* September 3, 1955, sec. 1, p. 2; "Urge Tolerance at Till Boy's Rites."

15. Bettye Collier-Thomas, *Jesus, Jobs, and Justice: African American Women and Religion* (New York: Random House, 2010), Kindle ed., KL 3465; James Fowler, *Stages of Faith: The Psychology of Human Development and the Quest for Meaning* (New York: HarperCollins, 1981), 17.

16. "Kin Tell How Murdered Boy Was Abducted."

17. Ibid.

18. "Southern Jury Indicts Two in Till Slaying," *Chicago Tribune,* September 7, 1955, sec. 1, p. 5; "Urge Tolerance at Till Boy's Rites"; "Will Mississippi Whitewash the Emmett Till Slaying?" *Jet,* September 22, 1955, 12.

19. Marty Richardson, "Mother of Lynched Boy Here to Open 1955 NAACP Drive," *Cleveland Call and Post,* September 17, 1955, A1–A2. For more information, see Clayborne Carson, David J. Garrow, Bill Kovach, and Carol Polsgrove, eds., *Reporting Civil Rights: American Journalism, 1941–1963* (New York: Library of America, 2003), 930, 942–43; Silver, *Mississippi;* Cobb, *The Most Southern Place on Earth;* Goodwin, *Black Migration in America;* and Isabel Wilkerson, *The Warmth of Other Suns: The Epic Story of America's Great Migration* (New York: Random House, 2010).

20. Moses J. Newson, "Minister Says He'll Leave Dixie," *Chicago Defender,* September 17, 1955, National, A1, A3; Robert Elliott, "Thousands at Rites for Till," *Chicago Defender,* September 10, 1955, National, A1.

21. Ethel Payne, "Says U.S. Can't Enter Till Murder Case," *Chicago Defender,* September 17, 1955, National, A1; "Mississippi Infamy," *Chicago Defender,* September 17, 1955, National, B9.

22. "Mississippi Terrorism," *Cleveland Call and Post,* September 17, 1955, D2. This piece used the word *supermen* rather than *superhuman.* The fact that the author chose to gender the statement showed the belief that men needed to take charge of the fight for civil rights.

23. "Thousands File Past Casket of Negro Boy Killed in South," *San Francisco Examiner,* September 4, 1955, sec. 1, p. 7; "Thousands at Rites for Slain Youth," *Los Angeles Times,* September 4, 1955, sec. 1, p. 4.

24. Buffalo Field Agent to J. Edgar Hoover, memorandum, January 11, 1956, F. J. Baumgardner to A. E. Belmont, memorandum, February 8, 1955, and Baltimore Field Agent to J. Edgar Hoover, memorandum, September 26, 1955, microfilm reel 2, *FBI File on the NAACP* (Wilmington, DE: Scholarly Resources, 1990).

25. Alvin Spivak, "Nixon Target for Stand on Soviet," *San Francisco Examiner,* September 11, 1955, sec. 3, p. 1.

26. "Mother to Attend Hearing," *Los Angeles Sentinel,* September 15, 1955, A1, A8.

27. Coleman, "Latest Atrocity in Mississippi"; "Sheriff Ready to Bury Victim

in Hole Dug in Graveyard of Church of Christ," *Philadelphia Tribune,* September 10, 1955, sec. 1, pp. 1–2.

28. "Bad News for NAACP," *Jackson (MS) Daily News,* September 8, 1955, Home final, sec. 1, p. 8.

29. "'Never into Any Meanness' in Their Lives, She Says," *Jackson (MS) Daily News,* September 2, 1955, Home final, sec. 1, p. 14; "'Were Never into Meanness' Says Accused Men's Mother," *Memphis Commercial Appeal,* September 2, 1955, final, A35; "Bryant's Brother Claims Charges Are All 'Politics,'" *Memphis Commercial Appeal,* September 3, 1955, final, A19.

30. "Search Halted for Woman in Negro Slaying," *Birmingham News,* September 3, 1955, A10; "Officer Fears Actions Build Up Resentment," *Jackson (MS) Daily News,* September 4, 1955, Home final, sec. 1, p. 1.

31. "Search Halted for Woman in Negro Slaying"; "Newspapers over State Blast Murder of Negro."

32. Sarah Hart Brown, "Redressing Southern 'Subversion': The Case of Senator Eastland and the Louisiana Lawyer," *Louisiana History* 43, no. 3 (2002): 295–314, 310–11.

33. Mrs. Charles Stewart, "Compares Till Case to Murder of White Woman," *Delta Democrat-Times* (Greenville, MS), September 15, 1955, Red Streak final, A7; "Lynching Post-Facto," *Delta Democrat-Times* (Greenville, MS), September 6, 1955, Red Streak final, A4.

34. "Splitting Hairs over 'Lynching,'" *Tri-State Defender* (Memphis), September 10, 1955, A2.

35. William Gordon, "The Way Europeans Look at Us," *Memphis World,* September 13, 1955, sec. 1, p. 8.

36. Roi Ottley, "Way of White Folks," *Tri-State Defender* (Memphis), September 17, 1955, sec. 1, p. 4.

37. "Mississippi Infamy," *Tri-State Defender* (Memphis), September 17, 1955, sec. 1, p. 7.

4. "M Is for Mississippi and Murder"

1. National Association for the Advancement of Colored People, "M Is for Mississippi and Murder," November 1955, microfilm reel 14, *Papers of the NAACP: Part 18 . . . Series C: General Office Files.*

2. Carson, Garrow, Kovach, and Polsgrove, eds., *Reporting Civil Rights,* 948–49.

3. "Mississippi: The Place, the Acquittal," *Newsweek,* October 3, 1955, 24; "*Daily Worker*'s Reporter at Trial in Mississippi," *Jackson (MS) Daily News,* September 20, 1955, sec. 1, p. 6; Abner W. Berry, "The Macbeths of Mississippi," *Daily Worker,* October 11, 1955, A3. See also James McBride Dabbs, *Who Speaks for the South?* (New York: Funk & Wagnalls, 1964), 3–8; and Silver, *Mississippi.*

4. "Henry Robinson Luce," 2012, *Columbia Electronic Encyclopedia*, http://www.infoplease.com/ce6/people/A0830534.html; "The Law," *Time*, October 3, 1955, 18; Cobb, *The Most Southern Place on Earth.*

5. Russell Harris, "Murder Town's Tension Hidden by Sleepy Look," *Detroit News*, September 18, 1955, A1, A6; Paul Holmes, "A Way of Life on Trial in Till Case," *Chicago Tribune*, September 18, 1955, sec. 1, pp. 1, 6.

6. Holmes, "A Way of Life on Trial"; Harris, "Murder Town's Tension"; "'Wolf Whistle' Murder Trial Opens in South," *St. Louis Post-Dispatch*, September 19, 1955, A17.

7. Harris, "Murder Town's Tension."

8. Ibid.

9. See David Donald, "The Proslavery Argument Reconsidered," *Journal of Southern History* 37 (1971): 3–18; Drew Gilpin Faust, *The Ideology of Slavery* (Baton Rouge: Louisiana State University Press, 1981); James C. Cobb, *Redefining Southern Culture: Mind and Identity in the Modern South* (Athens: University of Georgia Press, 1999); Daniel, *Lost Revolutions;* Ted Ownby, ed., *The Role of Ideas in the Civil Rights South* (Jackson: University Press of Mississippi, 2002); Hale, *Making Whiteness;* Jane Dailey, Glenda Elizabeth Gilmore, and Bryant Simon, eds., *Jumpin' Jim Crow: Southern Politics from Civil War to Civil Rights* (Princeton, NJ: Princeton University Press, 2000); and Charles M. Payne and Adam Green, eds., *Time Longer Than Rope: A Century of African American Activism, 1850–1950* (New York: New York University Press, 2003).

10. Tom Yarbrough, "Odds 10 to 1 for Acquittal; 'Intrusion' Resented in Mississippi Murder Trial," *St. Louis Post-Dispatch*, September 22, 1955, A2.

11. Russell Harris, "Mississippi Opens Wolf-Whistle Trial," *Detroit News*, September 19, 1955, A1, A4; Holmes, "A Way of Life on Trial."

12. Holmes, "A Way of Life on Trial"; Harris, "Murder Town's Tension."

13. "Slain Boy's Mother to Testify at Trial," *Chicago Sun-Times*, September 9, 1955, sec. 1, p. 26 (first three quotes); "Ex-FBI Agent to Aid Till Prosecution," *Chicago Sun-Times*, September 11, 1955, sec. 1, p. 5 (fourth quote); "2 Face Trial Sept. 19 in Dixie Slaying," *Detroit News*, September 10, 1955, A2; "Till's Mom to Take Stand, Attorney Says," *Chicago Tribune*, September 11, 1955, sec. 1, p. 10.

14. Harris, "Murder Town's Tension"; Holmes, "A Way of Life on Trial."

15. Harris, "Murder Town's Tension." See also Jacqueline Jones, *Labor of Love, Labor of Sorrow: Black Women, Work, and the Family from Slavery to the Present* (New York: Vintage, 1985); Herbert Gutman, *The Black Family in Slavery and Freedom, 1750–1925* (New York: Vintage, 1976); and Douglas A. Blackmon, *Slavery by Another Name: The Re-Enslavement of Black Americans from the Civil War to World War II* (New York: Doubleday, 2008).

16. Paul Holmes, "Uncle Tells How 3 Kidnapers Invaded Home and Seized Till," *Chicago Tribune*, September 19, 1955, sec. 1, p. 2; Harris, "Mississippi

Opens Wolf-Whistle Trial." In actuality, Moses Wright was not as poor as the papers portrayed. Of course, he was a pauper compared to Strider; however, compared to his peers, he was in a relatively good financial position. He lived in a three-room house and made a good living off his crop. Darryl Mace, interview with the Reverend Wheeler Parker, September 16, 2005.

17. Holmes, "Uncle Tells How 3 Kidnapers Invaded Home"; Harris, "Mississippi Opens Wolf-Whistle Trial."

18. On the lack of wealthy men on the jury, see Russell Harris, "3 Surprise Witnesses Hinted for Prosecution in Dixie Trial," *Detroit News,* September 20, 1955, A1, A4, A17.

19. "Mississippi Wolf Call Murder Trial under Way," *Pittsburgh Post-Gazette,* September 20, 1955, A1–A2; "Jury Is Chosen in Boy's Slaying," *Philadelphia Evening Bulletin,* September 20, 1955, sec. 1, p. 28; Murray Kempton, "Preacher, Preacher," *New York Post,* September 19, 1955, A3, A30; John N. Popham, "Racial Issues," *New York Times,* September 18, 1955.

20. "Mississippi Wolf Call Murder Trial under Way" (first quote); John N. Popham, "Slain Boy's Uncle on Stand at Trial," *New York Times,* September 22, 1955, A64 (second quote); "Whistle Trial Told Boy Was Kidnaped, Freed," *Pittsburgh Post-Gazette,* September 22, 1955, A1–A2 (third quote); "Mississippi Rests Its Case in Murder of Chicago Boy, 14," *Philadelphia Evening Bulletin,* September 22, 1955, sec. 1, p. 1.

21. James L. Kilgallen, "Racial Trial," *Philadelphia Evening Bulletin,* September 19, 1955; "Mississippi Democracy," *Philadelphia Evening Bulletin,* September 21, 1955, sec. 1, p. 22.

22. US Census Bureau, "Table 39. Mississippi—Race and Hispanic Origin: 1800–1990," September 13, 2002, http://www.census.gov; Kilgallen, "Racial Trial"; Crespino, "Mississippi as Metaphor" (2010), 100. For more on the Evers brothers, see *The Rise and Fall of Jim Crow,* episode 4, *Terror and Triumph,* dir. Bill Jersey and Richard Wormser (New York: Quest, Videoline, Educational Broadcasting Corp., 2002), DVD; and Richard Wormser, *The Rise and Fall of Jim Crow* (New York: St. Martin's, 2003).

23. "Boy, 14, Victim of Race Hate," *Pittsburgh Courier,* September 10, 1955, A1.

24. "Attorneys Studying Facts on Lynching," *Philadelphia Tribune,* September 13, 1955, A4.

25. George F. Brown, "Mom Wants Son's Murder Avenged," *Pittsburgh Courier,* September 17, 1955, A1, A4.

26. "Williams CME Church to Be Site of Protest," *New York Amsterdam News,* September 17, 1955, A1–A2.

27. James L. Kilgallen, "Trial of 2 for 'Wolf Whistle' Killing of Negro Starts Today," *San Francisco Examiner,* September 19, 1955, sec. 1, p. 10; "Trial Starts for Two in Mississippi Killing," *San Francisco Examiner,* September 20, 1955,

sec. 1, p. 6; "Trial Set in Slaying of Negro," *Denver Post,* September 18, 1955, A16; "State Opens Final Plea in Negro Boy Slay Case," *Denver Post,* September 23, 1955, A8.

5. Trial by Print

1. "The Law"; "Emmett Till's Day in Court," *Life,* October 3, 1955, 36.

2. Dan Wakefield, "Justice in Sumner," *The Nation,* 1 October 1955, 284.

3. Ibid. (first quote); "Slain Boy's Mother to Testify at Trial"; "The Accused," *Newsweek,* September 19, 1955, 38 (second and third quotes).

4. "History, 1910," n.d. (first quote), "About Us," *The Crisis,* http://www .thecrisismagazine.com/history.html; "Till Protest Meeting," *The Crisis,* November 1955, 546 (second quote); "Mississippi Barbarism," *The Crisis,* October 1955, 480–81 (subsequent quotes).

5. Paul Holmes, "2 Go on Trial in South for Till Murder," *Chicago Tribune,* September 20, 1955, sec. 1, pp. 1–2.

6. Ibid.; Harris, "3 Surprise Witnesses Hinted."

7. Holmes, "2 Go on Trial in South" (quotes); Harris, "3 Surprise Witnesses Hinted."

8. Holmes, "2 Go on Trial in South." On the bellicose nature of the South, see John Hope Franklin, *The Militant South, 1800–1861* (1956; reprint, Urbana: University of Illinois Press, 2002).

9. Holmes, "2 Go on Trial in South"; Harris, "3 Surprise Witnesses Hinted."

10. Paul Holmes, "Hunt Shadow Witnesses in Till Slaying," *Chicago Tribune,* September 21, 1955, sec. 1, p. 3; Russell Harris, "3 Terrified Witnesses," *Detroit News,* September 21, 1955.

11. Russell Harris, "Verdict Due in Whistle Trial Today," *Detroit News,* September 23, 1955, A1, A4; "Youth Tells Murder Jury He Saw Till as Captive," *Chicago Sun-Times,* September 23, 1955, sec. 1, pp. 5, 14. There was a history of black Mississippians courageously giving testimony that challenged white supremacy. Of note are the testimonies of Nathaniel Lewis and several other black people who gave damning statements in the U.S. Senate Committee's investigation of the racist Mississippi senator Theodore Bilbo. See John Dittmer, *Local People: The Struggle for Civil Rights in Mississippi* (Urbana: University of Illinois Press, 1995), 25, 92.

12. Harris, "Verdict Due in Whistle Trial Today." See also Paul Holmes, "Open Defense Fight in Till Slaying Trial," *Chicago Tribune,* September 23, 1955, sec. 1, pp. 1, 6; "Youth Tells Murder Jury He Saw Till as Captive."

13. James L. Hicks, "Fear for Lives of Two Playmates of Emmett Till," *Cleveland Call and Post,* September 24, 1955, A1–A2.

14. L. Alex Wilson, "Picking of Jury Delays Opening," *Chicago Defender,* September 24, 1955, National, A1–A2.

15. Roi Ottley, "Southern Style," *Chicago Defender,* October 10, 1955, National, B8.

16. James L. Hicks, "All-White Jury of Sharecroppers Ignores Evidence," *Cleveland Call and Post,* October 1, 1955, A1–A2. The jungle analogy was a play on traditional white depictions of black people. Whites saw African Americans as savages whom they had rescued from the jungles of Africa through the process of enslavement. Here, Hicks turned the jungle reference around and accused the Mississippians of being the savages. Thus, the institution of slavery stole black people from the peace of their African nations and thrust them into the jungles of the American South.

17. "'Vengeance Is Mine,' Sayeth the Lord," *Cleveland Call and Post,* October 1, 1955, D2.

18. John H. Sengstacke, *The Chicago Defender, the Negro Press, and You* (n.p., 1960), 5 (first quote); Nelson, *The Black Press;* "Sengstacke Comments on Verdict," *Chicago Defender,* January 10, 1955, National, A1 (second and third quotes); John Sengstacke to Dwight Eisenhower, September 1, 1955 (fourth quote), box 3113, Emmett Till, Alphabetical File, Dwight D. Eisenhower Papers, DDE's Records as President, Dwight D. Eisenhower Presidential Library, Abilene, KS; Roberts and Klibanoff, *The Race Beat,* 94–96 (interview with Emogene W. Wilson); Emogene W. Wilson, "Profile: L. Alex Wilson, T-SD [*Tri-State Defender*]," February 24, March 3, 1990, cited in ibid., 424.

19. Mattie Smith Colin, "Till's Mom, Diggs Both Disappointed," *Chicago Defender,* October 1, 1955, National, A1–A2; "Jailed to Bar Them from Trial," *Chicago Defender,* October 1, 1955, National, A1. In the 1950s, women were assumed to be in subservient positions. They were supposed to let men wage wars and speak for them. Despite this fact, the *Defender* decided to allow Mamie Till-Mobley to speak, seemingly without a male figure guiding her words.

20. Murray Kempton, "The Baby Sitter," *New York Post,* September 20, 1955, A5, A32.

21. Popham, "Racial Issues"; Murray Kempton, "The Future," *New York Post,* September 23, 1955, A3, A40.

22. "Defendant's Wife," *Pittsburgh Post-Gazette,* September 23, 1955, A1 (first quote); "Jurors Urged to Free 2 Tried in Boy's Killing," *Philadelphia Evening Bulletin,* September 23, 1955, sec. 1, pp. 1, 56 (second quote); "Mississippi Wolf Call Murder Trial under Way" (third quote). On the violence that occurred as a result of miscegenation fears and the rape complex, see also Michael D'Orso, *Like Judgment Day: The Ruin and Redemption of a Town Called Rosewood* (New York: Putnam's, 1996); Alfred L. Brophy, *Reconstructing the Dreamland: The Tulsa Riot of 1921: Race, Reparations, and Reconciliation* (Oxford: Oxford University Press, 2002); Carter, *Scottsboro;* Goodman, *Stories of Scottsboro;* David S. Cecelski and Timothy B. Tyson, eds., *Democracy Betrayed: The Wilmington Race Riot of 1898 and Its Legacy* (Chapel Hill: University of North Carolina

Press, 1998); and David Fort Godshalk, *Veiled Visions: The 1906 Atlanta Race Riot and the Reshaping of American Race Relations* (Chapel Hill: University of North Carolina Press, 2005).

23. "Mississippi Wolf Call Murder Trial under Way"; photograph captioned "Ordeal—Mrs. Roy Bryant pillows her head on husband's shoulder after testifying," *Pittsburgh Post-Gazette,* September 23, 1955, A1.

24. James Edmond Boyack, "'Men's Souls Are Torn by Hatred, Violence, Fear,'" *Pittsburgh Courier,* September 24, 1955, sec. 1, p. 5; P. L. Prattis, "Tears Instead of Money," *Pittsburgh Courier,* September 24, 1955, 6; "Sheriff Makes Search for Hidden Guns," *New York Amsterdam News,* September 24, 1955, A1, A3.

25. "Mississippians Are Acquitted in the Kidnap-Slaying of Boy," *Richmond (VA) Times-Dispatch,* September 24, 1955, A1; "Jury Acquits Pair," *Charlotte (NC) Observer,* September 24, 1955; John N. Popham, "Brothers Acquitted," *Atlanta Constitution,* September 24, 1955; "2 Acquitted of 'Whistle' Slaying in Mississippi," *Washington Post,* September 24, 1955, A1.

26. "A Drama Plays Out, but Its Full Meaning May Be Missed," *Charlotte (NC) Observer,* September 25, 1955, C2.

27. James L. Hicks, "Feared Reprisals for Telling Truth," *Baltimore Afro-American,* October 1, 1955, A1, A8. See also Carson, Garrow, Kovach, and Polsgrove, eds., *Reporting Civil Rights,* 930; and James L. Hicks, "Sheriff Kept Key Witness Hid in Jail during Trial," *Cleveland Call and Post,* October 8, 1955, A1, C8, "Hicks Says Key Witnesses in Jail during Till Case Hearing," *Atlanta Daily World,* October 4, 1955, A1–A4, and "Hicks Tells of Daring Efforts to Get Witnesses in Till Case," *Atlanta Daily World,* October 11, 1955.

28. Hicks, "Hicks Says Key Witnesses in Jail during Till Case Hearing."

29. Ibid.

30. Ibid.

31. Hicks, "Hicks Tells of Daring Efforts to Get Witnesses in Till Case."

32. Ibid.

33. Ibid.

34. James L. Hicks, "Hicks Arrested during Trial in Till Lynch-Murder Case," *Atlanta Daily World,* October 18, 1955, A1–A2.

35. Ibid.

36. Ibid.

37. Ibid.

38. Ibid.

39. "Mississippi Decision Nothing New," *Baltimore Afro-American,* October 1, 1955, A4. This ready excuse still exists. Most recently, Susan Smith, the white mother who drowned her children when she drove her car into a lake in Union, South Carolina, in 1994, originally claimed that a black man carjacked her and drove away with her children in the car.

40. "Mississippi Decision Nothing New"; "Facing the Cold Facts," *Atlanta Daily World,* September 25, 1955, A4.

41. "Congressman Diggs, Till's Mother in Attendance at Sumner Trial," *Jackson Advocate,* September 24, 1955, A1, A4.

42. "Facing the Cold Facts"; "Determined to Harvest Bumper Crop of Cotton," *Tri-State Defender* (Memphis), September 17, 1955, sec. 1, p. 1.

43. Raymond F. Tisby, "Lynch-Murder Victim's Mother Appears at Miss. Murder Trial," *Birmingham World,* September 23, 1955, sec. 1, pp. 1, 6. Juxtaposed with the courage of Congressman Diggs, Moses Wright, and Mamie Till-Mobley was, as the *World* publications lamented, the cowardice of those witnesses who refused to testify at the Brookhaven, Mississippi, trial of the men responsible for the lynching of the Mississippi black activist Lamar Smith. In that case, another all-white jury was unwilling and/or unable to produce an indictment. "Jury Reconvenes, Adjourns without Indictment in Courthouse Slaying," *Birmingham World,* September 23, 1955, sec. 1, p. 1.

6. Galvanizing the Emmett Till Generation

1. Hudson-Weems, *Emmett Till.*

2. Mosnier, interview with Booker and Newson.

3. Mr. and Mrs. D. E. Hansen, letter to the editor, *Time,* October 17, 1955, 19.

4. Robert A. Potter, letter to the editor, *Time,* October 24, 1955, 6; James J. Mertz, letter to the editor, *Life,* October 31, 1955, 6.

5. "500 at LYL Rally Urge Govt. Act in Mississippi," *Daily Worker,* December 19, 1955, A2; "5,000 in Los Angeles Rally, 1,600 in Boston Assail Lynching of Child," *Daily Worker,* October 13, 1955, A3; Roosevelt Ward Jr., "Harlemites Applaud Plan for 'March on Washington,'" *Daily Worker,* October 13, 1955, A3; "Wisconsin Democratic Convention Assails Injustice in Till Case," *Daily Worker,* October 14, 1955, A3, A8; "2,000 in Frisco Hit Till Murder; Rep. Roosevelt Urges U.S. Act," *Daily Worker,* October 19, 1955, A3; "Eastland Uses Secret Army Files to Aid Till Lynchers," *Daily Worker,* October 21, 1955, A1, A3; "Lynching Hit at Connecticut CIO Meet," *Daily Worker,* October 21, 1955, A3; "3,000 in Pittsburgh Rally," *Daily Worker,* October 26, 1955, A3; Richard Henry Barnes, "Introduce Till Resolutions into Pennsy Legislature," *Daily Worker,* October 27, 1955, A3.

6. Gloria Barton Morris, letter to the editor, *Time,* October 24, 1955, 6; Bennye Chatham, letter to the editor, *Time,* October 24, 1955, 6.

7. Hodding Carter to Anthony V. Ragusin, December 5, 1955, folder 13-5, Hodding Carter Correspondences 1955 (July–December), Hodding Carter II and Betty Werlein Carter Papers, Mitchel Memorial Library, Mississippi State University, Mississippi State, MS; Hodding Carter, "Racial Crisis in the Deep South,"

Saturday Evening Post, December 17, 1955, 26. See also Ann Waldron, *Hodding Carter: The Reconstruction of a Racist* (Chapel Hill, NC: Algonquin, 1993), Kindle ed., KL 3099–3100; and Hodding Carter to Gayle Waldrop, September 30, 1955, folder 13-14, Hodding Carter Correspondences 1955 (July–December), Carter Papers.

8. "'Ill-Chosen Symbol,'" *Time,* November 21, 1955, 21.

9. Ibid.

10. Roy Wilkins to Dwight Eisenhower, memorandum, September 16, 1955, microfilm reel 14, *Papers of the NAACP: Part 18 . . . Series C: General Office Files.* See also Crespino, "Mississippi as Metaphor" (2010), 100.

11. "The Predictable Verdict," *St. Louis Post-Dispatch,* September 25, 1955, B2.

12. Eugene M. Garner, "As to the Till Case," *St. Louis Post-Dispatch,* September 27, 1955, C2; A Disgusted White Reader, letter to the editor, *St. Louis Post-Dispatch,* September 27, 1955, C2; Norma Claywell, "Mississippi Justice," *St. Louis Post-Dispatch,* September 29, 1955, B2; Lee W. Davies, "Almost Impossible," *St. Louis Post-Dispatch,* September 30, 1955, C2; Mrs. Edw. Wagner, "Afterthoughts," *St. Louis Post-Dispatch,* October 2, 1955, C2.

13. "Statement by Mr. Wilkins RE Cancellation of NAACP-Sponsored Speaking Tour of Mrs. Mamie Bradley," November 7, 1955, microfilm reel 14, *Papers of the NAACP: Part 18 . . . Series A: Legal Department Files;* "Mrs. Bradley Says Fee NAACP Idea," *Chicago Defender,* November 19, 1955, National, A1–A2. Till-Mobley checked into a hospital after the murder trial, reportedly because she was exhausted. The stay lasted for a few days, and afterward she continued with her speaking engagements.

14. Roy Wilkins to Henry Moon, memorandum, November 18, 1955, and Roy Wilkins to Louis Martin, memorandum, November 18, 1955, microfilm reel 13, *Papers of the NAACP: Part 18 . . . Series A: Legal Department Files.*

15. "Deeply Hurt by NAACP Rebuke," *Chicago Defender,* November 26, 1955, National, A1–A2.

16. For evidence of Till-Mobley's close association with the *Defender,* see Mattie Smith Colin, "Slain Boy's Mother Lauds the Defender," *Chicago Defender,* September 17, 1955, National, A1, in which she praised the paper for its coverage of the events. The following year, when most newspapers had left the Till case behind, the *Defender* published a series of interviews with Till-Mobley. See Colin, "Slain Boy's Mother Lauds the Defender"; and Bradley, "Mamie Bradley's Untold Story, Installment I"; Mamie Bradley, "Mamie Bradley's Untold Story, Installment II, As Told by Ethel Payne," *Chicago Defender,* April 28, 1956, 5; Mamie Bradley, "Mamie Bradley's Untold Story, Installment III, As Told by Ethel Payne," *Chicago Defender,* May 5, 1956, 5; Mamie Bradley, "Mamie Bradley's Untold Story, Installment IV, As Told by Ethel Payne," *Chicago Defender,* May 12, 1956, 5; Mamie Bradley, "Mamie Bradley's Untold Story, Installment

V, As Told by Ethel Payne," *Chicago Defender,* May 19, 1956, 5; Mamie Brad-ley, "Mamie Bradley's Untold Story, Installment VI, As Told by Ethel Payne," *Chicago Defender,* May 26, 1956, 5; Mamie Bradley, "Mamie Bradley's Untold Story, Installment VII, As Told by Ethel Payne," *Chicago Defender,* June 2, 1956, 5; and Bradley, "Mamie Bradley's Untold Story, Installment VIII."

17. Max Lerner, "Southern Jury Justice," *New York Post,* September 25, 1955, M8.

18. "Case of Emmett Till," *New York Times,* September 26, 1955, A26; Donna Schultz, "Protests Verdict in Negro Boy Case," *Pittsburgh Post-Gazette,* September 27, 1955, A10; "Who of Us Doesn't Share in Guilt of Till Murder?" *Pittsburgh Post-Gazette,* September 29, 1955, A16; W.S., "Mississippi Mud," *New York Post,* September 26, 1955, A35. In the Cold War era, Americans were increasingly concerned with how the world viewed them. Additionally, the United States was competing with the Soviet Union for the trust, respect, and resources of non-white nations in Latin America, the Middle East, Asia, and Africa. In this tenuous environment, diplomats increasingly spoke of culture rather than race as the identifier of difference. However, race still dominated American domestic policy. In response, the federal government took an increasingly hard-line view when it came to racism and racial discrimination. See Thomas Borstelmann, *The Cold War and the Color Line: American Race Relations in the Global Arena* (Cambridge, MA: Harvard University Press, 2003); and Dudziak, *Cold War Civil Rights.*

19. "Acquittal in Mississippi," *Pittsburgh Post-Gazette,* September 27, 1955, A10.

20. Robert Conaway, "Till Case a Boon to Enemies of U.S.," *Pittsburgh Post-Gazette,* October 3, 1955, A8; Ruth Poritz, "Criticizes Editorial on Till Case Verdict," *Pittsburgh Post-Gazette,* October 3, 1955, A8. Poritz identified herself as a white person.

21. "Till Case Verdict Rapped by Reader," *Pittsburgh Post-Gazette,* September 30, 1955, A12; Robert E. Merry, "Praises Reprint of Magazine Article," *Pittsburgh Post-Gazette,* October 3, 1955, A8.

22. White American, "Jury in Till Case Scored by Reader," *Pittsburgh Post-Gazette,* October 4, 1955, A8.

23. Minister, "Answers Letter on Till Trial," *Pittsburgh Post-Gazette,* October 8, 1955, A6. For in-depth discussions of Cold War ideas of race, see Borstelmann, *The Cold War and the Color Line;* and Dudziak, *Cold War Civil Rights.*

24. Donna Schultz, "Protests Verdict in Negro Boy Case." It is important to note that the word *men* appeared in brackets in print.

25. Evelyn Cunningham, "Harlem Protests Lynching," *Pittsburgh Courier,* October 1, 1955, sec. 1, p. 4.

26. "Democrats Condemn Cracker Thugs Who Mutilated Victim," *Philadelphia Tribune,* September 27, 1955, 1.

27. James Edmund Boyack, "*Courier's* James Boyack Hangs Head in Shame,"

Pittsburgh Courier, October 1, 1955, sec. 1, p. 4 (first four quotes); "Mississippi Justice," *New York Amsterdam News,* October 1, 1955, A1 (remaining quotes). The term *fear complex* refers to the state of terror that southern blacks lived under. They feared for their lives constantly because white supremacy and racial oppression had no concrete laws. The only certainty was that the whites were in control and could exact whatever they deemed fitting in the way of "justice," with little fear of repercussions.

28. Boyack, *"Courier'*s James Boyack Hangs Head in Shame"; Robert M. Ratcliffe, "Opening Day of the Farce!" *Pittsburgh Courier,* October 1, 1955, 9.

29. Charles C. Diggs Jr., "Cong. Diggs: Emmett Till Trial Over but Negroes Should Never Forget Its Meaning," *Pittsburgh Courier,* October 8, 1955, sec. 1, p. 5.

30. T. R. M. Howard, "Dr. Howard: Situation in Mississippi Extremely Serious; Tension Is Continuing to Mount," *Pittsburgh Courier,* October 8, 1955, sec. 1, pp. 1, 4.

31. "Fight Miss. Bigots!" *New York Amsterdam News,* October 15, 1955, A10.

32. George F. Brown, "Mrs. Bradley Plans Suit," *Pittsburgh Courier,* September 22, 1955, 1.

33. "Mamie Apologizes!" *Pittsburgh Courier,* November 19, 1955, 1–2; "Mother of Till Bitter!" *Pittsburgh Courier,* December 24, 1955, sec. 1, p. 3.

34. "Mother of Till Bitter!" The report leaves the impression that Till-Mobley had been married only once, to Louis Till, when, in fact, at the time of the trial she was divorced from her second husband. She married her third husband only two years after the trial. In later years, she painted her first husband as a gambler and philander who did little to take care of his family and her second husband, Pink Bradley, as a philanderer and a wife beater. Interestingly, she had nothing but praise for her third husband, Gene Mobley, whom she remained with until his death. See Hudson-Weems, *Emmett Till,* 219–50; and Till-Mobley and Benson, *Death of Innocence,* 91.

35. R. C. Bolen, "Point Ignored in Till Case," *Charlotte (NC) Observer,* September 28, 1955, B2; Chalmers G. Davidson, "A Finger Pointed in the Till Case," *Charlotte (NC) Observer,* October 6, 1955, B2.

36. Alton E. Ogbern, "No Right to Pass Judgment on Justice," *Atlanta Constitution,* October 7, 1955, A4; R. L. Ponder, "Americans Demand Guilt Be Proven," *Atlanta Constitution,* October 8, 1955, A4.

37. Tom Adams, "The Big Issue, a Simplification," *Charlotte (NC) Observer,* October 10, 1955, B2. On relations between the races, see generally Elizabeth Fox-Genovese, *Within the Plantation Household: Black and White Women of the Old South* (Chapel Hill: University of North Carolina Press, 1988); John W. Blassingame, *The Slave Community: Plantation Life in the Antebellum South* (New York: Oxford University Press, 1979); and Lemire, *"Miscegenation."*

38. "Till's Father Was a Killer, Paper Reports," *Charlotte (NC) Observer,* October 15, 1955, A2.

39. Ibid.

40. Edmund G. Hyde, "In Mississippi, Pitiful Travesty," *Charlotte (NC) Observer,* October 5, 1955, B2; L. W. McKinley, "Place for Bigots Somewhere Else?" *Charlotte (NC) Observer,* October 4, 1955, B2; Robert T. Clark, "Deplores Outcome of Mississippi Trial," *Charlotte (NC) Observer,* October 11, 1955, B2.

41. La Verne Gordon, "For No Reason, a Boy Is Dead," *Charlotte (NC) Observer,* October 10, 1955, B2; Ernest Hinson, "Mississippi Trial Attacked by Georgian," *Atlanta Constitution,* October 4, 1955, A4.

42. H. H. Strong, "Comments on Trial Lauded by Negro," *Atlanta Constitution,* October 10, 1955, A4.

43. "Justice, 1955, in Mississippi, U.S.A., as Depicted in the Till Murder Case," *Norfolk (VA) Journal and Guide,* October 1, 1955, A10.

44. Ibid.

45. (Mrs.) M. E. Lee, "'Couldn't Have Treated a Dog That Cruelly,'" *Norfolk (VA) Journal and Guide,* October 8, 1955, A10.

46. A Disgusted Citizen, "Emmett Till's Death Will Be Avenged," *Norfolk (VA) Journal and Guide,* October 15, 1955, A10.

47. Mary Strafford, "'When I Find Time I'll Cry,' Till's Mother Tells *Afro,*" *Baltimore Afro-American,* October 29, 1955, A1–A2.

48. James L. Hicks, "Why Emmett Till's Mother and NAACP Couldn't Agree," *Baltimore Afro-American,* December 31, 1955, A2.

49. "Till's Mother Says No Effort Made to Find Eye Witness," *San Francisco Examiner,* September 24, 1955, sec. 1, p. 20; "Till's Mother Calls Trial in Mississippi 'Comedy,'" *San Francisco Examiner,* September 26, 1955, sec. 1, p. 8; "2 Till Kidnap Suspects' Bond Set at $10,000," *Denver Post,* September 30, 1955, A18.

50. "'Due Process' of Law?" *Denver Post,* September 28, 1955, A20.

51. Gladys Madden Vied, letter to the editor, *San Francisco Examiner,* September 27, 1955, sec. 1, p. 30.

52. Richard Haase, letter to the editor, *San Francisco Examiner,* September 27, 1955, sec. 1, p. 30. While organizations like the NAACP, the National Urban League, and the Congress of Racial Equity never officially subscribed to the Communist ideology, individual black Americans were members of the Communist Party. Often their Communist and socialist politics led to these African Americans being blacklisted by key civil rights organizations. For detailed discussions, see Nell Irvin Painter, ed., *A Narrative of Hosea Hudson: His Life as a Negro Communist in the South* (Cambridge, MA: Harvard University Press, 1981); Mark Naison, *Communists in Harlem during the Depression* (Urbana: University of Illinois Press, 1983); John D'Emilio, *Lost Prophet: The Life and Times of Bayard Rustin* (Chicago: University of Chicago Press, 2004); Daniel Levine, *Bayard*

Rustin and the Civil Rights Movement (New Brunswick, NJ: Rutgers University Press, 2000); and David Levering Lewis, *W. E. B. DuBois: The Fight for Equality and the American Century, 1919–1963* (New York: Holt, 2000).

53. Franklin Hichborn, "Southern Exposure," *San Francisco Examiner,* September 28, 1955, sec. 3, p. 2.

54. P. M. Snider, "Safely Returned," *Seattle Times,* October 6, 1955, Night Sports final, sec. 1, p. 8.

55. Bernice C. Johnston, "The Till Case," *Denver Post,* October 8, 1955, A7.

56. "Claim Eyewitnesses to Till Murder Held in Miss. Jail," *Los Angeles Sentinel,* October 6, 1955.

57. The articles dealing with this issue include "Mrs. Bradley Dropped from Speaking Tour," *Los Angeles Sentinel,* November 10, 1955, A1, A4; and Kenneth C. Field, "Miss., 'Nightmare of Terror,' Rev. Moses Wright Relates," *Los Angeles Sentinel,* November 17, 1955, A1.

58. "Mrs. Bradley Dropped from Speaking Tour."

59. Lester Bailey to Roy Wilkins, memorandum, August 31, 1955, Roy Wilkins to Sylvester Odum, memorandum, November 8, 1955, Frank Barnes to Roy Wilkins, memorandum, November 9, 1955 (quote), and Frank Barnes to Roy Wilkins, memorandum, November 8, 1955, microfilm reel 14, *Papers of the NAACP: Part 18 . . . Series C: General Office Files.*

60. "Emmett Till Case Gains All Out Aid for NAACP," *Los Angeles Sentinel,* September 29, 1955, A5; "Justice—'Ole Miss' Style," *Los Angeles Sentinel,* September 29, 1955, A9. The latter—likely written by Leon Washington, the *Sentinel*'s editor—was just one example of the scathing attacks on racism found in *Sentinel* editorials.

61. "Justice—'Ole Miss' Style."

62. Ibid.

63. "Will the NAACP Accept Blame?" *Delta Democrat-Times* (Greenville, MS), September 21, 1955, Red Streak final, A4.

64. Crespino, "Mississippi as Metaphor" (2006).

65. Jay Milner, "Delta Town Welcomes Quiet Following in Wake of Sensational Murder Trial," *Jackson (MS) Daily News,* September 25, 1955, Home final, sec. 1, p. 10 (first quote); "Legal Processes Continue," *Memphis Commercial Appeal,* September 24, 1955, final, A6 (second and third quotes); McCann L. Reed, "Ahlgren: Just as Big a Bigot," *Tri-State Defender* (Memphis), July 19, 1995, online; Walter Sillers Jr. to Frank Ahlgren, October 15, 1941, folder 12, box 6, Sillers Papers; "The Verdict at Sumner," *Jackson (MS) Daily News,* September 25, 1955, Home final, sec. 1, p. 8 (fourth and fifth quotes); "Acquittal," *Delta Democrat-Times* (Greenville, MS), September 25, 1955, Red Streak final, A4 (sixth quote).

66. Presley J. Snow, "Strong Pressure," *Memphis Commercial Appeal,* October 2, 1955, final, sec. 5, p. 3 (first quote); W. L. C. Griffin, "Who's Behind It?" *Memphis Commercial Appeal,* October 2, 1955, final, sec. 5, p. 3 (second quote).

67. "Time to Forget the Till Case," *Delta Democrat-Times* (Greenville, MS), October 30, 1955, Red Streak final, A4.

68. Morris Cunningham, "Till's GI Dad Hanged in Italy for Women Attacks in 1944," *Memphis Commercial Appeal,* October 16, 1955, final, sec. 1, p. 4.

69. John Herbers, "'Case Closed' as Jury Fails to Indict Pair for Till Kidnaping," *Delta Democrat-Times* (Greenville, MS), November 10, 1955, Red Streak final, A1.

70. "Justice in Leflore County," *Delta Democrat-Times* (Greenville, MS), November 10, 1955, Red Streak final, A4.

71. "The Till Case Verdict," *Jackson (MS) Advocate,* October 1, 1955, A4.

72. Chester M. Hampton, "World Shocked by Till Trial," *Birmingham World,* September 30, 1955, A6; "No White Man Given Death for Killing in Miss. since 1890, Writer Observes," *Birmingham World,* September 27, 1955, sec. 1, p. 6.

73. "1,000 Attend Paris Meeting to Protest Till Case," *Birmingham World,* October 4, 1955, sec. 1, p. 2; "Public Protest Mounts on Emmett Till Case," *Memphis World,* October 7, 1955, sec. 1, p. 1, 4; "Till Case Repercussions," *Tri-State Defender* (Memphis), November 5, 1955, sec. 1, p. 7.

74. "Miss. Reporter Says Witnesses 'Captive' in Chicago," *Birmingham World,* October 14, 1955, sec. 1, p. 5.

75. Ibid.

7. In Remembrance of Emmett Till

1. Both hypotheses can be found in Stanley Nelson, dir., *The Murder of Emmett Till* (PBS, 2003), videocassette.

2. Jesse L. Jackson Sr., "Appreciation," *Time,* November 7, 2005, 20.

3. Evers-Williams quoted in Christopher Metress, ed., *The Lynching of Emmett Till: A Documentary Narrative* (Charlottesville: University Press of Virginia, 2002), 247, 250.

4. Charles M. Payne, *I've Got the Light of Freedom: The Organizing Tradition and the Mississippi Freedom Struggle* (1995; reprint, Berkeley: University of California Press, 2007), 54.

5. Andrew Lewis, *The Shadow of Youth: The Remarkable Journey of the Civil Rights Generation* (New York: Hill & Wang, 2009), 363–77.

6. Spirit Trickey-Rowan, "Q&A: One of Little Rock 9 Speaks with Daughter, a History Maker in the Making," The Grio, February 8, 2010, http://thegrio.com; and "The Story of Emmett Till," n.d., *February One: The Story of the Greensboro Four, Independent Lens*, PBS, http://www.pbs.org/independentlens/februaryone/till.html.

7. Hudson-Weems, *Emmett Till,* 287, 292–93.

8. Metress, *The Lynching of Emmett Till,* 3.

9. William Bradford Huie, "The Shocking Story of Approved Killing in Mis-

sissippi," *Look,* January 24, 1956, 46. Huie continued to pay for information, most notably $40,000 to James Earl Ray for the exclusive on the assassination of Dr. Martin Luther King Jr. Huie was the author of twenty-one books and hundreds of articles on a wide variety of topics. Seven of his books became Hollywood movies. See also Hugh Stephen Whitaker, "A Case Study of Southern Justice: The Emmett Till Case" (M.A. thesis, Florida State University, 1963), 160.

10. Mace, interview with the Reverend Wheeler Parker; Hudson-Weems, *Emmett Till,* 225–26; Simeon Wright and Herb Brown, *Simeon's Story: An Eyewitness Account of the Kidnapping of Emmett Till* (Chicago: Chicago Review Press, 2010).

11. Huie, "The Shocking Story of Approved Killing," 47–50.

12. "Letters to the Editor," n.d., *The Murder of Emmett Till, The American Experience,* PBS, http://www.pbs.org/wgbh/amex/till/sfeature/sf_look_letters .html; David T. Beito and Linda Royster Beito, *Black Maverick: T. R. M. Howard's Fight for Civil Rights and Economic Power* (Urbana: University of Illinois Press, 2009); Amos Dixon, "Mrs. Bryant Didn't Even Hear Emmett Till Whistle," *California Eagle* (Los Angeles), January 26, 1956, A1 (all quotes).

13. Dixon, "Mrs. Bryant Didn't Even Hear." The story Dixon told was an age-old one. In a similar account from the early twentieth century, when Henry Watson, a well-to-do black farmer from Georgia, bought a car and drove his daughter into town, jealous white people "surrounded the car, forced Watson and his daughter out at gunpoint, and burned the vehicle." Furthermore, "Watson was told, 'From now on, you niggers walk into town, or use that ole mule if you want to stay in this city.'" This was just one account of the long history of white anger over black success. See Darlene Clark Hine, William C. Hine, and Stanley Harrold, *The African-American Odyssey* (Upper Saddle River, NJ: Prentice-Hall, 2006), 357–59.

14. Dixon, "Mrs. Bryant Didn't Even Hear" (first two quotes); Amos Dixon, "Till Case: Torture and Murder," *California Eagle* (Los Angeles), February 9, 1956, A1 (last two quotes).

15. Dixon, "Till Case" (first two quotes); Amos Dixon, "South Wins Out in Till Lynching Trial," *California Eagle* (Los Angeles), September 23, 1956, A1 (last quote).

16. William Bradford Huie, "What's Happened to the Emmett Till Killers?" *Look,* January 22, 1957, 63–66. This type of boycott has a long history. Ida B. Wells-Barnett organized protests and boycotts directly linked to the lynching death of three of her black friends who, in 1892, were attacked because they opened a grocery store that dared to compete with a white-owned store. Refusing to back down, these three, Thomas Moss, Calvin McDowell, and Henry Stewart, shot one of their attackers. As was customary in southern vigilante justice, the three were arrested and put in jail. That night, a lynch mob came, dragged the men out of jail, and lynched them. As a result of Wells-Barnett's work to highlight

the atrocity, the boycott was successful. In another example of African American boycotts, during the Great Depression black people bonded together in what was known as the "Don't buy where you can't work" campaign. In this effort, African Americans refused to buy products in the numerous white-owned stores found in black neighborhoods that refused to hire black workers. These efforts were also successful, and many merchants were forced to reconsider their hiring practices. See Patricia A. Schechter, *Ida B. Wells-Barnett and American Reform, 1880–1930* (Chapel Hill: University of North Carolina Press, 2001); and Michele F. Pacifico, "'Don't Buy Where You Can't Work': The New Negro Alliance of Washington," *Washington History* 6 (1994): 66–88.

17. Huie, "What's Happened to the Emmett Till Killers?" 65.

18. Ibid., 65–68.

19. Till-Mobley and Benson, *Death of Innocence,* 261–62 (all quotes); Devery Anderson, "Death of the Accused," n.d., *Emmett Till Murder,* http://www.emmetttillmurder.com.

20. Devery S. Anderson, interview with Mamie Till-Mobley, December 3, 1966, *Emmett Till Murder,* http://www.emmetttillmurder.com. Mamie Till-Mobley outlived most of the principals in the Till trial. For updates on the other key figures, see Whitaker, "A Case Study of Southern Justice," 163–65; and Devery Anderson, n.d., "Who's Who in the Emmett Till Case," *Emmett Till Murder,* http://www.emmetttillmurder.com.

21. Mamie Bradley, "Mamie Bradley's Untold Story, Installment VI, As Told by Ethel Payne," *Chicago Defender,* May 26, 1956, 5.

22. Ibid.

23. Bradley, "Mamie Bradley's Untold Story, Installment VIII"; Terkel, interview with Mamie Mobley; Bradley, "Mamie Bradley's Untold Story, Installment I"; and Anderson, interview with Mamie Till-Mobley.

24. Bradley, "Mamie Bradley's Untold Story, Installment VIII."

25. Bradley, "Mamie Bradley's Untold Story, Installment I"; Terkel, interview with Mamie Till-Mobley.

26. Till-Mobley and Benson, *Death of Innocence,* 229.

27. Ibid., 291, 242–43; Anderson, interview with Mamie Till-Mobley; Devery Anderson, "Emmett Till Foundation," n.d., *Emmett Till Murder,* http://www.emmetttillmurder.com.

28. Till-Mobley and Benson, *Death of Innocence,* 247–48.

29. Ibid., 254; "National Outrage at Texas Lynching," *Chicago Defender,* June 13, 1998, A1, A6.

30. J. N'deye Walton, "Emmett Till Remembered," *Chicago Defender,* July 25, 1992, A1, A14.

31. Till-Mobley and Benson, *Death of Innocence,* 265.

32. Debra Pickett, "Mamie Till Mobley Dies; Made Son's Slaying Meaning-ful," *Chicago Sun-Times,* January 7, 2003, online; Ana Mendieta, "500 Mourn

Mamie Till Mobley; Homegoing Service Celebrates Her Life; Funeral Set for Today," *Chicago Sun-Times,* January 11, 2003, online (first quote); "Remembering Mamie Till Mobley," *Ebony,* March 2003, 20.

33. See http://firelightmedia.tv/project/the-murder-of-emmett-till; Mace, interview with the Reverend Wheeler Parker.

34. Karen E. Pride, "Till Commemorations Fill 50th Anniversary Weekend," *Chicago Defender,* August 26, 2005, online, "Federal Officials Lead Exhumation of Emmett Till," *Chicago Defender,* June 2, 2005, online, and "Emmett Till Returned to His Final Resting Place," *Chicago Defender,* June 6, 2005, online; "FBI Till Findings May Be Out Next Month," *Chicago Tribune,* February 20, 2006, online; Earl O. Hutchinson, "Why the Emmett Till Case Still Matters," *Chicago Defender,* June 10, 2005, online; Devery Anderson, "News and Events," n.d., *Emmett Till Murder,* http://www.emmetttillmurder.com; "Emmett Till Group Want to Embrace the Truth, Spread the Word," *Natchez (MS) Democrat,* October 1, 2007, online.

35. Avis Thomas-Lester, "A Senate Apology for History of Lynching," *Washington Post,* June 14, 2005, A12; Jim Abrams, "Senate Apologizes for Past Failures to Pass Anti-Lynching Legislation," *Chicago Defender,* June 14, 2005, online; Hazel Trice Edney, "At Least Eight Senators Backed Anti-Lynching Measure After It Was Adopted," *Chicago Defender,* June 24, 2005, online.

36. "Washington: 'Cold Case' Squad for Civil Rights Killings," *New York Times,* September 15, 2005, online; Karen E. Pride, "Commemoration of Emmett Till Lynching Anniversary Includes Renaming Expressway Bridge," *Chicago Defender,* August 29, 2005, online; Don Babwin, "Officials, Others Hope Church Where Emmett Till's Funeral Will Bring Tourists," *Chicago Defender,* November 18, 2005, online. See also Charles Sheehan, "Till Rites Site Could Become a Landmark," *Chicago Tribune,* November 1, 2005, Metro sec., 1. Preservation Chicago is an organization founded in 2001 for the purpose of protecting Chicago's vast history. As part of its mission, this group tries to save historic buildings from demolition. One of the most effective ways to achieve this goal is to have buildings designated as landmarks because that distinction commits the city to preserving them. See "Roberts Temple Church of God: 4021 S. State—Civil Rights Monument Now Part of History—2006," n.d., *Preservation Chicago,* http://www.preservationchicago.org/success-story/11; Karen E. Pride, "South Side Park Named for Popular Alderman," *Chicago Defender,* January 11, 2005, online; and Mema Ayi, "Woodlawn School Renamed After Emmett Till," *Chicago Defender,* February 27, 2006, online.

37. Drew Jubara, "Decades Later, an Apology: Once an Icon of Racism, Town Plans to Say It's [*sic*] Sorry Near Where Emmett Till's Killers Were Freed," *Atlanta Journal-Constitution,* October 2, 2007, A1; "Emmett Till Museum," n.d., *The Village of Glendora,* http://www.glendorams.com; "Emmett Till Group Want to Embrace the Truth."

Bibliography

Primary Sources

Archives

Hodding Carter II and Betty Werlein Carter Papers. Mitchel Memorial Library, Mississippi State University, Mississippi State, MS.

Dwight D. Eisenhower Papers. Dwight D. Eisenhower Presidential Library, Abilene, KS. http://www.eisenhower.archives.gov.

FBI File on the NAACP. Wilmington, DE: Scholarly Resources, 1990.

Field Foundation Archives. Briscoe Center for American History, University of Texas at Austin.

C. A. McKnight Papers. Special Collections, J. Murrey Atkins Library, University of North Carolina at Charlotte.

Papers of the NAACP: Part 18: Special Subjects, 1940–1955: Series A: Legal Department Files. Bethesda, MD: University Publications of America, 1995.

Papers of the NAACP: Part 18: Special Subjects, 1940–1955: Series C: General Office Files. Bethesda, MD: University Publications of America, 1995.

Schomburg Center for Research in Black Culture. New York Public Library.

Walter Sillers Jr. Papers. Delta State University Archives and Museum, Delta State University, West Cleveland, MS. http://collections.msdiglib.org.

Robert F. Wagner Labor Archives. Tamiment Library, New York University.

Interviews

Anderson, Devery S. Interview with Mamie Till-Mobley. December 3, 1996. *Emmett Till Murder*, http://www.emmetttillmurder.com.

Mace, Darryl. Interview with the Reverend Wheeler Parker. September 16, 2005.

Mosnier, Joseph. Interview with Simeon Booker and Moses J. Newson. July 13, 2011. Civil Rights History Project Collection, Archive of Folk Culture, American Folklife Center, Library of Congress, Washington, DC.

Terkel, Studs. Interview with Mamie Mobley. November 30, 1999. *The Studs Terkel Program,* WFMT-FM, http://www.studsterkel.org/results.php?keywords=mobley.

Secondary Sources

"Abducted Boy Found Dead; Two Men Held." *Seattle Times,* August 31, 1955, Night Sports final, sec. 3, p. 48.

"Abducted Boy Found Slain." *Philadelphia Evening Bulletin,* August 31, 1955, sec. 1, p. 1.

Abrams, Jim. "Senate Apologizes for Past Failures to Pass Anti-Lynching Legislation." *Chicago Defender,* June 14, 2005, online.

"The Accused." *Newsweek,* September 19, 1955, 38.

"Acquittal." *Delta Democrat-Times* (Greenville, MS), September 25, 1955, Red Streak final, A4.

"Acquittal in Mississippi." *Pittsburgh Post-Gazette,* September 27, 1955, A10.

Adams, Tom. "The Big Issue, a Simplification." *Charlotte (NC) Observer,* October 10, 1955, B2.

"After-War Migration." *Savannah (GA) Tribune,* October 25, 1919, 4.

Anderson, Devery. "Death of the Accused." n.d. *Emmett Till Murder*, http://www.emmetttillmurder.com.

———. "Emmett Till Foundation." n.d. *Emmett Till Murder,* http://www.emmetttillmurder.com.

———. "News and Events." n.d. *Emmett Till Murder,* http://www.emmetttillmurder.com.

———. "Who's Who in the Emmett Till Case." n.d. *Emmett Till Murder,* http://www.emmetttillmurder.com.

Ashmore, Harry. *Hearts and Minds: A Personal Chronicle of Race in America.* Cabin John, MD: Seven Locks, 1988.

"Ask Ike to Act in Dixie Death of Chicago Boy." *Chicago Tribune,* September 2, 1955, sec. 1, p. 2.

"Ask Mississippi Governor to Denounce Killing of Boy." *Chicago Tribune,* September 1, 1955, sec. 1, p. 2.

"Attorneys Studying Facts on Lynching." *Philadelphia Tribune,* September 13, 1955, A4.

Ayi, Mema. "Woodlawn School Renamed After Emmett Till." *Chicago Defender,* February 27, 2006, online.

Babwin, Don. "Officials, Others Hope Church Where Emmett Till's Funeral Will Bring Tourists." *Chicago Defender,* November 18, 2005, online.

"Bad News for NAACP." *Jackson (MS) Daily News,* September 8, 1955, Home final, sec. 1, p. 8.

Barnes, Richard Henry. "Introduce Till Resolutions into Pennsy Legislature." *Daily Worker,* October 27, 1955, A3.

"Battered Body of Boy, 14, Found in River in Miss." *Birmingham World,* September 2, 1955, sec. 1, pp. 1, 8.

"Battered Body of Boy, 14, Found in River in Miss." *Memphis World,* February 2, 1955, sec. 1, pp. 1, 8.

Beito, David T., and Linda Royster Beito. *Black Maverick: T. R. M. Howard's Fight for Civil Rights and Economic Power.* Urbana: University of Illinois Press, 2009.

Berry, Abner W. "The Macbeths of Mississippi." *Daily Worker,* October 11, 1955, A3.

"Biographical Note." n.d. "A Guide to the Field Foundation Archives, Pt. 1," Field Foundation Archives, Briscoe Center for American History, University of Texas at Austin, http://www.lib.utexas.edu/taro/utcah/00091/00091-P.html.

The Birth of a Nation. 1915. Directed by D. W. Griffith. Image Entertainment, 1998. DVD.

Blackmon, Douglas A. *Slavery by Another Name: The Re-Enslavement of Black Americans from the Civil War to World War II.* New York: Doubleday, 2008.

Blassingame, John W. *The Slave Community: Plantation Life in the Antebellum South.* New York: Oxford University Press, 1979.

"Blood on Their Hands." *Chicago Defender,* September 10, 1955, A1.

Bolen, R. C. "Point Ignored in Till Case." *Charlotte (NC) Observer,* September 28, 1955, B2.

Borstelmann, Thomas. *The Cold War and the Color Line: American Race Relations in the Global Arena.* Cambridge, MA: Harvard University Press, 2003.

"Boy, 14, Victim of Race Hate." *Pittsburgh Courier,* September 10, 1955, A1.

"A Boy Goes Home." *Newsweek,* September 12, 1955, 32.

Boyack, James Edmund. "*Courier*'s James Boyack Hangs Head in Shame." *Pittsburgh Courier,* October 1, 1955, sec. 1, p. 4.

———. "'Men's Souls Are Torn by Hatred, Violence, Fear.'" *Pittsburgh Courier,* September 24, 1955, sec. 1, p. 5.

"Boy's Slaying Brings Wrath of Governor." *Charlotte (NC) Observer,* September 2, 1955, A2.

Bradley, Mamie. "Mamie Bradley's Untold Story, Installment I, As Told by Ethel Payne." *Chicago Defender,* April 21, 1956, 5.

———. "Mamie Bradley's Untold Story, Installment II, As Told by Ethel Payne." *Chicago Defender,* April 28, 1956, 5.

———. "Mamie Bradley's Untold Story, Installment III, As Told by Ethel Payne." *Chicago Defender,* May 5, 1956, 5.

———. "Mamie Bradley's Untold Story, Installment IV, As Told by Ethel Payne." *Chicago Defender,* May 12, 1956, 5.

———. "Mamie Bradley's Untold Story, Installment V, As Told by Ethel Payne." *Chicago Defender,* May 19, 1956, 5.

———. "Mamie Bradley's Untold Story, Installment VI, As Told by Ethel Payne." *Chicago Defender,* May 26, 1956, 5.

———. "Mamie Bradley's Untold Story, Installment VII, As Told by Ethel Payne." *Chicago Defender,* June 2, 1956, 5.

———. "Mamie Bradley's Untold Story, Installment VIII, As Told by Ethel Payne." *Chicago Defender,* June 9, 1956, 5.

Bradshaw, Michael. *Regions and Regionalism in the United States.* London: Macmillan, 1988.

Brophy, Alfred L. *Reconstructing the Dreamland: The Tulsa Riot of 1921: Race, Reparations, and Reconciliation.* Oxford: Oxford University Press, 2002.

Brown, George F. "Mom Wants Son's Murder Avenged." *Pittsburgh Courier,* September 17, 1955, A1, A4.

———. "Mrs. Bradley Plans Suit." *Pittsburgh Courier,* September 22, 1955, 1.

Brown, Sarah Hart. "Redressing Southern 'Subversion': The Case of Senator Eastland and the Louisiana Lawyer." *Louisiana History* 43, no. 3 (2002): 295–314.

"A Brutal Slaying." *Delta Democrat-Times* (Greenville, MS), September 2, 1955, Red Streak final, A4.

"Bryant's Brother Claims Charges Are All 'Politics.'" *Memphis Commercial Appeal,* September 9, 1955, final, A19.

Carson, Clayborne, David J. Garrow, Bill Kovach, and Carol Polsgrove, eds. *Reporting Civil Rights: American Journalism, 1941–1963.* New York: Library of America, 2003.

Carter, Dan T. *Scottsboro: A Tragedy of the American South.* 1969. Reprint, Baton Rouge: Louisiana State University Press, 1979.

Carter, Hodding. "Racial Crisis in the Deep South." *Saturday Evening Post,* December 17, 1955, 26.

"Case of Emmett Till." *New York Times,* September 26, 1955, A26.

Cecelski, David S., and Timothy B. Tyson, eds. *Democracy Betrayed: The Wilmington Race Riot of 1898 and Its Legacy.* Chapel Hill: University of North Carolina Press, 1998.

Chatham, Bennye. Letter to the editor. *Time,* October 24, 1955, 6.

"Chicago Boy Found Slain in Dixie." *Chicago Sun-Times,* September 1, 1955, sec. 1, pp. 1, 4.

"Chicago Boy, 14, Kidnaped by Miss. Whites." *Jet,* September 8, 1955, 4.

Civil Rights Historical Sites. "Reverend George Lee." 2005. *Bluejean's Place,* http://www.bluejeansplace.com/civil-rights-historical-sites/rev-george-lee.html.

"Claim Eyewitnesses to Till Murder Held in Miss. Jail." *Los Angeles Sentinel,* October 6, 1955.

"Claims Mississippi Has Executed White for Negro Murder." *Delta Democrat-Times* (Greenville, MS), September 23, 1955, Red Streak final, A1.

Clark, Robert T. "Deplores Outcome of Mississippi Trial." *Charlotte (NC) Observer,* October 11, 1955, B2.

Claywell, Norma. "Mississippi Justice." *St. Louis Post-Dispatch,* September 29, 1955, B2.

Cobb, James C. *Away Down South: A History of Southern Identity.* New York: Oxford University Press, 2005.

————. *The Most Southern Place on Earth: The Mississippi Delta and the Roots of Regional Identity.* Oxford: Oxford University Press, 1992.

————. *Redefining Southern Culture: Mind and Identity in the Modern South.* Athens: University of Georgia Press, 1999.

Coleman, Theodore. "Latest Atrocity in Mississippi Arouses Nation." *Pittsburgh Courier,* September 10, 1955, A1, A4.

Colin, Mattie Smith. "Mother's Tears Greet Son Who Died a Martyr." *Chicago Defender,* September 10, 1955, A1–A2.

————. "Slain Boy's Mother Lauds the Defender." *Chicago Defender,* September 17, 1955, A1.

————. "Till's Mom, Diggs Both Disappointed." *Chicago Defender,* October 1, 1955, A1–A2.

Collier-Thomas, Bettye. *Jesus, Jobs, and Justice: African American Women and Religion.* New York: Random House, 2010. Kindle ed.

Conaway, Robert. "Till Case a Boon to Enemies of U.S." *Pittsburgh Post-Gazette,* October 3, 1955, A8.

"Congressman Diggs, Till's Mother in Attendance at Sumner Trial." *Jackson Advocate,* September 24, 1955, A1, A4.

Crespino, Joseph. "Mississippi as Metaphor: Civil Rights, the South, and the Nation in the Historical Imagination." In *The Myth of Southern Exceptionalism,* ed. Matthew D. Lassiter and Joseph Crespino, 99–120. Oxford: Oxford University Press, 2010.

————. "Mississippi as Metaphor: State, Region, and Nation in the Historical Imagination." Paper presented at the conference "The End of Southern History," Emory University, Atlanta, March 23–24, 2006.

Crump, Robert A. "Negro Workers Lose $86,000 Daily in Ford Strike." *Kansas City (KS) Plain Dealer,* April 18, 1941, 2.

Cunningham, Evelyn. "Harlem Protests Lynching." *Pittsburgh Courier,* October 1, 1955, sec. 1, p. 4.

Dabbs, James McBride. *Who Speaks for the South?* New York: Funk & Wagnalls, 1964.

Dailey, Jane, Glenda Elizabeth Gilmore, and Bryant Simon, eds. *Jumpin' Jim Crow: Southern Politics from Civil War to Civil Rights.* Princeton, NJ: University of Princeton Press, 2000.

"*Daily Worker*'s Reporter at Trial in Mississippi." *Jackson (MS) Daily News,* September 20, 1955, sec. 1, p. 6.

Daniel, Peter. *Lost Revolutions: The South in the 1950s.* Chapel Hill: University of North Carolina Press, 2000.

Daughen, Joseph R. "A Personal Odyssey." In *Nearly Everybody Read It,* ed. Peter Binze, 111–26. Philadelphia: Camino, 1998.

Davidson, Chalmers G. "A Finger Pointed in the Till Case." *Charlotte (NC) Observer,* October 6, 1955, B2.

Davies, Lee W. "Almost Impossible." *St. Louis Post-Dispatch,* September 30, 1955, C2.

"Deeply Hurt by NAACP Rebuke." *Chicago Defender,* November 26, 1955, A1–A2.

"Defendant's Wife." *Pittsburgh Post-Gazette,* September 23, 1955, A1.

D'Emilio, John. *Lost Prophet: The Life and Times of Bayard Rustin.* Chicago: University of Chicago Press, 2004.

"Democrats Condemn Cracker Thugs Who Mutilated Victim." *Philadelphia Tribune,* September 27, 1955, 1.

"Determined to Harvest Bumper Crop of Cotton." *Tri-State Defender* (Memphis), September 17, 1955, sec. 1, p. 1.

Diggs, Charles C., Jr. "Cong. Diggs: Emmett Till Trial Over but Negroes Should Never Forget Its Meaning." *Pittsburgh Courier,* October 8, 1955, sec. 1, p. 5.

A Disgusted Citizen. "Emmett Till's Death Will Be Avenged." *Norfolk (VA) Journal and Guide,* October 15, 1955, A10.

A Disgusted White Reader. Letter to the editor. *St. Louis Post-Dispatch,* September 27, 1955, C2.

Dittmer, John. *Local People: The Struggle for Civil Rights in Mississippi.* Urbana: University of Illinois Press, 1995.

Dixon, Amos. "Mrs. Bryant Didn't Even Hear Emmett Till Whistle." *California Eagle* (Los Angeles), January 26, 1956, A1.

———. "South Wins Out in Till Lynching Trial." *California Eagle* (Los Angeles), September 23, 1956, A1.

———. "Till Case: Torture and Murder." *California Eagle* (Los Angeles), February 9, 1956, A1.

Dixon, Julian C. "Empowering African-American Organizations: Present and Future." *Congressional Record,* March 3, 1994. http://thomas.loc.gov/cgi-bin/query/z?r103:E01MR4-2:.

Dixon, Thomas. *Clansman: An Historical Romance of the Ku Klux Klan.* 1905. Lexington: University Press of Kentucky, 1970.

Donald, David. "The Proslavery Argument Reconsidered." *Journal of Southern History* 37 (1971): 3–18.

D'Orso, Michael. *Like Judgment Day: The Ruin and Redemption of a Town Called Rosewood.* New York: Putnam's, 1996.

"Doubts Body That of Till." *Charlotte (NC) Observer,* September 4, 1955, A16.

"A Drama Plays Out, but Its Full Meaning May Be Missed." *Charlotte (NC) Observer,* September 25, 1955, C2.

Dudziak, Mary L. *Cold War Civil Rights: Race and the Image of American Democracy.* 2000. Reprint, Princeton, NJ: Princeton University Press, 2002.

"'Due Process' of Law?" *Denver Post,* September 28, 1955, A20.

Dunning, William Archibald. *Essays on the Civil War and Reconstruction and Related Topics.* New York: Macmillan, 1897.

"Eastland Uses Secret Army Files to Aid Till Lynchers." *Daily Worker,* October 21, 1955, A1, A3.

Edney, Hazel Trice. "At Least Eight Senators Backed Anti-Lynching Measure After It Was Adopted." *Chicago Defender,* June 24, 2005, online.

Elliott, Robert. "Thousands at Rites for Till." *Chicago Defender,* September 10, 1955, A1.

"Emmett Till Case Gains All Out Aid for NAACP." *Los Angeles Sentinel,* September 29, 1955, A5.

"Emmett Till Group Want to Embrace the Truth, Spread the Word." *Natchez (MS) Democrat,* October 1, 2007, online.

"Emmett Till Museum." n.d. *The Village of Glendora,* http://www.glendorams.com.

"Emmett Till's Day in Court." *Life,* October 3, 1955, 36.

"Ex-FBI Agent to Aid Till Prosecution." *Chicago Sun-Times,* September 11, 1955, sec. 1, p. 5.

"Facing the Cold Facts." *Atlanta Daily World,* September 25, 1955, A4.

Faust, Drew Gilpin. *The Ideology of Slavery.* Baton Rouge: Louisiana State University Press, 1981.

"FBI Till Findings May Be Out Next Month." *Chicago Tribune,* February 20, 2006, online.

Field, Kenneth C. "Miss., 'Nightmare of Terror,' Rev. Moses Wright Relates." *Los Angeles Sentinel,* November 17, 1955, A1.

"Fight Miss. Bigots!" *New York Amsterdam News,* October 15, 1955, A10.

"Find Kidnaped Chicago Boy's Body in River." *Chicago Tribune,* September 1, 1955, sec. 1, p. 1.

Fitzgerald, Michael W. "'We Have Found Our Moses': Theodore Bilbo, Black Nationalism, and the Greater Liberia Bill of 1939." *Journal of Southern History* 63 (1997): 293–320.

"500 at LYL Rally Urge Govt. Act in Mississippi." *Daily Worker,* December 19, 1955, A2.

"5,000 in Los Angeles Rally, 1,600 in Boston Assail Lynching of Child." *Daily Worker,* October 13, 1955, A3.

Fleegler, Robert L. "Theodore Bilbo and the Decline of Public Racism, 1938–1947." *Journal of Mississippi History* 68, no. 1 (Spring 2006): 1–27.

Foster, M. Marie Booth. *Southern Black Creative Writers, 1829–1953.* Westport, CT: Greenwood, 1988.

"Fourth Race Victim in Mississippi; State Attempting to Shift Blame; Hundreds View Boy's Remains." *Norfolk (VA) Journal and Guide,* September 10, 1955, sec. 1, pp. 1–2.

Fowler, James. *Stages of Faith: The Psychology of Human Development and the Quest for Meaning.* New York: HarperCollins, 1981.

Fox-Genovese, Elizabeth. *Within the Plantation Household: Black and White*

Women of the Old South. Chapel Hill: University of North Carolina Press, 1988.

Franklin, John Hope. *The Militant South, 1800–1861.* 1956. Reprint, Urbana: University of Illinois Press, 2002.

Gallagher, Gary W. Introduction to *The Myth of the Lost Cause and Civil War History,* ed. Gary W. Gallagher and Alan T. Nolan, 1–10. Urbana: University of Illinois Press, 2010.

Garner, Eugene M. "As to the Till Case." *St. Louis Post-Dispatch,* September 27, 1955, C2.

Giroux, Vincent Arthur, Jr. "Theodore G. Bilbo: Progressive to Public Racist." Ph.D. diss., Indiana University, 1984.

Godshalk, David Fort. *Veiled Visions: The 1906 Atlanta Race Riot and the Reshaping of American Race Relations.* Chapel Hill: University of North Carolina Press, 2005.

Goodman, James E. *Stories of Scottsboro.* New York: Pantheon, 1994.

Goodwin, Marvin. *Black Migration in America from 1915 to 1960: An Uneasy Exodus.* Lewiston, NY: Edwin Mellen, 1990.

Gordon, La Verne. "For No Reason, a Boy Is Dead." *Charlotte (NC) Observer,* October 10, 1955, B2.

Gordon, William. "The Sins of Mississippi." *Atlanta Daily World,* September 4, 1955, A4.

———. "The Way Europeans Look at Us." *Memphis World,* September 13, 1955, sec. 1, p. 8.

"Gov. White Orders Trial in Boy's Kidnap-Slaying." *Atlanta Constitution,* September 2, 1955, A2.

"Governor Acts in Slaying of Boy, 15." *Los Angeles Times,* September 2, 1955, sec. 1, p. 14.

"Governor Orders Probe of Negro's Slaying." *Seattle Times,* September 1, 1955, Night Sports final, sec. 1, p. 16.

Gowran, Clay. "Urban League Asks Action in Till Case." *Chicago Tribune,* September 6, 1955, sec. 1, p. 8.

Grantham, Dewey. "Conceptualizing the History of Modern Southern Politics." *History Teacher* 17, no. 1 (1983): 9–31.

Griffin, W. L. C. "Who's Behind It?" *Memphis Commercial Appeal,* October 2, 1955, final, sec. 5, p. 3.

Gutman, Herbert G. *The Black Family in Slavery and Freedom, 1750–1925.* New York: Vintage, 1976.

Hale, Grace Elizabeth. *Making Whiteness: The Culture of Segregation in the South, 1890–1940.* 1998. Reprint, New York: Vintage, 1999.

Hall, Stuart. "Ideology and Communication Theory." In *Paradigm Issues.* Vol. 1 of *Rethinking Communication,* ed. Brenda Dervin, Larry Grossberg, Barbara J. O'Keefe, and Ellen A. Wartella, 40–52. Newbury Park, CA: Sage, 1989.

Halpern, Rick. *Down on the Killing Floor: Black and White Workers in Chicago's Packing Houses, 1904–1954.* Urbana: University of Illinois Press, 1997.

Hampton, Chester M. "World Shocked by Till Trial." *Birmingham World,* September 30, 1955, A6.

Hansen, Mr. and Mrs. D. E. Letter to the editor. *Time,* October 17, 1955, 19.

Harden, P. L. "Tennessee Attorney Attacks Bilbo on Negro Colonization in Liberia." *Kansas City (KS) Plain Dealer,* March 18, 1938.

Harris, Russell. "Mississippi Opens Wolf-Whistle Trial." *Detroit News,* September 19, 1955, A1, A4.

———. "Murder Town's Tension Hidden by Sleepy Look." *Detroit News,* September 18, 1955, A1, A6.

———. "3 Surprise Witnesses Hinted for Prosecution in Dixie Trial." *Detroit News,* September 20, 1955, A1, A4, A17.

———. "3 Terrified Witnesses." *Detroit News,* September 21, 1955.

———. "Verdict Due in Whistle Trial Today." *Detroit News,* September 23, 1955, A1, A4.

Heft, Harold. "'Strange' Evolution of Legendary Song: Jewish Composer Penned Tune Made Famous by Billie Holiday." *Jewish Daily Forward,* March 30, 2012, online.

Hendrickson, Paul. *Sons of Mississippi: A Story of Race and Its Legacy.* New York: Knopf, 2003.

"Henry Robinson Luce." 2012. *Columbia Electronic Encyclopedia,* http://www.infoplease.com/ce6/people/A0830534.html.

Herbers, John. "'Case Closed' as Jury Fails to Indict Pair for Till Kidnaping." *Delta Democrat-Times* (Greenville, MS), November 10, 1955, Red Streak final, A1.

Hichborn, Franklin. "Southern Exposure." *San Francisco Examiner,* September 28, 1955, sec. 3, p. 2.

Hicks, James L. "All-White Jury of Sharecroppers Ignores Evidence." *Cleveland Call and Post,* October 1, 1955, A1–A2.

———. "Fear for Lives of Two Playmates of Emmett Till." *Cleveland Call and Post,* September 24, 1955, A1–A2.

———. "Feared Reprisals for Telling Truth." *Baltimore Afro-American,* October 1, 1955, A1, A8.

———. "Hicks Arrested during Trial in Till Lynch-Murder Case." *Atlanta Daily World,* October 18, 1955, A1–A2.

———. "Hicks Says Key Witnesses in Jail during Till Case Hearing." *Atlanta Daily World,* October 4, 1955, A1–A4.

———. "Hicks Tells of Daring Efforts to Get Witnesses in Till Case." *Atlanta Daily World,* October 11, 1955.

———. "Sheriff Kept Key Witness Hid in Jail during Trial." *Cleveland Call and Post,* October 8, 1955, A1, C8.

———. "Why Emmett Till's Mother and NAACP Couldn't Agree." *Baltimore Afro-American,* December 31, 1955, A2.

Hine, Darlene Clark, William C. Hine, and Stanley Harrold. *The African-American Odyssey.* Upper Saddle River, NJ: Prentice-Hall, 2006.

Hinson, Ernest. "Mississippi Trial Attacked by Georgian." *Atlanta Constitution,* October 4, 1955, A4.

Hirsch, Arnold. *Making the Second Ghetto: Race and Housing in Chicago, 1940–1960.* Chicago: University of Chicago Press, 1998.

"History, 1910." n.d. "About Us," *The Crisis,* http://www.thecrisismagazine.com/history.html.

Holmes, Paul. "Hunt Shadow Witnesses in Till Slaying." *Chicago Tribune,* September 21, 1955, sec. 1, p. 3.

———. "Open Defense Fight in Till Slaying Trial." *Chicago Tribune,* September 23, 1955, sec. 1, pp. 1, 6.

———. "2 Go on Trial in South for Till Murder." *Chicago Tribune,* September 20, 1955, sec. 1, pp. 1–2.

———. "Uncle Tells How 3 Kidnapers Invaded Home and Seized Till." *Chicago Tribune,* September 19, 1955, sec. 1, p. 2.

———. "A Way of Life on Trial in Till Case." *Chicago Tribune,* September 18, 1955, sec. 1, pp. 1, 6.

hooks, bell. *Black Looks: Race and Representation.* Boston: South End, 1992.

———. *We Real Cool: Black Men and Masculinity.* New York: Routledge, 2004.

"Housing Target of Urban League." *New York Times,* September 6, 1955, A39, A52.

Howard, T. R. M. "Dr. Howard: Situation in Mississippi Extremely Serious; Tension Is Continuing to Mount." *Pittsburgh Courier,* October 8, 1955, sec. 1, pp. 1, 4.

Hudson-Weems, Clenora. *Emmett Till: Sacrificial Lamb of the Civil Rights Movement.* Troy, MI: Bedford, 1994.

Huie, William Bradford. "The Shocking Story of Approved Killing in Mississippi." *Look,* January 24, 1956, 46–49.

———. "What's Happened to the Emmett Till Killers?" *Look,* January 22, 1957, 63–68.

Hutchinson, Earl O. "Why the Emmett Till Case Still Matters." *Chicago Defender,* June 10, 2005, online.

Hyde, Edmund G. "In Mississippi, Pitiful Travesty." *Charlotte (NC) Observer,* October 5, 1955, B2.

"'Ill-Chosen Symbol.'" *Time,* November 21, 1955, 21.

"Impose Equal Justice." *Jackson (MS) Daily News,* September 19, 1955, Home final, sec. 1, p. 10.

Inventing LA: The Chandlers and Their Times. Directed by Peter Jones. Peter Jones Productions, 2009. DVD.

"An Investigation, Then What?" *Los Angeles Sentinel,* September 8, 1955, A9.

"It Now Becomes All Our Business." *Memphis World,* September 2, 1955, sec. 1, p. 8.

Jackson, David. "Image of Emmett Till." *Jet,* September 17, 1955, 8–9.

Jackson, Jesse L., Sr. "Appreciation." *Time,* November 7, 2005, 20.

"*Jackson News* Is Sold: Passes to *Clarion-Ledger* After Long Control Battle." *New York Times,* August 8, 1954, 84.

"Jailed to Bar Them from Trial." *Chicago Defender,* October 1, 1955, A1.

Johnston, Bernice C. "The Till Case." *Denver Post,* October 8, 1955, A7.

Jones, Jacqueline. *Labor of Love, Labor of Sorrow: Black Women, Work, and the Family from Slavery to the Present.* New York: Vintage, 1985.

Jordan, William G. *Black Newspapers and America's War for Democracy, 1914–1920.* Chapel Hill: University of North Carolina Press, 2001.

Jubara, Drew. "Decades Later, an Apology: Once an Icon of Racism, Town Plans to Say It's [*sic*] Sorry Near Where Emmett Till's Killers Were Freed." *Atlanta Journal-Constitution,* October 2, 2007, A1.

"Jurors Urged to Free 2 Tried in Boy's Killing." *Philadelphia Evening Bulletin,* September 23, 1955, sec. 1, pp. 1, 56.

"Jury Acquits Pair." *Charlotte (NC) Observer,* September 24, 1955.

"Jury Is Chosen in Boy's Slaying." *Philadelphia Evening Bulletin,* September 20, 1955, sec. 1, p. 28.

"Jury Reconvenes, Adjourns without Indictment in Courthouse Slaying." *Birmingham World,* September 23, 1955, sec. 1, p. 1.

"Justice in Leflore County." *Delta Democrat-Times* (Greenville, MS), November 10, 1955, Red Streak final, A4.

"Justice, 1955, in Mississippi, U.S.A., as Depicted in the Till Murder Case." *Norfolk (VA) Journal and Guide,* October 1, 1955, A10.

"Justice—'Ole Miss' Style." *Los Angeles Sentinel,* September 29, 1955, A9.

Kempton, Murray. "The Baby Sitter." *New York Post,* September 20, 1955, A5, A32.

———. "The Future." *New York Post,* September 23, 1955, A3, A40.

———. "Preacher, Preacher." *New York Post,* September 19, 1955, A3, A30.

"Kidnaped Boy." *Richmond (VA) Times-Dispatch,* September 1, 1955, A12.

"Kidnaped Boy Whistled at Woman: Friend." *Chicago Tribune,* August 30, 1955, sec. 1, p. 2.

"Kidnaped Negro." *Charlotte (NC) Observer,* September 1, 1955.

Kilgallen, James L. "Racial Trial." *Philadelphia Evening Bulletin,* September 19, 1955.

———. "Trial of 2 for 'Wolf Whistle' Killing of Negro Starts Today." *San Francisco Examiner,* September 19, 1955, sec. 1, p. 10.

Killian, Lewis M. "Consensus in the Changing South." *Phylon* 18, no. 2 (1957): 107–17.

"Kin Tell How Murdered Boy Was Abducted." *Chicago Tribune,* September 3, 1955, sec. 1, p. 11.

Kirby, Jack Temple. "Bioregionalism: Landscape and Culture in the South Atlantic." In *The New Regionalism,* ed. Charles Reagan Wilson, 19–44. Jackson: University Press of Mississippi, 1998.

Klarman, Michael J. "The White Primary Rulings: A Case Study in the Consequences of Supreme Court Decision Making." *Florida State University Law Review* 29 (2001): 55–102.

Kleppner, Paul. *Chicago Divided: The Making of a Black Mayor.* DeKalb: Northern Illinois University Press, 1985.

Kusmer, Kenneth L. *A Ghetto Takes Shape: Black Cleveland, 1870–1930.* Urbana: University of Illinois Press, 1976.

Lassiter, Matthew D., and Joseph Crespino. "Introduction: The End of Southern History." In *The Myth of Southern Exceptionalism,* ed. Matthew D. Lassiter and Joseph Crespino, 3–23. Oxford: Oxford University Press, 2010.

"The Law." *Time,* October 3, 1955, 18.

"Law Moves Ahead." *Memphis Commercial Appeal,* September 7, 1955, sec. 1, p. 6.

Lawson, Stephen F. "Long Origins of the Short Civil Rights Movement, 1954–1968." In *Freedom Rights: New Perspectives on the Civil Rights Movement,* ed. Danielle L. McGuire and John Dittmer, 9–38. Lexington: University Press of Kentucky, 2011.

Lee, (Mrs.) M. E. "'Couldn't Have Treated a Dog That Cruelly.'" *Norfolk (VA) Journal and Guide,* October 8, 1955, A10.

"Legal Processes Continue." *Memphis Commercial Appeal,* September 24, 1955, final, A6.

Lemire, Elsie Virginia. *"Miscegenation": Making Race in America.* Philadelphia: University of Pennsylvania Press, 2002.

Lerner, Max. "Southern Jury Justice." *New York Post,* September 25, 1955, M8.

"Letters to the Editor." n.d. *The Murder of Emmett Till, The American Experience,* PBS, http://www.pbs.org/wgbh/amex/till/sfeature/sf_look_letters.html.

Levine, Daniel. *Bayard Rustin and the Civil Rights Movement.* New Brunswick, NJ: Rutgers University Press, 2000.

Lewis, Andrew. *The Shadow of Youth: The Remarkable Journey of the Civil Rights Generation.* New York: Hill & Wang, 2009.

Lewis, David Levering. *W. E. B. DuBois: The Fight for Equality and the American Century, 1919–1963.* New York: Holt, 2000.

Lubin, Alex. *Romance and Rights: The Politics of Interracial Intimacy, 1945–1954.* Jackson: University Press of Mississippi, 2005.

"Lynching Hit at Connecticut CIO Meet." *Daily Worker,* October 21, 1955, A3.

"Lynching Post-Facto." *Delta Democrat-Times* (Greenville, MS), September 6, 1955, Red Streak final, A4.

"Lynching Resumed." *Philadelphia Tribune,* September 3, 1955, A4.

"Mamie Apologizes!" *Pittsburgh Courier,* November 19, 1955, 1–2.

"Mayor Daley Protests Slaying of Chicagoan." *Chicago Sun-Times,* September 2, 1955, sec. 1, p. 3.

McCombs, Maxwell. "News Influence on Our Picture of the World." In *Media Effects: Advances in Theory and Research,* ed. Jennings Bryant and Dolf Zillmann, 1–16. Hillsdale, NJ: Erlbaum, 1994.

McCombs, Maxwell, and Tamara Bell. "The Agenda-Setting Role of Mass Communication." In *An Integrated Approach to Communication Theory and Research,* ed. Michael Salwen and Donald Stack, 93–110. Hillsdale, NJ: Erlbaum, 1996.

McGuire, Danielle L., and John Dittmer, eds. *Freedom Rights: New Perspectives on the Civil Rights Movement.* Lexington: University Press of Kentucky, 2011.

McKinley, L. W. "Place for Bigots Somewhere Else?" *Charlotte (NC) Observer,* October 4, 1955, B2.

McLaughlin, Malcolm. *Power, Community, and Racial Killing in East St. Louis.* New York: Palgrave Macmillan, 2005.

McLemore, Richard A. *A History of Mississippi.* 2 vols. Jackson: University Press of Mississippi, 1973–81.

Meeropol, Abel. "Bitter Fruit." *New York Teacher,* January 1937.

Meier, August, and Elliott Rudwick. *Black Detroit and the Rise of the UAW.* New York: Oxford University Press, 1979.

Mendiata, Ana. "500 Mourn Mamie Till Mobley; Homegoing Service Celebrates Her Life; Funeral Set for Today." *Chicago Sun-Times,* January 11, 2003, online.

Merry, Robert E. "Praises Reprint of Magazine Article." *Pittsburgh Post-Gazette,* October 3, 1955, A8.

Mertz, James J. Letter to the editor. *Life,* October 31, 1955, 6.

Metress, Christopher, ed. *The Lynching of Emmett Till: A Documentary Narrative.* Charlottesville: University Press of Virginia, 2002.

Milner, Jay. "Delta Town Welcomes Quiet Following in Wake of Sensational Murder Trial." *Jackson (MS) Daily News,* September 25, 1955, Home final, sec. 1, p. 10.

Minister. "Answers Letter on Till Trial." *Pittsburgh Post-Gazette,* October 8, 1955, A6.

"Miss. Reporter Says Witnesses 'Captive' in Chicago." *Birmingham World,* October 14, 1955, sec. 1, p. 5.

"Mississippi Barbarism." *The Crisis,* October 1955, 480–81.

"Mississippi Decision Nothing New." *Baltimore Afro-American,* October 1, 1955, A4.

"Mississippi Democracy." *Philadelphia Evening Bulletin,* September 21, 1955, sec. 1, p. 22.

"Mississippi Infamy." *Chicago Defender,* September 17, 1955, B9.

"Mississippi Infamy." *Tri-State Defender* (Memphis), September 17, 1955, sec. 1, p. 7.

"Mississippi Justice." *New York Amsterdam News,* October 1, 1955, A1.

"The Mississippi Lynch-Murder." *Atlanta Daily World,* September 2, 1955, A4.

"The Mississippi Lynch-Murder." *Birmingham World,* September 9, 1955, sec. 1, p. 6.

"The Mississippi Lynch-Murder." *Memphis World,* September 2, 1955, sec. 1, p. 8.

"Mississippi Nabs 2 in Death of Boy." *Philadelphia Inquirer,* September 1, 1955.

"Mississippi Rests Its Case in Murder of Chicago Boy, 14." *Philadelphia Evening Bulletin,* September 22, 1955, sec. 1, p. 1.

"Mississippi Terrorism." *Cleveland Call and Post,* September 17, 1955, D2.

"Mississippi: The Place, the Acquittal." *Newsweek,* October 3, 1955, 24.

"Mississippi Will Probe Boy's Slaying." *Richmond (VA) Times-Dispatch,* September 2, 1955, A10.

"Mississippi Wolf Call Murder Trial under Way." *Pittsburgh Post-Gazette,* September 20, 1955, A1–A2.

"Mississippians Are Acquitted in the Kidnap-Slaying of Boy." *Richmond (VA) Times-Dispatch,* September 24, 1955, A1.

"Mississippi's Governor Orders Probe of Killing." *Daily Oklahoman* (Oklahoma City), September 2, 1955, A18.

Moore, Jesse Thomas, Jr. *A Search for Equality: The National Urban League, 1910–1961.* University Park: Pennsylvania State University Press, 1981.

Morris, Gloria Barton. Letter to the editor. *Time,* October 24, 1955, 6.

Morris, Willie. *The Ghosts of Medgar Evers: A Tale of Race, Murder, Mississippi, and Hollywood.* New York: Random House, 1998.

"Mother of Till Bitter!" *Pittsburgh Courier,* December 24, 1955, sec. 1, p. 3.

"Mother to Attend Hearing." *Los Angeles Sentinel,* September 15, 1955, A1, A8.

"Mrs. Bradley Dropped from Speaking Tour." *Los Angeles Sentinel,* November 10, 1955, A1, A4.

"Mrs. Bradley Says Fee NAACP Idea." *Chicago Defender,* November 19, 1955, A1–A2.

Muller, Will. "New 'Klan in Tuxedos' Fights Desegregation." *Detroit News,* September 1, 1955, A49.

"Murder in Mississippi." *New York Amsterdam News,* September 10, 1955, A14.

"'Murder,' White Says; Promises Prosecution." *Chicago Defender,* September 10, 1955, A1.

Naison, Mark. *Communists in Harlem during the Depression.* Urbana: University of Illinois Press, 1983.

"Nation Horrified by Murder of Kidnaped Chicago Youth." *Jet,* September 8, 1955, 6.

"National Indignation Seen as Nationwide Editorial Comment Condemns Slaying of 14-Year-Old Negro Boy in Wolf-Whistle Incident at Money, Mississippi." *Jackson (MS) Advocate,* September 10, 1955, A1–A2.

"National Outrage at Texas Lynching." *Chicago Defender,* June 13, 1998, A1, A6.

"Negro Boy." *New York Post,* September 1, 1955.

"Negro 14, Called Insulter." *Atlanta Constitution,* September 1, 1955, A1.

"Negro Youth, 14, Slain; Two White Men Jailed." *Denver Post,* September 1, 1955, A8.

"Negro Youth's Killing Probed." *Pittsburgh Post-Gazette,* September 2, 1955, A1–A2.

Nelson, Stanley, dir. *The Black Press: Soldiers without Swords.* San Francisco: California Newsreel, 2000. DVD.

———. *The Murder of Emmett Till.* PBS, 2003. Videocassette.

"'Never into Any Meanness' in Their Lives, She Says." *Jackson (MS) Daily News,* September 2, 1955, Home final, sec. 1, p. 14.

Newport, Frank, David W. Moore, and Lydia Saad. "The Most Important Events of the Century from the Viewpoint of the People." December 6, 1999. Gallup News Service, http://www.gallup.com.

Newson, Moses J. "Minister Says He'll Leave Dixie." *Chicago Defender,* September 17, 1955, A1, A3.

"Newspapers over State Blast Murder of Negro." *Jackson (MS) Daily News,* September 3, 1955, Home final, sec. 1, p. 1.

"No. Three in Reign of Terror." *Cleveland Call and Post,* September 10, 1955, A1.

"No White Man Given Death for Killing in Miss. since 1890, Writer Observes." *Birmingham World,* September 27, 1955, sec. 1, p. 6.

Odum, Howard W., and Harry Estill Moore. *American Regionalism: A Cultural-Historical Approach to National Integration.* New York: Holt, 1930.

Odum-Hinmon, Maria. "The Cautious Crusader: How the *Atlanta Daily World* Covered the Struggle for African American Rights from 1945 to 1985." Ph.D. diss., University of Maryland, 2005.

"Officer Fears Actions Build Up Resentment." *Jackson (MS) Daily News,* September 4, 1955, Home final, sec. 1, p. 1.

Ogbern, Alton E. "'No Right to Pass Judgment on Justice.'" *Atlanta Constitution,* October 7, 1955, A4.

"1,000 Attend Paris Meeting to Protest Till Case." *Birmingham World,* October 4, 1955, sec. 1, p. 2.

Ottley, Roi. "Southern Style." *Chicago Defender,* October 10, 1955, B8.

———. "Way of White Folks." *Tri-State Defender* (Memphis), September 17, 1955, sec. 1, p. 4.

"Overview of the Seattle Times." n.d. *Seattle Times,* http://www.seattletimescompany.com/communication/overview.htm.

Ownby, Ted, ed. *The Role of Ideas in the Civil Rights South.* Jackson: University Press of Mississippi, 2002.

Pacifico, Michele F. "'Don't Buy Where You Can't Work': The New Negro Alliance of Washington." *Washington History* 6 (1994): 66–88.

"Painful Progress." *Denver Post,* September 6, 1955, A16.

Painter, Nell Irvin, ed. *A Narrative of Hosea Hudson: His Life as a Negro Communist in the South.* Cambridge, MA: Harvard University Press, 1981.

Payne, Charles M. *I've Got the Light of Freedom: The Organizing Tradition and the Mississippi Freedom Struggle.* 1995. Reprint, Berkeley: University of California Press, 2007.

Payne, Charles M., and Adam Green, eds. *Time Longer Than Rope: A Century of African American Activism, 1850–1950.* New York: New York University Press, 2003.

Payne, Ethel. "Says U.S. Can't Enter Till Murder Case." *Chicago Defender,* September 17, 1955, A1.

Peplow, Michael W. *George S. Schuyler.* Boston: Twayne, 1980.

Phillips, Ulrich B. *American Negro Slavery: A Survey of Supply, Employment and Control of Negro Labor as Determined by the Plantation Regime.* 1918. Reprint, Baton Rouge: Louisiana State University Press, 1960.

Pickett, Debra. "Mamie Till Mobley Dies; Made Son's Slaying Meaningful." *Chicago Sun-Times,* January 7, 2003, online.

Ponder, R. L. "Americans Demand Guilt Be Proven." *Atlanta Constitution,* October 8, 1955, A4.

Popham, John N. "Brothers Acquitted." *Atlanta Constitution,* September 24, 1955.

———. "Racial Issues." *New York Times,* September 18, 1955.

———. "Slain Boy's Uncle on Stand at Trial." *New York Times,* September 22, 1955, A64.

Poritz, Ruth. "Criticizes Editorial on Till Case Verdict." *Pittsburgh Post-Gazette,* October 3, 1955, A8.

Potter, Robert A. Letter to the editor. *Time,* October 24, 1955, 6.

Prattis, P. L. "Tears Instead of Money." *Pittsburgh Courier,* September 24, 1955, 6.

"The Predictable Verdict." *St. Louis Post-Dispatch,* September 25, 1955, B2.

Pride, Karen E. "Commemoration of Emmett Till Lynching Anniversary Includes Renaming Expressway Bridge." *Chicago Defender,* August 29, 2005, online.

———. "Emmett Till Returned to His Final Resting Place." *Chicago Defender,* June 6, 2005, online.

———. "Federal Officials Lead Exhumation of Emmett Till." *Chicago Defender,* June 2, 2005, online.

———. "South Side Park Named for Popular Alderman." *Chicago Defender,* January 11, 2005, online.

————. "Till Commemorations Fill 50th Anniversary Weekend." *Chicago Defender,* August 26, 2005, online.

"Prince of the Peckerwoods." *Time,* July 1, 1946, 23.

"Protest Killing of Negro Boy." *Milwaukee Journal,* September 1, 1955, sec. 1, p. 9.

"Public Protest Mounts on Emmett Till Case." *Memphis World,* October 7, 1955, sec. 1, pp. 1, 4.

Race: The Power of an Illusion. Episode 3, *The House We Live In.* Directed by Llewellyn M. Smith. San Francisco: California Newsreel, 2003. Videocassette.

Ratcliffe, Robert M. "Opening Day of the Farce!" *Pittsburgh Courier,* October 1, 1955, 9.

Reed, McCann L. "Ahlgren: Just as Big a Bigot." *Tri-State Defender* (Memphis), July 19, 1995, online.

"Remembering Mamie Till Mobley." *Ebony,* March 2003, 20.

Richardson, Marty. "Mother of Lynched Boy Here to Open 1955 NAACP Drive." *Cleveland Call and Post,* September 17, 1955, A1–A2.

The Rise and Fall of Jim Crow. Episode 4, *Terror and Triumph.* Directed by Bill Jersey and Richard Wormser. New York: Quest, Videoline, Educational Broadcasting Corp., 2002. DVD.

Roberts, Gene, and Hank Klibanoff. *The Race Beat: The Press, the Civil Rights Struggle, and the Awakening of a Nation.* New York: Knopf, 2006.

"Roberts Temple Church of God: 4021 S. State—Civil Rights Monument Now Part of History—2006." n.d. *Preservation Chicago,* http://www .preservationchicago.org/success-story/11.

Robinson, Charles F. *Dangerous Liaisons: Sex and Love in the Segregated South.* Fayetteville: University of Arkansas Press, 2003.

Roth, John K., ed. *American Diversity, American Identity: The Lives and Works of 145 Writers Who Define the American Experience.* New York: Holt, 1995.

Sartre, Jean-Paul. *Existentialism and Human Emotions.* New York: Wisdom, 1957.

Schechter, Patricia A. *Ida B. Wells-Barnett and American Reform, 1880–1930.* Chapel Hill: University of North Carolina Press, 2001.

Schroeder, John D. "Summit, IL." 2005. *Encyclopedia of Chicago,* http://www .encyclopedia.chicagohistory.org.

Schultz, Donna. "Protests Verdict in Negro Boy Case." *Pittsburgh Post-Gazette,* September 27, 1955, A10.

Schuyler, George S. *Black No More: Being an Account of the Strange and Wonderful Workings of Science in the Land of the Free, A.D. 1933–1940.* College Park, MD: McGrath, 1969.

"Search Halted for Woman in Negro Slaying." *Birmingham News,* September 3, 1955, A10.

"The Seeds of Terror Are Planted." *Charlotte Observer,* September 8, 1955, B2.

Senechal, Roberta. *The Sociogenesis of a Race Riot: Springfield, Illinois in 1908.* Urbana: University of Illinois Press, 1990.

Sengstacke, John H. *The Chicago Defender, the Negro Press, and You.* N.p., 1960.

"Sengstacke Comments on Verdict." *Chicago Defender,* January 10, 1955, A1.

"The Shape of Things." *The Nation,* September 17, 1955, 234–35.

Sheehan, Charles. "Till Rites Site Could Become a Landmark." *Chicago Tribune,* November 1, 2005, Metro sec., 1.

"Sheriff Makes Search for Hidden Guns." *New York Amsterdam News,* September 24, 1955, A1, A3.

"Sheriff Ready to Bury Victim in Hole Dug in Graveyard of Church of Christ." *Philadelphia Tribune,* September 10, 1955, sec. 1, pp. 1–2.

"Sheriff Says Body Found May Not Be Chicago Boy." *Richmond (VA) Times-Dispatch,* September 4, 1955, A7.

Shortbridge, James R. "Persistence of Regional Labels in the United States." In *The New Regionalism,* ed. Charles Reagan Wilson, 45–70. Jackson: University Press of Mississippi, 1998.

Siegel, Michael. "Principal States of Origin of the Migrants, 1910–1930." 2005. *In Motion: The African American Migration Experience,* Schomburg Center for Research in Black Culture, New York Public Library, http://www.inmotionaame.org.

Silver, James W. *Mississippi: The Closed Society.* 1964. Reprint, New York: Harcourt, Brace & World, 1966.

Simmons, Charles A. *The African American Press: A History of News Coverage during National Crises, with Special Reference to Four Black Newspapers, 1827–1965.* Jefferson, NC: McFarland, 1998.

Simone, Nina. Vocal performance of "Mississippi Goddam." On *Nina Simone in Concert,* Philips Records, 1964, ISRC GBAWA0652908.

Skates, John Ray. *Mississippi: A History.* New York: Norton, 1979.

"Slain-Boy's Body Arrives Here; Sets Off Emotional Scene at Depot." *Chicago Sun-Times,* September 3, 1955, sec. 1, p. 4.

"Slain Boy's Mother to Testify at Trial." *Chicago Sun-Times,* September 9, 1955, sec. 1, p. 26.

Smeed, Howard. *Blood Justice: The Lynching of Mack Charles Parker.* New York: Oxford University Press, 1996.

Snider, P. M. "Safely Returned." *Seattle Times,* October 6, 1955, Night Sports final, sec. 1, p. 8.

Snow, Presley J. "Strong Pressure." *Memphis Commercial Appeal,* October 2, 1955, final, sec. 5, p. 3.

Sorrels, William. "Murder Indictment to Be Asked of Slain Negro Boy." *Memphis Commercial Appeal,* September 2, 1955, final, A1.

"South Pushes Murder Trial." *Philadelphia Evening Bulletin,* September 1, 1955, sec. 1, p. 44.

"Southern Jury Indicts Two in Till Slaying." *Chicago Tribune,* September 7, 1955, sec. 1, p. 5.

Spivak, Alvin. "Nixon Target for Stand on Soviet." *San Francisco Examiner,* September 11, 1955, sec. 3, p. 1.

"Splitting Hairs over 'Lynching.'" *Tri-State Defender* (Memphis), September 10, 1955, A2.

"State Opens Final Plea in Negro Boy Slay Case." *Denver Post,* September 23, 1955, A8.

Stewart, Mrs. Charles. "Compares Till Case to Murder of White Woman." *Delta Democrat-Times* (Greenville, MS), September 15, 1955, Red Streak final, A7.

"The Story of Emmett Till." n.d. *February One: The Story of the Greensboro Four, Independent Lens,* PBS, http://www.pbs.org/independentlens/februaryone/till .html.

Strafford, Mary. "'When I Find Time I'll Cry,' Till's Mother Tells *Afro.*" *Baltimore Afro-American,* October 29, 1955, A1–A2.

Street, William. "Murder Trial Publicity Irks Placid Town." *Memphis Commercial Appeal,* September 18, 1955, final, sec. 5, p. 10.

Strong, H. H. "Comments on Trial Lauded by Negro." *Atlanta Constitution,* October 10, 1955, A4.

Stroupe, Phil. "Delta Residents Expected Indictments and Want Justice Done in Till Case but Outside Interference Resented." *Jackson (MS) Daily News,* September 7, 1955, Home final, sec. 2, p. 3.

Sugrue, Thomas J. *The Origins of the Urban Crisis: Race and Inequality in Postwar Detroit.* Princeton, NJ: Princeton University Press, 1996.

Thomas-Lester, Avis. "A Senate Apology for History of Lynching." *Washington Post,* June 14, 2005, A12.

"Thousands at Rites for Slain Youth." *Los Angeles Times,* September 4, 1955, sec. 1, p. 4.

"Thousands Crowd into Church to See Body of Slain Boy." *Milwaukee Journal,* September 3, 1955, sec. 1, p. 2.

"Thousands File Past Casket of Negro Boy Killed in South." *San Francisco Examiner,* September 4, 1955, sec. 1, p. 7.

"Thousands Pass Bier of Slain Negro Boy." *Washington Post,* September 4, 1955, A3.

"3,000 in Pittsburgh Rally." *Daily Worker,* October 26, 1955, A3.

"Till Case Repercussions." *Tri-State Defender* (Memphis), November 5, 1955, sec. 1, p. 7.

"The Till Case Verdict." *Jackson (MS) Advocate,* October 1, 1955, A4.

"Till Case Verdict Rapped by Reader." *Pittsburgh Post-Gazette,* September 30, 1955, A12.

"Till Protest Meeting." *The Crisis,* November 1955, 546.

Till-Mobley, Mamie, and Christopher Benson. *Death of Innocence: The Story of the Hate Crime That Changed America.* New York: Random House, 2003.

"Till's Father Was a Killer, Paper Reports." *Charlotte (NC) Observer,* October 15, 1955, A2.

"Till's Mom to Take Stand, Attorney Says." *Chicago Tribune,* September 11, 1955, sec. 1, p. 10.

"Till's Mother Calls Trial in Mississippi 'Comedy.'" *San Francisco Examiner,* September 26, 1955, sec. 1, p. 8.

"Till's Mother Says No Effort Made to Find Eye Witness." *San Francisco Examiner,* September 24, 1955, sec. 1, p. 20.

"Time to Forget the Till Case." *Delta Democrat-Times* (Greenville, MS), October 30, 1955, Red Streak final, A4.

"Timeline of Polling History: Events That Shaped the United States, and the World." n.d. Gallup News Service, http://www.gallup.com.

Tisby, Raymond F. "Lynch-Murder Victim's Mother Appears at Miss. Murder Trial." *Birmingham World,* September 23, 1955, sec. 1, pp. 1, 6.

"T. M. Hederman, 73; A Longtime Editor in Southern Capital." *New York Times,* January 8, 1985, B6.

"Trial Set in Slaying of Negro." *Denver Post,* September 18, 1955, A16.

"Trial Starts for Two in Mississippi Killing." *San Francisco Examiner,* September 20, 1955, sec. 1, p. 6.

Trickey-Rowan, Spirit. "Q&A: One of Little Rock 9 Speaks with Daughter, a History Maker in the Making." *The Grio,* February 8, 2010. http://thegrio.com.

Trotter, Joe William, Jr. *Black Milwaukee: The Making of an Industrial Proletariat, 1915–1945.* Urbana: University of Illinois Press, 1985.

Tuttle, William. *Race Riot: Chicago in the Red Summer of 1919.* New York: Atheneum, 1970.

"2,500 at Rites Here for Boy, 14, Slain in South." *Chicago Tribune,* September 4, 1955, sec. 1, p. 2.

"Twenty-Six Lynchings in 1923 as against 61 in 1922." *Broad Axe* (Chicago), December 29, 1923, 2.

"2 Acquitted of 'Whistle' Slaying in Mississippi." *Washington Post,* September 24, 1955, A1.

"2 Face Trial Sept. 19 in Dixie Slaying." *Detroit News,* September 10, 1955, A2.

"Two Governors Demand Inquiry in Race Killing." *St. Louis Post-Dispatch,* September 2, 1955, A12.

"2 Held for Trial in Slaying of Boy." *New York Times,* September 7, 1955, A19.

"Two Held in Connection with Chicago Lad's Death." *Atlanta Daily World,* September 1, 1955, A1.

"Two Indicted in the South for Boy's Death." *Pittsburgh Post-Gazette,* September 7, 1955, A1.

"2,000 in Frisco Hit Till Murder; Rep. Roosevelt Urges U.S. Act." *Daily Worker,* October 19, 1955, A3.

"2 Till Kidnap Suspects' Bond Set at $10,000." *Denver Post,* September 30, 1955, A18.

The Untold Story of Emmett Till. Directed by Keith Beauchamp. New York: Thinkfilm, 2006. DVD.

"Urge Tolerance at Till Boy's Rites." *Chicago Sun-Times,* September 4, 1955, sec. 1, pp. 1, 3.

U.S. Census Bureau. "Table 39. Mississippi—Race and Hispanic Origin: 1800–1990." September 13, 2002. http://www.census.gov.

"'Vengeance Is Mine,' Sayeth the Lord." *Cleveland Call and Post,* October 1, 1955, D2.

"The Verdict at Sumner." *Jackson (MS) Daily News,* September 25, 1955, Home final, sec. 1, p. 8.

"Virginius Dabney, Pulitzer Winner, Dies as Historian, Author, Richmond Editor, He Challenged Views on Race and History." *Virginian-Pilot* (Norfolk, VA), December 29, 1995, A9.

Wagner, Mrs. Edw. "Afterthoughts." *St. Louis Post-Dispatch,* October 2, 1955, C2.

Wakefield, Dan. "Justice in Sumner." *The Nation,* October 1, 1955, 284.

Waldrep, Christopher. *African Americans Confront Lynching: Strategies of Resistance from the Civil War to the Civil Rights Era.* Lanham, MD: Rowman & Littlefield, 2009.

Waldron, Ann. *Hodding Carter: The Reconstruction of a Racist.* Chapel Hill, NC: Algonquin, 1993. Kindle ed.

Walton, J. N'deye. "Emmett Till Remembered." *Chicago Defender,* July 25, 1992, A1, A14.

Ward, Roosevelt, Jr. "Harlemites Applaud Plan for 'March on Washington.'" *Daily Worker,* October 13, 1955, A3.

"Washington: 'Cold Case' Squad for Civil Rights Killings." *New York Times,* September 15, 2005, online.

"'Were Never into Meanness' Says Accused Men's Mother." *Memphis Commercial Appeal,* September 2, 1955, final, A35.

"Whistle Trial Told Boy Was Kidnaped, Freed." *Pittsburgh Post-Gazette,* September 22, 1955, A1–A2.

Whitaker, Hugh Stephen. "A Case Study of Southern Justice: The Emmett Till Case." M.A. thesis, Florida State University, 1963.

White American. "Jury in Till Case Scored by Reader." *Pittsburgh Post-Gazette,* October 4, 1955, A8.

"Who of Us Doesn't Share in Guilt of Till Murder?" *Pittsburgh Post-Gazette,* September 29, 1955, A16.

Wilkerson, Isabel. *The Warmth of Other Suns: The Epic Story of America's Great Migration.* New York: Random House, 2010.

"Will Mississippi Whitewash the Emmett Till Slaying?" *Jet,* September 22, 1955, 12.

"Will the NAACP Accept Blame?" *Delta Democrat-Times* (Greenville, MS), September 21, 1955, Red Streak final, A4.

"Williams CME Church to Be Site of Protest." *New York Amsterdam News,* September 17, 1955, A1–A2.

Wilson, Charles Reagan, ed. *The New Regionalism.* Jackson: University Press of Mississippi, 1998.

Wilson, L. Alex. "Picking of Jury Delays Opening." *Chicago Defender,* September 24, 1955, A1–A2.

"Wisconsin Democratic Convention Assails Injustice in Till Case." *Daily Worker,* October 14, 1955, A3, A8.

"'Wolf Whistle' Murder Trial Opens in South." *St. Louis Post-Dispatch,* September 19, 1955, A17.

Wolseley, Roland Edgar. *The Black Press, U.S.A.* Ames: Iowa State University Press, 1990.

Wormser, Richard. *The Rise and Fall of Jim Crow.* New York: St. Martin's, 2003.

Wright, Simeon, and Herb Brown. *Simeon's Story: An Eyewitness Account of the Kidnapping of Emmett Till.* Chicago: Chicago Review Press, 2010.

W.S. "Mississippi Mud." *New York Post,* September 26, 1955, A35.

Wyatt, Edward. "D. Tennant Bryan, 92, Chief of Newspaper and TV Empire." *New York Times,* December 12, 1998, online.

Yarbrough, Tom. "Odds 10 to 1 for Acquittal; 'Intrusion' Resented in Mississippi Murder Trial." *St. Louis Post-Dispatch,* September 22, 1955, A2.

"Youth Tells Murder Jury He Saw Till as Captive." *Chicago Sun-Times,* September 23, 1955, sec. 1, pp. 5, 14.

Zhang, Aimin. *The Origins of the African-American Civil Rights Movement, 1865–1956.* New York: Routledge, 2002.

Index

Civil Rights and the Struggle for Black Equality
in the Twentieth Century

Series Editors
Steven F. Lawson, Rutgers University
Cynthia Griggs Fleming, University of Tennessee

Freedom's Main Line: The Journey of Reconciliation and the Freedom Rides
Derek Charles Catsam

Subversive Southerner: Anne Braden and the Struggle for Racial Justice in the Cold War South
Catherine Fosl

Constructing Affirmative Action: The Struggle for Equal Employment Opportunity
David Hamilton Golland

River of Hope: Black Politics and the Memphis Freedom Movement, 1865–1954
Elizabeth Gritter

Sidelined: How American Sports Challenged the Black Freedom Struggle
Simon Henderson

Becoming King: Martin Luther King Jr. and the Making of a National Leader
Troy Jackson

Civil Rights in the Gateway to the South: Louisville, Kentucky, 1945–1980
Tracy E. K'Meyer

In Peace and Freedom: My Journey in Selma
Bernard LaFayette Jr. and Kathryn Lee Johnson

Democracy Rising: South Carolina and the Fight for Black Equality since 1865
Peter F. Lau

Civil Rights Crossroads: Nation, Community, and the Black Freedom Struggle
Steven F. Lawson

CPSIA information can be obtained at www.ICGtesting.com
Printed in the USA
BVOW03*1540300514

354778BV00001B/2/P

9 780813 145365